Quotable

"Everyone has the obligation to ponder well his own specific traits of character. He must also regulate them adequately and not wonder whether someone else's traits might suit him better. The more definitely his own a man's character is, the better it fits him."
- Marcus Tullius Cicero. Roman philosopher, statesman (d. 42 BC).

"To measure the man, measure his heart."
- Malcolm Forbes. Publisher of Forbes magazine (d. 1990)

The Vision Of An Unknown Indian Muslim

The Quranic phrase *"I take refuge in God"* written in *tughra* form by the Turkish calligrapher Mustafa Rakim (d. 1767).

Also by Jamal Khwaja

* Living The Quran In Our Times

* Authenticity and Islamic Liberalism

* Five Approaches to Philosophy

* Quest For Islam

* The Call Of Modernity And Islam

* Essays On Cultural Pluralism

* Numerous articles and scholarly essays

To learn more about the author, visit
www.JamalKhwaja.com
Download free Digital Books, Lectures, Essays and more …

The VISION OF AN UNKNOWN INDIAN MUSLIM

My Journey to Interfaith Spirituality

Jamal Khwaja
Member of the Lok Sabha,
(1957-62)

ALHAMD PUBLISHERS, LLC

Los Angeles

Copyright © by Jamal Khwaja 2015

All rights reserved. Copyright under Berne Copyright Convention, Universal Copyright Convention, and Pan American Copyright Convention. No part of this book may be reproduced, stored in a retrieval system, or transmitted in any form or by any means, electronic or mechanical or otherwise, including photocopying and recording, without prior written permission of the publisher, except for the inclusion of brief quotations in a review.

For permission to reproduce selections from this book contact the Publisher.

Published and distributed worldwide by ALHAMD Publishers, LLC.
3131 Roberts Avenue, Culver City, CA 90232, USA.
www.AlhamdPublishers.com

Printed and bound in the United States of America
Book and Jacket Design by Sandeep Sandhu and Raisa Shafiyyullah.
Author Photo by Kenny Zepeda

More information about the Author and his works can be found at www.JamalKhwaja.com
Look for FREE Downloads of Essays & Articles written by the Author.

ISBN 13 978-1-935293-60-6 (Hardcover)
ISBN 13 978-1-935293-96-5 (Softcover)
ISBN 13 978-1-935293-58-3 (EPUB)

BISAC
BIO026000 Biography & Autobiography : Personal Memoirs
BIO002000 Biography & Autobiography : Cultural Heritage
SOC039000 Social Science: Sociology of Religion

Publisher's SAN #: 857-0132

In the name of God, the Beneficent, the Merciful.

Dedicated to the future leaders and builders of the new India, committed to the ideals of authenticity, interfaith spirituality and fraternity of the human family.

Quotable

"The ultimate measure of a man is not where he stands in moments of comfort, but where he stands at times of challenge and controversy."

- *Martin Luther King, Jr. American human rights icon (d. 1968)*

Table Of Contents

Preface xi

Part 1: Stages of My Life

Chapter 1:
ROOTS: With Humility and Gratitude 3

Chapter 2:
ALLAHABAD AND ALIGARH: Early Education 9

Chapter 3:
CAMBRIDGE: Free Enquiry 31

Chapter 4:
FROM A.M.U. TO LOK SABHA: Wider Horizons 51

Chapter 5:
ALIGARH ONCE AGAIN: Slow Maturity, Part 1 77

Chapter 6:
ALIGARH ONCE AGAIN: Part 2 109

Chapter 7:
HIMALAYAN RETREAT: Discovery Of Self 129

Chapter 8:
THE INNER CALL: Contented Self 139

Part 2: My Image of India

Chapter 9:
India in Medieval Times 157

(Continued)

Contents

Chapter 10:
British Rule in Modern India and the Transfer of Power in 1947 189

Chapter 11:
Candid Reflections on the Indian Political Scene, 1947-1992 209

Chapter 12:
The Dream of an Indian Muslim 245

Appendix 1:
Facsmiles of Three Letters Addressed to the Author 255

Appendix 2:
Some Random Personal Memories of Abdul Majeed Khwaja 259

Appendix 3:
About the Author 293

Index 297

PREFACE

Born and bred as an Indian Muslim I have always had a bi-polar identity and I regard this as a blessing. Love of Islam and love of my motherland were instilled into my consciousness without any sense of conflict between the two. We, as children, often heard father saying that the question whether he was Indian first and Muslim second, or the other way round was like asking whether he was the son of his mother or the son of his father. Our family always had close social relations and lasting friendships with members of all communities. The only taboo was inter-marriage between the two.

My father, a liberal Muslim and also a true Gandhian, wanted me to study science but I opted for philosophy. My study of philosophy at Aligarh, Cambridge, and Munster universities and my interacting with several prominent Indian public figures (because of my father's prominent role in the Indian freedom struggle under Gandhiji's leadership) led to my getting elected to the Indian Parliament (*Lok Sabha*) at the rather early age of thirty-one*. However, I soon realized that politics was not my 'cup of tea' and my life work lay elsewhere.

I vividly recall that I, as a youth, always admired Asoke and Akbar and also Aurangzeb, as outstanding monarchs who had brought about the unification of the ancient land, but I felt inwardly uneasy at some of the stories in circulation that the latter was a bigot who destroyed Hindu temples and re-imposed the *jizya*, after Akbar had abolished it. I was, of course, too young and immature to understand the complex issues involved, but I never took sides and continued to respect the great men of my country. I never thought that Hinduism or other religions were worthless or monstrous bundles of falsehood but I did believe that Islam was perfect and Muslims were the

---

* Jamal Khwaja was born in Delhi on August 12, 1926. However, most official records mistakenly show 1928 as the year of birth.

'chosen people' while all other religions partook of some defect or other, hence, all religious groups ought to convert to Islam of their own free will. This, for me, logically implied that I ought to evangelize and try to make them see the beauty of Islam. Beyond the pious hope that sooner or later this will come to pass in a peaceful and gradual manner I was comfortable and at ease with people of all faiths and castes and regions of my great country.

As I grew up and my critical powers developed and the range of my studies widened I began to realize the full complexity of the human situation in space and time. My quest for truth, which started in Aligarh (under the limitations mentioned in Part A), blossomed in Cambridge and the search is still on to date. I would rather have the search continue till my last breath even though I have reached a state of inner peace in my spiritual journey. I have recounted important facets of the story of my inner intellectual and spiritual growth. It is the story of how, a, relatively, dogmatic model or paradigm of Islam developed into the model that I now accept. I have explained fully my reasons for doing so in my recent work, *Living the Quran in Our Times* (2010) and *Quest for Islam* (1977) and also other writings.

In one sentence, my journey has taken me from an honest acceptance that Muslims alone will win salvation to an equally honest acceptance of the beauty and validity of inter-faith spirituality. More importantly, my reasons for accepting so are derived not merely from my study of philosophy, but also, and very much so, from the study of the Quran in the perspective of history. My paradigm of Quranic Islam may be termed as Spirit-centered Humanism to distinguish it from Neutral or Scientific Humanism. And I submit that this interpretation of Islam is amply supported by numerous Quranic texts. However, as is well known, Muslims, as an organized religious group in the course of history have enormously diluted, even distorted, the original vibrant living core of Spirit-centered Humanism. This has happened to other religions also.

Every religion is born and develops in a social matrix and absorbs the ideas and ideals of the age into the new creative vision of truth, goodness and beauty that the founder or founders project uphold. Likewise, every individual is born into a particular milieu, learns the mother tongue, acquires bits of factual information and also assimilates a basic perspective on life as a whole. This basic 'world view' includes a set of spiritual, moral and aesthetic values. The members of the group accept all bits of information, evaluations and prescriptions as absolutely right, without any critical scrutiny. However, critical insight into the tradition is essential for ensuring that faith remains really alive and authentic and does not turn into mere lip profession for some reason or other.

Many Muslim believers hold that real believers do not need any enquiry, reasoning or study of history etc. in addition to the guidance contained in the Quran and the sayings of the Prophet. This approach is highly simplistic and misleading. There is a clear distinction between the infallible *'Word of God'* and the all too human (hence varied and fallible interpretations, in the natural course of time) of the unchanged Quranic texts. Without free enquiry and loving tolerance of dissent no religious, spiritual or intellectual tradition can survive and retain its primal force of conviction due to new ideas and ideals that are bound to emerge in human society.

Several brilliant Western intellectuals and scientists devalue any intensive concern with religious issues because they are never free from controversy and even the most rigorous or intensive enquiry fails to provide certainty. This is the position of ultra-scientific Positivists. But the human spirit moves on.

In Part A, I give a brief account of my intellectual and spiritual growth at different stages of my life. In Part B, I briefly describe my image of India based on critical history. I have no words to express my gratitude to my teachers, specially, at Cambridge University, where I learnt my first lesson in independent thinking and the over-riding value of spiritual autonomy and tolerance. I owe a special debt of gratitude to John Wisdom and I.T. Ramsey, my teachers at Cambridge, and J. Ritter, my teacher and mentor at Munster.

My vision of medieval and modern Indian history is indebted to eminent historians who were liberal humanists by conviction and, relatively, politically detached—such as Jadunath Sarkar, Tara Chand, M.Habib, Pannikar, Moreland, Penderel Moon, and Romilla Thapar, *et al*. Historians must have empathy for the entire human family, not just their own in-group. In the recent past I came across several writings of (late) Dr. Rafiq Zakaria on Muslim politics in modern India and I have come to admire them. His son, Farid Zakaria, is now brilliantly carrying on the torch lit by his father.

As one who had the good fortune of coming into close contact with Jawaharlal Nehru, Indira Gandhi and some other tall figures of modern India I thought that recollecting the stages of my mental and spiritual development may be of some help to the present and the upcoming generations in their own independent search for truth. My work is not an autobiography in the complete sense, but only a story of my mental and spiritual development and my transition from a simple liberal Islam to inter-faith spirituality with firm roots in the Quran and *Theopathic Sufism*.

Jamal Khwaja
June , 2015

PART 1

STAGES OF MY LIFE

Quotable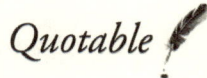

"Nearly all men can stand adversity, but if you want to test a man's character, give him power."
- *Abraham Lincoln. Iconic American President (d. 1865).*

"Fame is a vapor, popularity an accident, riches take wing, and only character endures."
- *Horace Greeley. Editor of the 'New York Tribune' (d. 1872)*

Chapter 1
Roots: With Humility and Gratitude

There are no printed or written records in my possession dealing with my ancestors. Whatever follows is, of necessity, confined to my parents, grandparents, paternal and maternal, and to my maternal great grandfather, Molvi Sami Ullah (d. 1908). I, however, understand that my ancestors on the father's side are the descendants of Khwaja Ubaidullah Ahrar, the renowned saint from Tashkent in the 16th century, and, reportedly, the spiritual mentor of Babar. Our first ancestor who lies buried in the family graveyard in Aligarh city is Khwaja Abdul Qadir. His ancestors had earlier lived in village Sasni, about twelve kilometers from Aligarh city.

My grandfather, Khwaja Muhammad Yusuf (d. 1902), one of the top lawyers and landowners of Aligarh, was a strong and influential supporter of the Aligarh Movement under the leadership of Sir Syed Ahmad Khan. Most of the rich and powerful landlords of the region were still reluctant, at that point of time, to go along with Sir Syed's mission of Western education and Islamic liberalism. They supported Western education more out of pressure from the British rulers rather than out of inner conviction. But Muhammad Yusuf, out of genuine conviction in the correctness of Sir Syed's vision, generously donated large sums to the *College Fund Committee*. He was also very active in the affairs of the *Scientific Society*. He had no objection to matrimonial alliances between different ethnic groups among the Muslims, something that was not looked upon as socially proper among traditional Muslims. He did not allow his beliefs and convictions to stand in the way of his warm friendships with Hindus and others or in adopting

Western ways in several social matters. Though *purdah* (seclusion) was practiced by the family womenfolk Muhammad Yusuf was the first Khwaja of Aligarh to impart English education to his sons.

Muhammad Yusuf was very close to his close friend and relative, Sami Ullah, a scion of the Muslim elite of Mughal Delhi and an accomplished oriental scholar and later District and Sessions Judge in Rai Bareilly in Uttar Pradesh. The Viceroy had lent his services to Lord Cromer in Egypt to facilitate the liberal reform movement in the region. This was the task Sir Syed had undertaken in India under the auspices of the Aligarh Movement, and both had been close friends and comrades. Sami Ullah introduced Shibli Nomani, as a young man, to Sir Syed who inducted him in the service of the MAO College. The famous advocate of Pan-Islamism in those days, Jamaluddin Afghani, bracketed Sir Syed and Sami Ullah together and denounced them as stooges of British imperialism.

Sir Syed and Sami Ullah were close comrades, but unfortunately, differences arose between the two due to some personal reasons as well as some policy matters relating to College affairs. The friends became estranged in the late 1880's. It was an ordeal for my grandfather, Khwaja Muhammad Yusuf, who was their common friend, to choose sides. His conscience compelled him to side with Sami Ullah. Our family lore has it that Sir Syed failed to appreciate the anguish and dilemma of a sincere friend and honest colleague. Sami Ullah withdrew himself from Aligarh affairs and made Allahabad the focus of his educational mission through founding of the *Muslim Boarding House* as part of the famous University of Allahabad. His son, Hamied Ullah, and, subsequently, his grandsons, Muhammad Ullah and Mahmud Ullah, remained closely associated with the *Muslim Boarding House* for the rest of their lives. Muhammad Ullah, my maternal uncle and a Cambridge graduate in Law, later on became a renowned author of several books on Anglo-Muslim family law.

My father, Abdul Majeed Khwaja, shifted the prefix, 'Khwaja' to the end of the name. He was the younger of the two sons of Khwaja Muhammad Yusuf. The elder son, Yahya, died as a young man. Father went up to Cambridge in 1906 as a member of Christ's College. He graduated in history and was called to the Bar in 1910. Jawaharlal Nehru, Sir Shah Sulaiman, the eminent jurist, and Iqbal, the poet, were among his contemporaries in Cambridge. It was in Cambridge that father first saw and heard Barrister M.K.Gandhi of South African fame and, then, a great admirer of British liberalism.

Returning home my father built up a flourishing legal practice first at the District Court, Aligarh and later at Patna High Court. At the call of Gandhiji he gave up his practice in 1919, joined the non-cooperation and *Khilafat* movements, and suffered six months' imprisonment. He was one of the founding fathers of the *Jamia Millia Islamia*, which was the brainchild of Maulana Muhammad Ali, M.A.Ansari, and Hakim Ajmal Khan. Muhammad Ali was the first Principal of the College, but due to his intense political activism, he decided to abdicate in favor of his close friend and associate, Khwaja Sahab. The young and dynamic Zakir Husain was the most prominent student leader of the MAO College to join the *Jamia* at its very inception and formation, and his zeal and commitment to the cause led him to join the staff as an honorary instructor. However, he soon left for Germany to study Economics in order to dedicate his life, after his return, to the *Jamia*. A little earlier, K.A.Hamied, another dynamic young man, and my father's favorite nephew, had done the same. Dr. Hamied, as he later came to be known, became famous as an industrial chemist and founder of the renowned pharmaceutical firm, Cipla, at Mumbai. Khwaja Sahab was thus left all alone to nurse the *Jamia* baby in the interim period. Father was, thus, Principal, Managing Trustee and Financier all rolled into one.

The greatest measure of moral and material support came from Gandhiji through his generous disciple, G.D.Birla. But there were other sources of sustenance also, such as Hakim Ajmal Khan, Dr. M.A.Ansari, and several dedicated teachers at the *Jamia*, like Aslam Jairajpuri, Shafiqur Rahman Kidwai, Kalat Sahab and Aqil Sahab among others. Perhaps, the most memorable episode of this period is the convocation address by Sir P.C.Ray in 1923. In this learned address (of which only two or three printed copies are now available) the eminent scientist and scholar recounted the contribution of Muslim thinkers, historians and scientists to world culture.

In 1925 father shifted the *Jamia* baby from Aligarh to Karol Bagh, Delhi and then handed over charge to Zakir Sahab who thenceforth became the soul of the *Jamia*. He later on shifted the small but steadily growing campus to its present site at Okhla.

Father resumed his legal practice at the Allahabad High Court in 1926, and remained there till 1944. After the death of Dr. Ansari in 1936 and at Zakir Sahab's insistence the mantle of Chancellorship of the *Jamia* fell on the shoulders of Khwaja Sahab.

My father was uncompromising in his commitment to Islamic liberalism and secular nationalism under the leadership of Mahatma Gandhi. Gandhiji was the only Indian leader father looked up to for inspiration and guidance. Those he cared for, next to Gandhi, were C.R.Das, Dr. M.A.Ansari, T.A.K.Sherwani and Sir Tej Bahadur Sapru. After suffering a heart attack in 1942 he gave up his legal practice and returned to Aligarh in 1944. From this date onwards right till the partition of the country he strove for a united India from the platform of the newly founded umbrella body of secular Muslims, the *All India Muslim Majlis*.

The martyrdom of Gandhji, soon after independence, shattered father politically. Despite his intimate friendship with Jawaharlal Nehru, he never thrived in the politics of the Nehruvian era. Some of his close friends and colleagues achieved far greater political success and recognition, but he never bothered about such matters. His strong point was his Islamic liberalism and secular politics even in the teeth of opposition from Muslims who had been carried away by the slogan of Pakistan. He always retained a passionate and selfless concern for his *alma mater*, the *Aligarh Muslim University*, at every stage of its career. He also had ample poetic gifts but was rather careless in preserving and publishing his poetry. He died in 1962.

Coming to my mother's side, our grandfather, Hamied Ullah (later Nawab Sarbuland Jung) was the eldest son of Molvi Sami

Ullah. Hamied Ullah was the first to be enrolled as a student of the MAO College and was the second member of the larger family of Sir Syed and Sami Ullah to proceed to Christ's College, Cambridge for higher studies. The first was none other than Sir Syed's son, Syed Mahmud, who became the first ever-Indian judge of the Allahabad High Court.

Hamied Ullah eventually became Chief Justice of the Nizam's High Court at Hyderabad. But he took early retirement and settled down at Allahabad. A religious and political liberal of a retiring nature, he shunned publicity and politics and preferred the quiet of the library to the polemics of the Courtroom or of the Assembly chamber. However, he was among the very distinguished early Presidents of the Muslim Educational Conference. He died in 1930. I have a very faint memory of him sitting in a wheel chair.

Our grandmother, Begum Akhtar Sarbuland Jung, survived grandfather by a quarter of a century. She had very little formal education. However, she was a poetess and writer and had traveled a lot in India, Europe and the Middle East. A pleasant conversationalist and charming hostess she conversed confidently with royalty as well as spiritual leaders. Queen Mary had given an audience to her when she visited London.

Mother was the first born of her parents. She too had no formal education beyond the Junior Cambridge level. But she had the immense benefit of learning from the enlightened and cultured atmosphere of her family and a circle of distinguished personalities of the day. Perhaps, the most famous among this circle was Sarojini Naidu and her daughter, Padmaja, who was mother's classmate at school in Hyderabad.

Mother was a good and efficient domestic manager. In addition, under the influence of father, she did a lot of constructive social work at Aligarh during the days of non-cooperation. During this period mother was torn between divided loyalties to her father, a Westernized liberal aristocrat, and her husband who, under Gandhiji's inspiration, had made a bonfire of his expensive and fashionable English suits and switched over to khadi kurta pyjama. She founded and ran successfully a *Women's Khadi Bhandar* at Aligarh and also edited an Urdu magazine, *Hind*. Gandhiji wrote his first ever letter in Urdu to mother on a postcard. I have misplaced the prized letter but I am hopeful of retrieving it. To the best of my knowledge, my mother was the first lady in Aligarh to come out of *purdah*. Begum Sajjad Haider and Begum Muhammad Habib later on joined her.

After our family shifted to Allahabad in 1926 she remained in touch with the Nehrus and had a large circle of friends among all communities, including the Christian missionary circle. She was the first among the Muslims to get her daughters admitted as boarders in the famous St. Mary's Convent, Allahabad. The young Indira Nehru was also a student at the Convent for a short period. Mother founded and managed the *Hamidia Girls School* in the interior of the city of Allahabad to promote education among the relatively weaker section of Muslim women. This was in the early 1930's. The primary school eventually grew into a Degree College under the fostering care of her daughter, Akhtar, married to Dr. A.H.Khan, who retired as Civil Surgeon of Allahabad.

Mother died in 1981 at the ripe age of eighty seven. She ever showered very tender maternal affection on me, as a son, after six daughters. Two more brothers, Rasheed and Ajmal, followed me. Rasheed, much later, changed his name to Raveend. My elder sister, Taj Apa, who was twelve years older, used to chide me in the hearing of the family that my mother's love had spoilt me. I still don't know the truth.

CHAPTER 2

ALLAHABAD AND ALIGARH: EARLY EDUCATION

I was born at Delhi in August 1926*. Shortly afterwards my parents shifted from our ancestral home at Aligarh to Allahabad. In 1919 my father, Abdul Majeed Khwaja (1885-1962) had given up his flourishing legal practice at Patna in response to Gandhiji's call for non-cooperation. After six years of dedicated service to the community and the nation he resumed his long interrupted legal practice at the Allahabad High Court. Though he was not actively involved in politics from 1926 to 1944 he retained his close association with Gandhiji and the national movement and also generously contributed to Congress funds. In 1944 he again plunged into the thick of politics for the sake of the unity and integrity of the country.

Firmly adhering to the fundamentals of Quranic Islam, father had long outgrown the orthodox stress upon *Hadis* literature, and popular beliefs in the supernatural powers of saints and mystics. A sort of Islamic rationalist and modernist, like his friend and associate, Maulana Azad, he affirmed the essential unity of all religions and gave great importance to inter-religious understanding and harmony. A confirmed and ardent Muslim as he was, he repudiated the mixing of religion with politics, even though he firmly stood for the ethical approach to politics as championed by Gandhiji who remained his mentor for life. This was the climate of thought and feeling in which

---
* Jamal Khwaja was born in Delhi on August 12, 1926. However, most official records mistakenly show 1928 as the year of birth.

I grew up in my childhood and youth.

Father held that the Quran was sufficient as a permanent source of guidance to humanity and that the traditional stress on the literature of *Hadis* and Islamic jurisprudence was not called for. He doubted the authenticity of several traditionally accepted reports of the Prophet's sayings or actions but he had his own repertoire of the same. He loved to relate them and they genuinely inspired him. He frequently reiterated in conversation with family and friends and also in public pronouncements that he had found Gandhi, among the moderns, to be nearest in purity of character to Prophet Muhammad. Father also taught his children to revere the *Bhagwad Gita* as a great scripture.

Pandit Sundarlal, noted Gandhian writer and freedom fighter, frequently visited father. I made it a point to be present as I loved to listen to his discourses on Hindu-Muslim unity, the essential unity of all religions and the wisdom of the great *Sufis*. There were numerous other visitors too with whom father exchanged his views on religious and cultural themes. My younger brother, Raveend, and I were often present. As young boys we remained silent hearers but we learnt a lot in this way. One of the things we learnt is that the custom in India to give a so-called Muslim or Islamic name to a child born in a Muslim family or to one who converts to Islam is, by no means, a doctrinal requirement of Islam, but rather a custom that evolved in several Muslim societies.

I can never forget the powerful impact of father's oft-repeated rhetorical question: Did the Holy Prophet require or demand that his fellow Arabs change their names after converting to Islam? Father used to impress upon his circle of visitors and friends that just as the early Muslims had freely absorbed Persian names and cultural heroes and themes the Indian Muslims too should do likewise in regard to Sanskrit and Hindi names and heroes without any fear that this would compromise their religion. Indeed, father went so far as to say that the practice of idol worship among the Hindus did not mean that Hinduism denied the ultimate unity of the Supreme Being.

An entirely different stream of influence came from my maternal grandmother, Begum Sarbuland Jung. She had widely traveled in the Muslim world and Europe and had repudiated the traditional veil. However, she was much given to visiting *Sufi* shrines and saints and performed selective litanies and also practiced meditation. She firmly believed that saints, both living and dead, granted favors and boons to the faithful. It is, perhaps, due to her influence that I continue to be keen on meeting and associating with holy men, even though I have no faith left in boons or miracles. My mother did not directly influence my mental or spiritual development. But I cannot help believing that her intense protective love for a male child (after six successive daughters) is the psychogenic cause of my exaggerated need for attention and affection from others. I also think that my pronounced sensitivity to human pain and suffering is the result of my mother's over protective concern and tenderness for her fist born male child.

I have hardly any recollections of my eldest sister who died early in life. My third elder and favorite sister, Atoo Apa, eleven years older than me, used to tell me stories and fairy tales and also motivated me to try to excel in life. My ethical idealism has its emotional roots not only in my parent's teachings but also in my sister's loving exhortations and didactic stories. But my second eldest sister, Taj Apa, who is now no more, was a strict disciplinarian. She, as mother's deputy, claimed to exercise full authority on her three younger brothers. I never questioned her claim that all her strictness was meant for my own good. A very trying form of her strictness was the compulsory cup of milk I just had to take at bedtime. I dared not lie to her if she questioned me, as she often did, whether I had taken the milk or not. I gradually hit upon the strategy of taking just one gulp and then imploring the caring and reluctant maidservant to consume the rest of the contents, as a great favor to me. This was my way of escaping from the dilemma of either submitting to 'forced feeding', or giving a false reply next morning, when she asked me the dreaded question: did you take milk last night?

As a child of seven or so I was filled with wonder at the idea of the everlasting happiness and bliss that Muslims would enjoy in heaven. I rejoiced at having been born in a Muslim home. I recall having told my elder sisters once or twice that I had dreamt of being in heaven. My sisters kept quiet. I also believed that I could prove by reasoning that Islam was the one true faith. My classmate and friend, Mahendranath, a Kashmiri Pandit, had other ideas. We frequently debated the issue, but this had no effect upon our warm friendship.

The social ties and bonds between Hindus and Muslims were very close in our circle. Perhaps, nothing could better illustrate this than a true story. When my eldest sister was about to be married in the early thirties a close family friend (the venerable father of the eminent lawyer and statesman, Kailash Nath Katju) called on the family and lovingly advised my sister to read a well known religious work in Urdu, *Heavenly Ornaments*, on the virtues and duties of a married Muslim woman. The author was Maulana Ashraf Ali Thanvi, an eminent traditional Muslim theologian. This small incident reflects the spirit of the intimate and close social and cultural ties between the Kashmiri Hindus and the Muslim community. It must be pointed out that the Kashmiri Hindus for all their exposure to Urdu and Persian literature had preserved their glorious Sanskrit cultural heritage. This had led to a remarkable humanistic cultural synthesis having a universal appeal, especially after its fusion with modern Western thought and culture. Perhaps Tej Bahadur Sapru could be said to be a symbol of this universal culture.

My earliest schooling took place in *Saint Mary's Convent*, Allahabad. My sisters also studied there. I was considered intelligent and hard working, but not talented or gifted in any sense. However, I secured high marks in all subjects, including Bible Studies. My secondary education was completed in the *City Anglo-Vernacular High School*, at that time a highly reputable institution of Allahabad. I consistently remained among the first three in all school examinations, securing high marks in all subjects without exception. But I did not display any special talent. My reading was confined to the prescribed course books. However, I took the initiative, entirely on my own, of writing two letters in Persian to father. He must have been pleased at this since his children had not been exposed to classical Arabic and Persian studies as he had been as a child. My ability to write in Persian was the result of the loving interest taken by our resident family tutor, Molvi Haidry Sahab, who was an accomplished traditional scholar. Unfortunately, I gave up studying Persian after clearing the secondary school level.

When I was a student of class seven or eight at the *City Anglo-Vernacular High School*, an incident occurred which made me feel compromised. A class test was being held, and like most others students I wanted to go through some 'important' portions of the textbook concerned. I was one of the best students in the class and there was no question of my resorting to any unfair means for scoring high marks. I was busy refreshing my memory when the invigilator entered the room and started distributing the paper. I quite naturally and innocently put the book inside the desk and got busy answering the question paper. Shortly thereafter a student was found copying from some book or notes in his possession, and the invigilator decided that the desks of all the students will have to be checked. Though I had not indulged in any cheating I did have a book inside my desk. My case was also reported to the Headmaster for necessary action. I felt my honor had been compromised, though none ever doubted my integrity.

My cousin, a senior student in the same school, took me to the Headmaster who readily cleared me and closed the issue as far as I was concerned. In retrospect, I think I have always been extremely sensitive on the matter of personal reputation. I have tried not only to be above board, in fact, but also appear to be so in the eyes of others. While the concern for a clean image is natural and also essential for social health it should never be allowed to outweigh the concern for the 'real thing'.

In 1941 I passed my High School Examination in the first division. I honestly believed that if I worked hard and also prayed for God's help I would stand first in the State. However I had not been able to work as hard as I had wanted to. Nevertheless, I went on praying, even after the examination was over, and felt rather disappointed that I had failed to secure any position in the merit list despite my earnest petitions to Allah.

I joined the prestigious Government Intermediate College, Allahabad. Ever since early childhood I was good in subjects that required abstract logical reasoning or skill of literary composition. However, I was rather poor in handling physical objects or tasks that required manual skill, including sports and athletics. Though I was pretty good in Mathematics at the school level I was rather scared of performing laboratory experiments in Physics or Chemistry. I was very keen to offer the Intermediate Arts stream at College, but out of deference to father's wishes I, after much reluctance, opted for the science stream.

I ought to have focused on science and tried to obtain high grades in my pre-university studies in science. This was the wise and natural thing to do having once resigned my will to father's wishes. Thereafter, I could have switched over to my beloved logic and philosophy at the university level. Unfortunately, I either sulked or spent all my time reading books on Psychology, religion and history. When examination time came near I lost my nerve. I had to choose between certain failure or dropping out of my Board examination. I chose the latter course. Meanwhile, father had a serious heart attack in 1942 and the family moved from Allahabad to the ancestral home at Aligarh. I had to join the first year of Intermediate Arts all over again in 1943 at the Aligarh Muslim University.

We, brothers and sisters, cannot be too grateful to our parents for their consistent emphasis on the supreme necessity of truthfulness in all matters. Our parents taught us this truth by both precept and example, and I can say, in all humility, that their training and love contributed to make the virtue of always telling the truth, without fear of consequences, almost my second nature. However, two clear instances of my deliberately deviating from truth stand out in my memory. These two instances exclude two or three others where I was constrained to be somewhat inaccurate because of altruistic motives, rather than any personal or material gain.

I spoke my first deliberate lie when I, as a young school going boy, accompanied my college going elder cousin to a matinee cinema show, and, subsequently, gave out to my family members that I had gone to see a cricket match. The lie was occasioned as I was not sure whether I will be given parental permission to go to the cinema show. The second occasion arose a decade and a half later when I was studying at the *University of Munster* in Germany after having graduated from Cambridge. But it might, well, be mentioned here. While on an educational tour by bus in Germany I met a German girl student studying at some place other than Munster. She suddenly and casually asked me if I was married. On the spur of the moment I replied in the negative, though, in fact, I had got married soon before leaving for Cambridge, but my wife had to stay behind with my parents due to domestic compulsions. Guilt feelings arose inside me for having given a false reply to her query. I later expressed my regrets through a postcard. Thereafter there was no interaction.

The traditional form of *purdah* was not practiced in our family even though our family was strictly opposed to free mixing and higher education for girls. In my belief that a good Muslim should not look at the opposite sex I always lowered my gaze during conversation. For the same reason I refused to hear music or sing popular songs, even though there was no parental restriction on these scores. This puritanical phase lasted for only a brief period, say, a year or so.

Being a natural 'idealist' in every matter I aspired to lead a disciplined and regulated life according to a fixed time schedule. But I never succeeded; no matter how persistently I tried. I read numerous books on self-improvement and the art of living and also prayed for God's help. But the pattern of my life remained irregular and was marked by chronic procrastination.

ALIGARH

I also had to face the emotional stresses and strains of adolescence without any sympathetic and informed guidance from elders or teachers. These problems had already cropped up at Allahabad where I had entered the threshold of adolescence. My early fascination for the study of religions, including Vedantic Hinduism, had drawn me powerfully to the ideal of brahmacharya. But I had felt helpless against the elemental force of the sex instinct.

In my innocence I had fervently prayed to God during my Allahabad days to help me in acquiring full control over my sex instinct and escaping unscathed from the pitfalls of the age of adolescence. But I stood repeatedly rebuffed. Doubts began to assail me if I had true faith in Islam and my self-esteem stood shaken. Sometimes I began to wonder if the belief in God was not really a belief in a glorified Santa Claus, after all. I had become superficially acquainted with both Marx and Freud and I could not help taking serious note of the possibility that religion was either an illusion or the opium of the masses. However, I dared not share my inner struggles with anybody. I suffered in loneliness and silence. I kept on saying my Islamic prayers and reading of the Quran in Arabic and also in English translation. My reverence for saints and seers of all religions survived though I was never drawn to seek their help for worldly gains.

The cultural climate at Aligarh was markedly different from the liberal humanist climate at Allahabad, thanks, to the High Court and the University graced by a galaxy of intellectuals and statesmen. I did very well in my academic studies at Aligarh and also in college debates. But I also came under the influence of ideas emanating from the peculiar qualified Islamic rationalism of Abul Ala Mawdudi. This was in spite of the liberal Islamic approach of my father.

The hold of *shariah* became so strong that I stopped watching movies. When my friends or brothers pressed me to accompany them to a movie I tried to excuse myself on some pretext or other. When I just could not wriggle out I went but just sat in the seat without looking at the screen, but merely hearing the dialogues. Of course, I never told my friends about my self-imposed 'Islamic' discipline. This was, however, not the general picture of Islamic piety at Aligarh.

An incident might give a better idea of the mindset of the majority of the Aligarh community of those days. The daughter of a family friend was interested, as a private candidate, in offering music as an optional subject at the Intermediate examination. When I enquired from the office of the university Registrar whether music was a subject of study at the AMU a fairly senior officer expressed his surprise at my ignorance or innocence in expecting that music could at all have been included in the syllabus of a Muslim institution.

To mention another interesting experience of mine soon after joining the Aligarh Muslim University at the pre-university level, the teacher who taught us Islamic history asked me on the first day I attended his lecture what other subjects I had offered for study. On my telling him that philosophy was one of my subjects he sincerely advised, or rather warned me to be very careful lest I slide into disbelief through the study of a subject 'dangerous' to religious faith.

I would also like to share another experience, which is still fresh in my memory. Somebody had read a paper on Islamic history dealing with the first four pious *Caliphs*. The meeting was held in the Philosophy Department shortly after I had joined the AMU. During question time a senior post-graduate student, Noorul Arfin, requested the speaker to throw some light on the differences that had cropped up between the third and the fourth *Caliph*. The Chairman of the meeting disallowed the question on the ground that proper deference to the pious Islamic personalities concerned requires that the faithful remain silent rather than discuss or presume to judge their conduct.

Turning to my own story of mental growth when I was still at the pre-university stage, I can never forget the overpowering impact of a famous work, *The Martyrdom of Man*, by Winwood Reade. A senior friend, Khurshid ul-Islam, who later on became an eminent Urdu critic and poet, recommended the book to me. Reade had mounted a brilliant and powerful attack on conventional theism and religion in general. I went through lucid and powerful passages, which seemed to tear apart the validity of beliefs I held precious and dear. I could not help feeling terrified at what might become of my faith. As and when I came upon some unusually brilliant or powerful argument or presentation I, in all sincerity, prayed to God to protect my Islamic faith lest I be carried away by the sophistry of a brilliant atheist.

When I joined the AMU, the Department of Philosophy was presided over by the venerable and rather forbidding Professor Zafrul Hasan, an Oxonian. He lived in an ivory tower capped by the clouds of Germanic and Islamic wisdom, which occasionally descended as gentle rain on some senior students but never reached lower levels. After he retired Professor M.M. Shareef, a Cantabrian, thoroughly revised the syllabus and brought in fresh air from several quarters.

I was a frequent visitor to Professor Zafrul Hasan's son, Ahmad, who was my classmate. In keeping with Indian tradition I often paid my respects to his father with whom I, as a junior student, had no contact at the university. Though I was diffident in public I was not at all tongue-tied in private one to one conversation. I was keen to seek enlightenment from the famous philosopher. But whenever I sought any enlightenment from him he just nodded and instructed me to read before raising any questions or seeking any discussion. This made me feel rather small and incompetent. The attitude of Professor M.M. Shareef was quite different. He stood just next in seniority and reputation to the Oxford philosopher. Shareef Sahab willingly conversed with me on philosophical themes and answered my questions. He also lent me books from his personal collection. I was, however, too immature to benefit much from his help.

The issues which consistently gripped my mind were proofs for God's existence, the nature of mystical experience, the justification of pain and suffering in a universe created by an all powerful and loving Creator, Darwin's theory of evolution, incompatibility between the freedom of the will and predestination, the philosophical problem of perception, the modern Western rationalistic criticism of traditional Islamic social ethics and the idea of the perfection and infallibility of the Holy Prophet. I am afraid my teachers in the Philosophy Department could not help me much in attaining clarity and intellectual satisfaction.

All through my student days at Aligarh I felt like a traveller condemned to search, in semi darkness, for a path promising to lead me to truth and the portals of a *'peace that passeth all understanding'*. I felt like a lonely traveler despite the presence around me of my elders, teachers, fellow students and the facilities of the University library. I was not, by that time, knowledgeable or mature enough to realize clearly the fact (usually ignored) that all attempts at rational justification of one's religious convictions partake more of defensive rationalization (in the Freudian sense) rather than of pure reasoning or rational thought. Yet, I vaguely sensed this crucial truth in my own case. But I could share my spiritual perplexities with nobody else, including my father (who held liberal views) or with other teachers or students.

To give just one or two instances, I spent sleepless nights over the problem of unmerited suffering and evil in society and nature when the Creator God is omnipotent and all-loving. No explanation worked. I read, I prayed, but all was in vain. My anguish remained, but I had to keep silent. Likewise, I had come to sense that the marriage of the Holy Prophet at a fairly advanced age with a minor girl posed the problem of the sense in which he was perfect, or his actions were infallible. Yet, I dared not share my perplexity with anybody.

Berkeley's theory of 'Subjective Idealism' was another anathema to me. I could never imagine how on earth the existence, as such, of solid things or objects, as distinguished from their perception, depended on their being perceived by some mind. I certainly did believe in God's existence, but I could never appreciate Bishop Berkeley's argument for God's existence. Yet, I was inclined to think that the fault lay with my poor power of reasoning rather than with the reasoning of a great thinker like Berkeley. The point is that there was nobody to guide and encourage a young, ill informed but enquiring mind how to think independently or to practise free enquiry without fear.

A measure of constructive guidance came from the eminent historian, Professor M.Habib, who was an old family friend. His elder brother, Muhammad Wasim, the eminent Lucknow barrister, had been father's close friend at Cambridge. Uncle Habib, as I called him, took great interest in my intellectual development. He advised me that a good path leading to real and solid intellectual growth was to select one great writer and then study every word ever penned by him. As far as I now remember he had suggested the names of Carlyle, John Morely, and H.G. Wells for this purpose. He actually made me read Well's *History of the World*, Nehru's *Glimpses into World History*, and H.A.L. Fisher's *History of Europe*. He also encouraged me to think for myself on all matters. Much later when I had become a teacher I immensely benefited from his critical studies dealing with the authenticity of medieval Indian *Sufi* writings, and his interpretation of the role and character of Mahmud of Ghazni.

The only other teacher (in my circle) who stimulated students to think for themselves was the then, rather young A.A.Suroor who later on became an eminent Urdu critic and a great liberal intellectual among Indian Muslims. He taught us Urdu, which had been my weak point due to my early education in an English school. But, to my misfortune and the fortune of others, Suroor Sahab soon left Aligarh to become Principal of the State College at Rampur. I was, thus, deprived of benefiting from his immense learning and conversational charm. However, I came in close contact with the then, even younger Masud Husain (later to become Vice-Chancellor, *Jamia Millia Islamia*, Delhi) who was a research scholar in Urdu. Despite being much older and senior to me he treated me as an equal and our long intellectual chats fostered my mental growth.

Another person, whom I must not fail to mention here is (late) Noorul Arfin, who was a senior post-graduate student of History when I joined the Aligarh Muslim University. He later on became an eminent lawyer and famous judge in Pakistan. He greatly encouraged me to travel on the road of independent thinking and free enquiry. Arfin and some other liberal minded senior students had formed a *Speakers and Writer's Club*, which I regularly attended. Participation in debates and discussions at this forum greatly helped in my mental and spiritual growth. I recall with genuine pride and humility that I had the courage to express at this forum my honest disagreement with the two-nation theory the Muslim League had put forward in its campaign for Pakistan.

The general intellectual climate at the AMU did not encourage the young to think independently or to cultivate the spirit of free enquiry. Classroom lectures were not supplemented by intensive seminars or discussion. There was no question of any student voicing any doubt or dissenting opinion on sensitive issues of faith. The tutorial system of Oxford and Cambridge was, no doubt, technically practiced at the Aligarh Muslim University. But the spirit of the system was absent for two reasons.

First, the tutorial class, though much smaller than the normal lecture classes was far from being (as at Cambridge and Oxford) a one to one 'Socratic' type of discussion or interaction lasting an hour between teacher and pupil. Second, the teachers at Aligarh read and corrected the essays brought by students in the class itself instead of doing this job prior to the tutorial period as such. At Cambridge students submit their essays a couple of days ahead of the due date and the tutor carefully evaluates the essay and subsequently discusses it with the student. There is an informed consensus that such small and informal discussions are for more educative and stimulating than formal lectures. Most important of all, the elders and teachers, at least in my youth, did not have or show sufficient respect and empathy for their students. The young people were afraid to think for themselves and were also afraid to unburden themselves of perplexities or queries arising in their minds. Moreover, since Indian teachers in general do not treat undergraduate students as more or less equals, teacher's here hardly care to initiate junior students into the proper methods or techniques of study (such as preparation of notes, making index cards etc.). I submit the scientific method of study, at different levels of education should be an integral part of the syllabus.

My undergraduate years at Aligarh from 1943 to 1947 were years of trying isolation from the mainstream thinking at the Aligarh Muslim University. As is well known, this was the heyday of the demand and struggle for the partition of the country. A handful of students, led by my brother, Raveend, gallantly but vainly tried to rebut the arguments and basic approach of the Muslim League. But the Aligarh community, hypnotized, as it were, by the personality of the '*Quaide Azam*' (Supreme Leader) and the sentimental talk of a Muslim homeland (rather foolish and suicidal for the Muslims of Uttar Pradesh, Bihar and other Muslim minority states in undivided India) barely listened to the sane advice of the liberal humanist leaders, Muslim or Hindu.

I was myself not politically active, though I also openly opposed the idea of Pakistan based on the two-nation theory. It was painful for a handful of nationalist Muslims to be dubbed as traitors to Islam and the lackeys of the 'Hindu Congress'. These students were hooted and threatened and at times were also socially boycotted by the more ardent champions of Pakistan.

The overwhelming majority among the Aligarh Muslim University community had been politically seduced by the slogan of Pakistan, as is well known. However a microscopic minority had stood firm in their sincere convictions in the realm of politics, which they kept quite apart from their religion. This small section included my younger brother, Raveend, and some others. I must mention, in particular, Ziaul Hasan (nephew of the renowned divine and freedom fighter, Maulana Husain Ahmad Madni), Jameel Siddiqui, and Usman Adhami. They took the bold initiative of organizing the small number of Congress minded or 'nationalist' Muslim students for doing active election work on behalf of the Congress in the crucial pre-independence general elections for the state Assemblies and the Central Assembly at Delhi. Dr. Hashim Kidwai, a well-known student leader at Lucknow University, had recently joined the Aligarh Muslim University as a temporary lecturer in the Department of History and Politics. He acted as a link between the Aligarh students and the Congress leadership at Lucknow.

As the general elections approached it became necessary to prepare a directory of names and addresses of the activists and sympathizers of the Congress or other allied parties. A classmate of Raveend offered his services for this task, and Raveend handed over all the information he already had and asked his friend to complete the task at hand. A few days later it turned out that the new enthusiastic Congress activist was a spy sent by the AMU branch of the Muslim League to gather inside information from the 'enemy' camp. After this disclosure Raveend and I accused the student concerned of having played a dirty trick against unsuspecting friends and fellow students. He strongly justified his behavior as 'espionage' for a public cause, not for any personal gains. The student later on became a senior and well-respected teacher at the Aligarh Muslim University and won a reputation for his integrity.

The campaign for Pakistan reached its peak in 1946. The handful of 'nationalist' students were subjected to increasing pressure and ridicule. I recall, more with amusement than bitterness, the times when the more militant among the champions of the Pakistan movement abused us right in our faces as 'Congress dogs' or as 'slaves of the Hindus'. At times when we crossed each other at a public place, usually the railway station of Aligarh, and a dog happened to be sitting or strolling on the platform they would spit as they uttered, 'Congress dog'.

Eventually Raveend became a target of official resentment in a more serious sense. As a student leader unwilling to give up allegedly, disruptive anti-Muslim activities right inside the 'arsenal' of the Pakistan movement, Raveend was expelled from the Aligarh Muslim University on some flimsy charge of having organized a strike against the University authorities. I do not remember with sufficient accuracy the details of the charge, but Raveend is thinking of mentioning the details in his memoirs. Raveend migrated to Allahabad University and lost one full academic year in the process. There he became a student leader and office bearer of the Students Union.

THE RETURN OF RAJA MAHENDRA PRATAP

Mahendra Pratap (d. 1979) was the legendary patriot and freedom fighter who had gone into voluntary exile in Afghanistan, Japan and other countries. He was a roving fighter for freedom of the country from British rule and had his own ideas and followed his own methods in politics, religion and economics. He was father's schoolmate at Aligarh during the times of Sir Syed and there were close ties between our families. When Nehru formed the provisional government at Delhi in 1946 the Raja returned home to a hero's welcome wherever he went. I was present with my father at the grand reception given him at Aligarh. Gandhiji and Nehru associated themselves with the public sentiment, though I guess they were not very comfortable with the unconventional stance of the famous revolutionary.

As a sincere and passionate humanist who believed in the oneness of the human family, the Raja had no reservations whatsoever on the choice of a suitable groom for his daughter, Bhakti. She was a mere child when her father had gone into a long exile and was now of marriageable age. Not at all perturbed by the raging fever of Hindu-Muslim antagonism in the sphere of politics, the Raja inserted a matrimonial ad in an Indian national daily (probably *The Hindustan Times*) inviting an alliance irrespective of religion, caste or creed. In 1946 this was quite a radical stand for a father who was an Indian prince. The ad led to a flutter but no alliance.

More than ten years after his return the Raja was elected as an independent candidate to the *Lok Sabha* from Mathura. Too much of an individualist, he was extremely loving and generous. An ardent prophet of world federation and the universal *Religion of Love*, the Raja remained honestly critical of the Congress under Nehru's leadership.

MUHAMMAD ALI JINNAH AT THE AMU

I vividly remember Muhammad Ali Jinnah's visits to the AMU. I had first seen and heard the 'supreme leader' at the plenary session of the Muslim League at Allahabad in 1941. The once great 'Muslim Gokhle', now turned into the foremost champion of a separate homeland for Muslims, Pakistan, was far from being a hero to me: a youth brought up to revere Gandhi, Nehru, and Azad *et al*. Nevertheless, a good opportunity arose for me to see and hear Jinnah Sahab at Allahabad. Around 1937 Barrister Muhammad Wasim of Lucknow had become a powerful pillar of the resurgent Muslim League under Jinnah and Liaquat Ali Khan. This, however, had made no difference to the warmth and sincerity between him and my father. Uncle Wasim intimated to father that he would be his guest at Allahabad during the 1941 plenary session of the Muslim League. This was the first session after the fateful Lahore session of 1940 where the League had passed the famous Pakistan resolution. The views of my father and Uncle Wasim were sharply divergent, but he just informed his dear friend that he would put up with him during his stay at Allahabad. And my father gladly played the host. When I asked Uncle Wasim if he could take me to the session he gladly agreed, even welcomed the idea. And this is how I first saw and heard, at very close quarters, the great leader of the League, once a great leader of the Congress.

Later I heard Jinnah speak several times at the Aligarh Muslim University. I was struck by his magnetic personality, and even more so, by his magnetic voice that compelled attention and respect. His extraordinary voice still rings in my ears though I never came under its spell, even in the hey-day of the two-nation theory that I have always held as the height of absurdity and folly. Here I must recount an argument to support partition, reportedly, advanced by Jinnah. The argument was doing the rounds at Aligarh and several Muslim circles elsewhere during my student days at Aligarh.

The *Quaid's* reported argument was based on the analogy of a ship caught in a violent storm when the lives of only some but not all passengers could possibly be saved with the help of the available lifeboats. The conclusion was that it is better that some lives be saved rather than all be lost. Those who could be saved were the Muslims belonging to the Muslim majority provinces or states, and the Muslims in the rest of the country (amounting to almost 45% of the total Muslim population) should, therefore, willingly sacrifice themselves for the good of the majority of their co-religionists. The analogy and the argument were both fallacious, but most unfortunately, the urban Muslims even in Uttar Pradesh, Bihar and elsewhere were politically seduced by religious pedagogy.

During this crucial period I often heard from father that the idea of Pakistan conceived as the largest sovereign Muslim state in the world, would, automatically, give birth to the idea of India as a Hindu state. My father used to say that whatever Indian Muslims may say about Jinnah being their greatest benefactor, as the prospective founder of the largest Muslim state in the world, the establishment of Pakistan will also make him the greatest benefactor of narrow Hindu communalism. My father used to warn Muslims both privately and publicly that Muslims in the Hindu majority provinces would have to pay a heavy price, in 'installments' for supporting partition. All the prominent Muslim leaders in the Congress and allied parties were unanimous on this score. But partition came all the same.

Here I cannot resist mentioning an anecdote recently reported to me by an Aligarh Congressman, Babu Abdul Rasheed, though I cannot vouch for the accuracy of the report. My informant related to me several years after 1947 a strange true story. A local Hindu friend of his with RSS (Rashtriya Swayamsevak Sangh) views had hung in his house a picture of Jinnah alongside those of Savarkar, and Golwalkar *et al.* One day Rasheed, in all good faith, told his friend that he was much puzzled to see Jinnah's picture alongside those of the RSS giants in the house. His friend replied that without Jinnah's contribution all the efforts of the Hindu heroes would have been in vain. I was so struck by this report that I asked my informant, Rasheed, if he could take me to the house of his friend. Rasheed replied that his friend had died several years ago and his family members had completely changed the decor of the house and the room in question.

Before concluding this section I would also like to refer to Bahadur Yar Jung of Hyderabad who had come to be known as *'Quaide Millat'*. He also used to visit and address the students of the Aligarh Muslim University. Famed for his Urdu oratory he was the leading light of Islamic politics in Hyderabad. His untimely death a year or two before 1947 brought to the centre stage, Qasim Razvi, whose irresponsible pedagogy eventually brought about the fall of the Nizam in 1948.

As an immature student I could not help being fascinated by the oratory of the *Quaide Millat* and his passionate commitment to Islam as a complete guide to life. I was, however, hardly aware of the full implications and nuances of his Islamic vision of politics. These came to my knowledge only recently after reading a scholarly and incisive article on the fall of Nizam's Hyderabad written by the internationally renowned Islamist, Cantwell Smith. Smith points out that the *Quaide Millat* seriously held as late as 1946 that the non-Muslim subjects of the Nizam's state (constituting more than 90% of the total state population) would be treated as *zimmis* (protected non-Muslim subjects in an Islamic state) rather than as equal citizens of a modern democratic state. The great Islamic leader honestly believed that the life, honor and property of the protected Hindu subjects of an Islamic state would be fully guaranteed. Hence, the venerable ideologue of an Islamic Hyderabad could not understand why Narasinha Rao and other Hindu leaders in Hyderabad felt scared about their fate in an independent and sovereign Hyderabad. Well, in retrospect I feel shocked and pained that an eminent Muslim leader could have been so out of tune with the democratic temper of the age.

This atmosphere of rejection and ridicule, however, gave me, and others in the same position, the inner strength and courage to be in a minority, or even stand alone, in the literal sense. We learnt how to resist the pressure to conform to majority dictates. The years of frustration became a school for spiritual growth. When at last freedom came it came under the dark shadow of the partition of the country and the disintegration of millions of homes and hearths on both sides of the border.

The advent of the Zakir Husain era in 1948 in the history of the Aligarh Muslim University marks a turning point. A true teacher and educationist, he did the utmost to raise standards and improve methods of teaching and research. He encouraged independent thinking and free enquiry and stood for large-hearted tolerance. He held that the old maxim that the young respect the elders and the elders shower affection upon the young was only a half-truth. Zakir Sahab often remarked that the elders must also learn to respect the individuality and autonomy of the young. He also often voiced his conviction that providing proper education to youth was the most crucial duty of the state. In retrospect, I cannot help lamenting that neither the Indian Muslims nor the Indian state paid sufficient heed to these basic truths.

Shortly after Zakir Sahab became Vice Chancellor of the Aligarh Muslim University, I left for Cambridge for further study in Philosophy. I was twenty-one and was thirsting to study and think independently and reach inner conviction and peace of mind in an atmosphere of free enquiry without any fear. I had grown sick of the defensive thinking that prevailed even in well-educated Muslim society in India. I was deeply committed to my Islamic faith, but I was intellectually puzzled and confused, and afraid of inner freedom, as defined by Erich Fromm. Cambridge was to give me both courage and clarity.

Here I recall Dr. Syed Mahmud's loving role in encouraging and also helping me to go to Cambridge where his youngest son, Sayeed, had already gone to study Physics. Both my father and my maternal grandfather had graduated from *Christ's College, University of Cambridge*. My father was naturally interested in my going up to 'the' place. But at that time the family finances were a hindrance. Uncle Mahmud, as we all called the well-known Congress personality, was a very close and old friend of father, and persuaded him not to hesitate in this regard. My father took the plunge and never looked back.

Before reaching Cambridge I had a rather tense but instructive experience I shall never forget. Our steamer 'Jal Azad', anchored for three or four hours in the night at the small port of Suez in Egypt. The passengers, mostly Indian students, were allowed to go sight-seeing or shopping at the mainland for a few hours. Return tickets for the motorboat trip were issued to us. Due to some misunderstanding the motorboat, on its return trip, left before the announced time. I found myself all alone, in the dead of night, stranded at the mainland, frantically seeking help to reach the steamer before its departure time. I found only three or four Egyptians roaming at the harbor site, and we could not communicate due to the language barrier. The scheduled departure time of the ship was perilously near, and I was at my wit's end. Somehow I managed to explain and a local motorboat carried me back to the steamer against a heavy charge. This episode made me realize, deep at the emotional level, the falsity of equating religious faith with nationhood. The crucial role of language and culture counts no less than religion. My thoughts flashed back to the blunder and tragedy of the partition of India.

CHAPTER 3

CAMBRIDGE: FREE ENQUIRY

MY NEW ALMA MATER

At Cambridge my avowed objective was Socratic free enquiry and, at the conscious level at least, I was prepared to follow the argument no matter where it may lead, despite the fact that I continued to remain a practicing Muslim, whose concrete content of faith was shaped under the combined influence of Sir Syed, Amir Ali, and Maulana Azad *et al*. I was already familiar with Freud's concept of defensive thinking and rationalization and was keen to avoid intellectual self-deception. In other words, my roots were in the domain of faith, while my aspirations beckoned me to the domain of pure reason. Above all, I yearned to be honest to myself.

As stated already, my prime inner perplexity was how to reconcile the vast extent of human pain and suffering (prima facie quite sporadic and unmerited) with my traditional faith that an almighty and loving God was the Creator and Sustainer of the universe. Suffering as a punishment for evil deeds was quite understandable as a natural or logical recompense as well as a means of education or reform of the evil doer. But this could not justify the suffering of children and also of morally good or virtuous persons in the case of gruesome accidents, diseases, natural calamities, crimes, etc. The difficulty could be removed if we were to qualify our initial belief in the innocence or goodness of the children or the adults concerned. But this appeared stretching the argument too far just in order to support or defend one's faith, and this procedure had little appeal for me, once I had started on the path of reasoned free enquiry. It was in this frame of mind that I had arrived at Cambridge. The problem continued to haunt me, but I persisted in patient reflection and analysis, helped by my Cambridge teachers and the wealth of books recommended by them.

Let me give a few concrete illustrations of the lines of analysis contained in the oral discussions and books in this context. One line was that God 'tested' the faith of the individual through subjecting him to pain and suffering. Immediately I was led to ask why should an all-knowing God have to test His creation? Another line of argument was that, through suffering, God educated or developed human character. But why should an all-powerful Creator use such a tortuous and painful method? Yet another line of thinking for justifying human suffering was that, through the suffering of children or innocent adults, God vicariously punished those who were really guilty. But why should a just and all loving God 'use' innocent beings for the good of society? The above pattern of arguments led me nowhere and I found myself stuck in a dark tunnel of confusion and perplexity. In the free atmosphere of Cambridge I found myself attracted to the Hindu concept of '*karma*' and rebirth as an alternative and, prima facie, a more satisfactory explanation of the phenomenon of human and animal suffering in a universe created and presided over by God. This point needs a little elaboration.

The 'problem' of unmerited suffering has its genesis in our inner conviction that innocent and good people should not suffer in a universe created by an all loving, all just and all powerful God, while the doers of evil may well be punished. Thus, the suffering of children whom we deem to be innocent or the suffering of the virtuous adults lands us into existential perplexity regarding our notions of Divine love and providence. If, however, the innocent child or the virtuous adult does not have one single life but his soul gets incarnated time and again according to his '*karma*' the prima facie unmerited suffering in the present life can consistently and conveniently be viewed as due punishment for wrongs done by the person in some previous incarnation. This postulate or faith is the bedrock of all faiths of Indian origin. It is pertinent to point out here that faiths of Semitic origin also have a common postulate, namely, the Final Day of Reckoning and Judgment. This postulate also greatly helps in resolving the inherent riddles and paradoxes of Divine love and justice when one dispassionately and impersonally reviews the human situation as a whole. The point, however, is that both the existential beliefs or postulates are, in essence, culturally conditioned, and that there is no way to confirm their truth, through reasoning, once a person, for some reason or other, falls into the state of 'existential' doubt or uncertainty. It was quite plain and evident to me that the arguments commonly cited to show or prove the phenomena of rebirth were far from being conclusive. In any case, the concept or postulate of '*karma*', in the Hindu sense of repeated rebirths and deaths, until the final release from a protracted cycle was not a, strictly, universal conviction, like the conviction of an underlying Supreme Power/Unifying Principle behind the flux of all that exists and happens. Even 'atheists' universally hold this latter conviction, in some sense or other.

I concentrated on widening my intellectual and cultural horizons, which, I discovered to my dismay, were far more parochial and limited than I ever could have suspected. The parameters of Western thought I was familiar with were limited to the study of Kant, Hegel, Bradley and Russell. I had also greatly benefited from Broad before joining Cambridge and was eager to attend his lectures at Cambridge. He was also my official supervisor. At my first meeting with him at Trinity College he asked me to write an essay on any subject of my choice and to leave it in his college mailbox a few days prior to our next meeting date.

The next meeting remains virginally fresh in my memory. A great world famous thinker had carefully gone through and made written comments on a student's essay running into fifteen or twenty hand written notebook pages. The subject was '*The Freedom of the Will*'. I had done my best and I believed that my language was very clear and precise. However, Broad's powerful and sharp mind made me realize the utter folly of my belief. What I had supposed to be transparently clear now began to appear to me as capable of several possible interpretations that Broad proceeded to spell out, one by one, in his even, measured but rather halting manner. This was Broad's typical philosophical behavior. When listening to my talk or reading some word or expression I used he quietly interrupted me and with disarming innocence asked me to explain the exact sense I had in mind, and I was hard pressed to do so. Later on I learnt that Broad never rejected or dismissed even the most absurd view or theory without first coolly and respectfully analyzing all its implications.

In other words I was just blissfully unaware of the spectrum of meanings hidden in ordinary words or philosophical theories. I, therefore, decided to focus all my studies on Broad's method of rigorous analysis of philosophical term and theories far more exactly than I had ever done before. Broad's famous pupil, John Wisdom, had done precisely the same in his early phase (before Wittgenstein entered his life) in his early work, *Problems of Mind and Matter*.

Broad who was an extremely cautious and balanced thinker also powerfully influenced my thinking in another way. He impressed upon me the philosophical significance of authentic psychic phenomena. He strongly disapproved of the tendency in 'hard' scientific circles to dismiss reports of spiritual or paranormal occurrences as sheer superstition, delusion or fraud. Sidgwick and Myers, before him, had already founded in Cambridge the famous *Society for Psychical Research* for the systematic and scientific study of such phenomena. Broad ably carried forward this work. He pointed out that hard-boiled skeptics fall into dogmatism when from some proved instances of the fraud or deception of mediums and spiritualists they generalize about all psychic phenomena, as such. Broad affirmed that critical enquiry consisted of two distinct tasks, one exploring the authenticity of the paranormal events or occurrences, and two, arriving at their valid religious or philosophical explanation or theory. To reject the very possibility of such phenomena, on the ground that they violated scientific theories or postulates of the present day was a case of reverse dogmatism. This amounted to an *a priori* denial of the complexity of the universe and to a one-dimensional approach to Reality. Likewise, to accept that some reported or investigated cases were authentic does not amount to proving the truth of any particular religious or philosophical belief or beliefs.

The new wave in the realm of Philosophy

Not very long after my first exposure to Cambridge philosophy I found that the famous trinity of Cambridge Philosophical Analysts: Moore, Russell and Broad had become rather dated and sterile and that the philosophical landscape in Cambridge had been totally transformed. New issues and problems, or new ways of dealing with old philosophical issues had come to occupy the centre stage of philosophy. The author of this radical change was Ludwig Wittgenstein, of Austrian origin, who much earlier had been a pupil of Bertrand Russell and Moore. The new approach to philosophy consisted of intensive linguistic analysis of ordinary language, and this analysis was used as a tool for clarifying technical concepts or theories of philosophy. This type of analysis was very different from the analytical method of Moore, Russell and Broad.

Wittgenstein had fathered this new approach in his second phase of philosophical activity at Cambridge in the middle thirties. In his first phase in the twenties of the 20th century he had authored *Tractatus Logico-Philosophicus*, which had declared all metaphysical talk or theories as 'nonsense'. He had qualified his position in the second phase and it was the later Wittgenstein who had become the father figure of the new Ox-Cam philosophy after the Second World War.

The method of this philosophy was creatively developed in the late thirties and the early forties by John Wisdom of Cambridge and Gilbert Ryle of Oxford. This method led to the revolutionary conclusion that classical philosophical theories were alternative ways of defining basic concepts, and further, that every definition or theory was illuminating or misleading in its own way. The implication was that the proper method of doing philosophy was not to attempt to prove any philosophical theory as either true or false, but rather to show in what way or ways each theory drew attention or laid stress upon some feature or aspect of a highly complex states of affairs. The proper approach, therefore, was to 'dissolve' philosophical issues or controversies rather than a futile attempt to solve them in the classical mode of analysis and unverifiable speculation. This approach led to results, in some respects, similar to the Logical Positivist rejection of Metaphysics. However, the mature and developed form of linguistic analysis in the manner of Wittgenstein, and John Wisdom *et al* was essentially different from the summary and total elimination of Metaphysics as 'nonsense'. In fact, it stood, relatively, nearer the ancient Socratic dialectic, or the Indian Jaina doctrine *Siyadvada*.

Having studied Western Philosophy in India in the classical mode (as a systematic exposition and evaluation of alternative and exclusive theories in the areas of Metaphysics, Epistemology, Ethics etc.) I was totally at sea in the new philosophical climate at Cambridge. By the time I reached there Wittgenstein had resigned his post due to the onset of cancer and permanently shifted to Oxford. He died there in 1950. Listening to the lectures of John Wisdom who had acquired world fame, next only to Wittgenstein himself, and reading his extremely terse and closely argued articles helped me greatly to enter gradually into the spirit of the Copernican revolution in philosophy. I also had the privilege of several hour-long tutorial sessions with Professor Wisdom, the resident *'Guru'* of the new movement. He was extremely considerate to me. However, my intellectual growth was a slow, halting and rather difficult process and this almost crippled my ability to put my own, as yet, nebulous thoughts and views in writing.

The new approach to philosophy had a corrosive effect upon my religious convictions which, liberal as they were, presupposed that religious and ethical truth claims, if valid at all, were objective truths, even if they could not be proved logically or empirically. I was still standing at the threshold of the new approach to philosophy and I clung to the classical epistemological approach that judgments were either subjective or objective and that the expressions, 'subjective judgment' and 'objective judgment' had a fixed determinate meaning. I was unaware that, under the impact of modern science and the collapse of traditional Christian value system after the first world war an 'existentialist' revolution had taken place in philosophy, chiefly in France and Germany, in addition to the 'linguistic' which was, primarily, a British contribution to contemporary philosophy.

There was yet another difficulty I encountered in my quest for certainty and truth relating to the riddle of unmerited human suffering. The philosophical atmosphere at Cambridge was gradually drilling into me a philosophical faith in the crucial importance of following the correct philosophical method in one's quest for truth. The essence of the Cambridge approach was first, to seek the maximum possible conceptual clarity in what one purported to hold or believe, and next, to ask the person making a particular truth claim to spell out the proper method of verifying or establishing the truth or 'validity' of the said claim. Now when I attempted to apply this method to the '*karma*' theory or belief I got stuck in confusion. It was difficult, if not impossible, to make out what, exactly, was meant when it was said that a congenitally deformed male patient was, a fresh incarnation of a ravishing princess who was punished for her haughty behavior towards others. The inherent lack of clarity increased sharply when one tried to analyze the belief that a scorpion or ant that I perceived was, in a previous incarnation, a horse or a philosopher. The idea or notion of punishment as well as of reward was also far from being clear when rebirth took the form of the metamorphosis of one species into another. Neither the concept of '*karma*' in this sense was clear, nor the hypothesis of ' *karma*' could be verified.

My inner spiritual and intellectual struggles finally made me realize that religious faith was not the subject matter of logical proof or scientific certainty, but that it was a matter of cultural conditioning. The latter, however, could, and in some cases, did evolve into existential certainty and authentic commitment. Though the concept of '*karma*' attracted me, it never became for me an irresistible 'whisper of the soul'. In the final analysis I found myself pushed into the arms of the Theology of Mystery and a philosophical humanistic version of liberal Islam.

INFLUENCE OF I.T. RAMSEY

Another source of my philosophical and religious conflicts and perplexity was the influence of another Cambridge teacher, I.T. Ramsey. He was my tutor and later became Professor of the Philosophy of Christian Religion at Oxford and Bishop of Durham. More important and significant is the fact that he was an extremely noble and loving person. My close contact with him gradually led me to question some of the beliefs and attitudes that were a part of my conventional Islamic upbringing. For instance, the belief that eating pork or taking alcohol leads to moral degradation. Here was a man who was extremely learned, had a very sharp intellect and logical mind but he held sincere beliefs quite different from mine. Likewise, he took pork and alcohol, but he remained remarkably honest and compassionate.

Not only Professor Ramsey, but numerous students and others regularly took pork and alcohol, had sex attitudes and morals vastly different from the Islamic, and yet they were admirably honest, responsible and dutiful persons. They were so honest that the Seminar library of the Department of Philosophy functioned effectively without the services of an issue clerk. Students borrowed books for studying at home simply by entering the relevant details in the issue register placed near the exit. When they returned books they made the proper entry on the same page. There were no losses or thefts, or, if there were any, they were so negligible that it hardly mattered.

Yet another matter, which began to intrigue me, was the realization that performing the five Islamic obligatory prayers in the prescribed collective manner, inevitably, hampered normal working activities in several parts of the globe. For example, in Cambridge itself during the winter months the days were so short (due to the early setting of the sun) that three of the five daily obligatory prayers had to be squeezed in the space of two and a half hours. In summer the nights were so short due to the very early rising and late setting of the sun that the gap between the last night prayer and the dawn prayer next day was a mere four hours.

I gradually began to realize that many of my beliefs and attitudes, as a Muslim, were what they were, not because they were demonstrable or self-evident, or 'natural' in the strict sense (as I had been taught) but that I cherished them because of cultural conditioning. A good Christian or Hindu was in the same position. The difference between me and a typical conventional Muslim was that I had honestly internalized the Islamic ethos, while the majority of believers were given to only external discipline. Though I never rejected the core of my Islamic faith, it got transformed into an 'existential commitment' to Islamic basics, rather than to the entire gamut of Islamic belief and practice, just as Ramsey's Christian faith was an existential commitment to Christian basics.

In his great novel, *Of Human Bondage*, Somerset Maugham tells how the hero, as a young man, one day suddenly awoke to the realization that his Christian convictions were, in the final analysis, derived from his childhood training, and this insight had a profound impact on him for the rest of his life. Maugham also refers to the paradox that arises when bad things happen to good people, in other words, the religious difficulty of reconciling unmerited pain and suffering with belief in an all powerful and all loving Creator. Dostoyevsky has raised this problem in the most powerful and poignant manner in his great novels, especially the masterpiece, *Brothers Karamazov*. I was to read these novels much later on. But my mindset and basic approach to religion had crystallized in this period.

From Cambridge to Munster, Germany

From Cambridge I proceeded to Munster University, Germany, after obtaining my Honors degree in the 2.2 grade. This was not much of an academic achievement. However, I felt I had not done badly, since I had a lot to unlearn, by way of the uncritical philosophical methodology I had earlier acquired. I had first to be awakened from my own 'dogmatic slumbers' even as each one of us has to go through a 'shaking of the foundations'. No less an authority than Bertrand Russell has observed that students who had not previously studied Aristotelian logic learnt Mathematical logic faster than those who had, precisely because the latter had first to unlearn many wrong unconscious assumptions deeply embedded in their mind.

My mentor at Munster University was Professor J.Ritter. He was well known in academic circles of the continent and also abroad, though he was not as famous as Heidegger or Jaspers. During my year long stay at Munster my main purpose was to learn the German language and get familiar with continental philosophy. In those days very little of the original French and German literature on philosophy had been translated into English. I also studied a lot of general works on history, sociology, psychology and religion though I could not profit from the original writings of the great living German thinkers. My studies at Munster, however, convinced me that linguistic analysis of the Cambridge school was absolutely necessary for philosophy, but that it was not sufficient by itself. Any philosopher who reduced philosophy to any single dimension of philosophical activity fell into a trap even as metaphysicians did who played 'language games' in Wittgenstein's sense without being aware of what they were doing.

My debt to Cambridge is beyond words. It is my *alma mater* in the literal sense. I honestly try to seek truth without fearing where the argument might lead me because of my apprenticeship at Cambridge. It was in Cambridge that I saw through the essential thinness of the self-deception that often goes by the name of firmness in faith. The faithful are required to do the right thing at the right moment, irrespective of their depth beliefs or inner attitudes, or any latent contradictions in them. I maintain that latent contradictions will not rise to the surface of individual awareness if the believer systematically represses them due to some reason or other. For instance, it is quite common to hear pious Muslims criticize marriages where there is a pronounced age difference between the spouses, but they do so without any awareness whatsoever of the full implications of this stand.

I also began to realize the essential weakness of the attempted defense of the weak spots in traditional Muslim political, economic and social institutions, such as the continuance of slavery, gender inequality, failure to grant full equality of human rights etc. Likewise, I was amazed to find conventional Muslims holding that Europeans were bound to be promiscuous and immodest as they consumed pork. I developed a lasting aversion to intellectual dishonesty in its various garbs, the most subtle being religious apologetics, no matter what the religion may be. However, I never became a total skeptic or even an agnostic during an extended period of my questioning of conventional Islam.

The shift in my religious perspective was, in part, also due to my growing interest in comparative religion and mysticism. This made me see three simple but liberating truths. First, that religious faith, be it Islamic or otherwise, can never be proved. Second, that faith is, essentially, culturally conditioned, just like the mother tongue, though faith may also be acquired due to external influence or inner growth. Third, that cultural diversity is the natural condition of the human family, and any form of religious piety that aspired to do away with this cultural plurality did more harm than good to the human family.

The above convictions, at which I arrived, thanks to my apprenticeship at Cambridge, became the pivot of my intellectual and spiritual life. They liberated me from parochialism and ethnocentricity without pushing me into atheism or sheer indifference to religion or spirituality. I, however, continued to be deeply troubled due to my utter inability to find any solution to the problem of pain and suffering in the universe. No attempted solution, including the Indian concept of '*karma*' in previous births of the soul could overcome my perplexity or 'existential opaqueness' on this score.

My association, both at Cambridge and Munster, with several persons who were men of both great ability and integrity but professed different religious beliefs or held different views on secular issues taught me to respect all religions, even atheism. It became transparent to me that the simple goodness of the heart or human decency cut across religious beliefs, that it was the quality of one's inner life and character rather than one's religious label, that was supremely important in human affairs. In other words, excellence of character and inner goodness were not the monopoly of any religion. Indeed, even skeptics and atheists could be good and compassionate human beings.

There were two other basic things I learnt during my Cambridge days: the value of music and of democracy. Father had always valued music and dance despite restrictions placed by orthodox Islam. However, his defence of music was a rather partial and halting apology for *Sufi* or religious music in general. This was a far cry from the high place both Western and Indian thought give to music in the scheme of the good life. Both these traditions hold that music has the power to bring man to almost the ecstasy of mystical experience. The prestige of the Faculty of Music at British and European universities made me read the lives of some of the great Western composers and changed my perspective on matters concerning art in general. However, I never had the opportunity to attend concerts until my visit to Germany.

I experienced democracy in action for the first time in Cambridge when I noticed the extremely kind and courteous behavior of students to the college waiters and other attendants. Likewise, renowned University teachers, no less than the town shopkeepers, office assistants and bank managers all treated the students with utmost courtesy and consideration. What struck me most was the incredible courtesy shown by car drivers to the pedestrian traffic. All this was in sharp contrast to conditions in my own country.

OXFORD AND CAMBRIDGE: SOME GENERAL OBSERVATIONS

Before I conclude this chapter I would like, first, to make a few general observations on Cambridge, and then to share four significant experiences without going into their concrete details.

Cambridge: Free Enquiry

Cambridge is world famous for its College 'backs'. The term 'backs' refers to the extensive lawns, gardens and meadows forming part of the banks of the river 'Cam' running right through the university campus. Great English poets have described the pastoral charm and peace which pervades the lush green meadows decorated by daffodils in the center and weeping willows on the banks of the Cam gracefully flowing down the ages, quite innocent of the contributions made by a Milton, a Newton, or a Darwin inside the colleges of solid brown stone, adjoined by equally solid and artistic bridges of stone across the pensive Cam. The moment one enters into the old colleges one feels transported into the medieval era of castles and meadows. However, the new red brick building of the Central Library on the other side of the Cam serves as a reminder that the age of Newton has now passed over into the age of Einstein. Having had the good fortune of visiting several famous universities like Oxford, Edinburgh, Paris, Heidelberg, and Harvard etc. I would impartially give top marks to my *alma mater* on the score of scenic ambience. However, I am told some university campuses in China and Sri Lanka are even better.

The friendly rivalry between the two oldest and premiere centers of learning and culture in Britain, Oxford and Cambridge is well known. I was, therefore, rather keen on visiting the 'other place' or the 'wrong place' as the Oxonians and Cantabrians refer to each other in jest. In order to judge things for myself I, along with two friends, went on a four-day tour of Oxford and the adjoining Shakespeare country, as it is called. We friends agreed that on the whole the college buildings at Oxford had an edge over the colleges at Cambridge, but there was no equivalent of the river Cam and college backs at Oxford. As for academic excellence, both of my friends (who happened to be studying Economics) never had any doubt of the much greater importance of the Cambridge contribution. I too was convinced that it was the Cambridge thinkers who, under the impact of modern science and Mathematical Logic, had given a creative and immensely influential turn to the modern way of doing philosophy. At this point I cannot resist sharing a popular joke at Cambridge at the expense of Oxford dons.

The Vision of an Unknown Indian Muslim: Part 1

An Oxford don was asked to explain what makes one drunk. He took a drink of whisky and soda and got drunk. Next day he took some brandy and soda and again he got drunk. The third time he mixed gin and soda and got drunk again. The Oxford don was familiar with the Cambridge logician and philosopher, Mill, and his famous logical method of agreement for finding out causal connections. The learned Oxford don promptly applied the method and concluded that since soda was the common factor in all three cases of getting drunk, soda was the cause. So much for Oxford powers of reasoning! The even more amusing part of the joke is that the Oxford version of the same joke locates the learned don in Cambridge.

Shakespeare's birthplace, Stratford upon Avon, is an enchanting little town whose architecture and ambience a thoughtful and grateful nation has preserved for future generations. No high-rise buildings have been permitted to dwarf the modest cottages of the poet's time. However, a memorial theatre attracts millions of visitors from Britain and abroad. Booking of seats is done a year in advance, though a small quota is reserved for spot booking by tourists. This facility leads to the formation of nightlong queues. We had to stand in the queue, by turns, as we were keen to watch the play that was on at the time.

Coming back to Cambridge, the college shower baths were located in a separate annex to the main building. There were no separate cubicles for taking showers in privacy. British students did not mind at all this arrangement. But I, as an Indian felt quite embarrassed to bathe completely in the nude before my college mates. I, therefore, arranged with the bath attendant to have a shower before the official admission time. This seemed to work for some time, but it was rather inconvenient having to rush to the college baths in the very early hours of the morning or at other odd times. The bath attendant felt rather amused and surprised at my oriental notion of shame in the presence of the same sex. I briefly told him that customs differ. However, I soon found myself acting upon the maxim to do in Rome as the Romans do.

My experience inside the college was just the reverse. I had never used a dressing gown in India. However, a good Indian friend of mine who was a year senior to me in Cambridge advised me never to be seen by any lady or even a gentleman without my dressing gown on. To be seen in pajamas or a night suit amounted, in polite society, to being seen in the nude, he warned me. Nudity in the college baths was quite different from moving in one's own room or house without a proper dressing gown, according to British etiquette. However, when I left Cambridge and joined Munster University in Germany I found that nobody cared for the dressing gown inside the hostels or student homes.

An old tradition at Oxford and Cambridge is that students be present at a minimum number of college dinners during their period of stay at the university. No record of attendance at lectures is kept, though students are required to submit weekly or fortnightly essays assigned to them by their college tutors. My last College dinner is still fresh in my memory for a strange reason. But, first, I must mention a few things about the institutional dinners at Oxford and Cambridge universities, which lay great stress upon corporate living and development of character. The teachers or fellows of colleges and the students are required to live and eat together though their level of comforts and of food naturally vary. The fellows sit at the high table on comfortable dining chairs, while the students sit on wooden benches at a lower level. The quality of the food served is also different. Before dinner is served the fellows assemble in the senior common room for drinks and then, at a fixed appointed time, enter the common dining hall in a procession. A student recites the customary Christian prayer before the start of the meal.

Students are permitted to order drinks to be served with dinner and they take turns in ordering them through signing vouchers, as is the standard practice in clubs. I had totally abstained from alcohol for two academic years and my friends had come to respect my Islamic or puritan ways in this regard. At this last college dinner a very good and warm hearted American friend rather surprised me by ordering a drink for me without first asking me. He then, literally, implored me to take it and not break his heart at this last dinner together. Well, after some hesitation I gave in to his pleading as to who knows we would ever meet again and dine together. I tasted a few drops of the drink and started wondering if I would get drunk and start behaving in funny ways on the last day in college. My fear amused my friends. I confess that my breaking one of the Islamic commandments did not produce in me any feelings of guilt. Here I cannot resist relating what, several years later, I came to hear from the venerable savant, Pandit Sundarlal, whom I had revered from my boyhood days.

In the early fifties Prime Minister Nehru asked Pandit Sundarlal to go on a goodwill visit to Nagaland. The Pandit was a true Gandhian radiating love and compassion for all. His hosts were greatly impressed that their distinguished guest freely mingled with them. But the hosts were rather disappointed since they could not offer their choicest items of food to the Pandit who took neither meat nor alcohol. However, on one special occasion the host poured a few drops of the Naga drink on Sundarlalji's cupped palm and he sipped them along with the host. Likewise, the host placed a piece of dried beef on the guest's palm and Panditji tasted the salt left after returning the portion of beef to the host. After relating this incident to me in his characteristically emotional manner Panditji went on to quote the famous line in Persian that winning over the human heart is the greatest *Hajj* or Islamic pilgrimage.

When I was studying in Munster after my graduation from Cambridge some friends belonging to different nationalities thought we would share each other's striking impressions of some foreign culture or society, one may have lived in for some length of time. When my turn came I recounted how strongly I was impressed with the democratic society of Britain. No sooner had I made this remark than a friend who happened to be an Australian burst into laughter. He expressed surprise that I could call a society democratic when one had to tip waiters, hairdressers, taxi drivers, doormen, porters etc. He proudly added if a customer ever dared to tip a waiter in Australia for services rendered in a restaurant the waiter would reprimand the customer for his crude condescending behavior and his delusive air of superior social status. Ever since this conversation I seem to have developed a strange inhibition related to tipping. At times I suffer from an inner conflict whether to tip or not. Much later in the course of my general reading I learnt that Socialist morality also censured tipping as a Capitalist vice. Nevertheless, tipping persisted as a fact in Soviet society like numerous other evils.

Four Significant Experiences and Lessons

A Muslim student from East Pakistan (presently Bangla Desh) lodged in a rather remote part of Cambridge town and had great difficulty in performing his prayers according to the strict timings. He was a deeply religious soul and a person of great integrity, which had much impressed me. He asked me whether he could offer his prayers in my college rooms (which were very centrally located), and I gladly agreed. We soon became good friends. One day he sadly complained that his Muslim compatriots from West Pakistan studying at Cambridge made fun of his religiosity and he was not comfortable in their society. This was more than twenty years before the Bangla Desh war led to the separation of East Pakistan.

Another instance concerns a person who later on became a Nobel Laureate in Physics. I refer to my friend, Dr. Abdus Salam. He was not only extremely brilliant but also a very good human being deeply committed to the Ahmadi version of Islam. I always admired him and deeply sympathized with the mental agony of those who sincerely and honestly claimed to be Muslims but who were unceremoniously declared non-Muslims by the majority establishment. Salam felt very unhappy at the intolerance shown to his community in Pakistan. Experiences like these confirmed for me my liberal Humanism and secular approach to politics. After a long gap of some thirty years I felt very happy and proud when the great physicist was awarded an honorary Doctorate by the AMU at a special convocation.

The universities of Cambridge and Oxford have always been known for their extra-curricular students voluntary associations and clubs. I reluctantly consented to become the President of the *Muslim Society* for one term in my final year. Dr. Fazlur Rahman of Oxford had recently been appointed Lecturer in Islamic Philosophy at Durham University. His book on Ibn Sina's philosophy had already made him well known. I, therefore, invited him to give a talk on the great Muslim savant of the medieval age. Eminent Cambridge scholars such as Professor Arberry and Professor Levi graced the occasion and the meeting was well attended and successful.

Several years later President Ayub of Pakistan asked Dr. Fazlur Rahman to head the newly established *Institute of Islamic Research* at Islamabad. Unfortunately, the author's liberal views, expressed in his excellent scholarly work, *Islam*, led to his severe victimization and eventual expulsion from Pakistan. The University of Chicago, however, offered him a Professorship. The Muslim world has yet to understand that suppression of honest views, whether the suppression be direct or indirect, is the enemy of both truth and faith. Intolerance breeds hypocrisy and sickness of the soul, never authentic faith or goodness.

The third experience took place when I was returning home from Cambridge. It was late 1952 and the 'Lysenko controversy' concerning scientific evidence for the genetic transmission of acquired traits in the species was at its peak. Under orders from the Communist High Command scientific data in Russia was distorted and suppressed to prove the thesis dear to the Party. A Communist sympathizer who was a Pakistani strongly defended the Communist party line even though he agreed that the stand of Lysenko was scientifically wrong. He held that telling lies was justified if it helped Communism. Nothing could be more different from my own commitment to the ethical approach to politics and the separation of both politics and science from religion.

My belief in the ethical approach to politics and to democracy became firmly rooted during my stay in Cambridge, and to date it has remained my spiritual anchor, despite its being under severe attack from many quarters ranging from Marxist intellectuals to conservative Muslims. I have always conceded the limitations of democracy, but pointed out that its alternatives are even worse.

The last experience I would like to share with the reader concerns the perplexity I felt several times whenever I attended Christian churches in search of spiritual enrichment, even though I never subscribed to Christian theology. The music and spirituality of the place of worship was my obvious attraction. Whenever the church people went round to collect monetary contributions from those present at the service I did not know what to do as a believing Muslim. Deep down in me I had some reservations about a Muslim materially helping a faith in some way tarred with 'polytheism'.

The answer came to me in a rather dramatic manner several years later when I saw a beautiful mosque and cultural centre in the heart of the diplomatic enclave of Washington. The builder was a white American Christian. I was astonished and felt somewhat amused at my religious perplexity and immaturity of my days at Cambridge.

The core views that took birth in my Cambridge days, followed by a year at Munster, slowly developed over the years and became articulate enough for publication in two works, *Five Approaches to Philosophy*, 1965, and *Quest For Islam*, 1977. Though a lot of reading and hard thinking on the issues involved was done by me at Aligarh over long years the core of my ideas was shaped at Cambridge and Munster.

Chapter 4
AMU to Lok Sabha: Wider Horizons

My Appointment as Lecturer, Department of Philosophy, AMU

I returned home from Cambridge at the end of 1952. Shortly afterwards I was appointed lecturer in Philosophy at my old university. I was given more recognition than usual, perhaps, because of my prestigious Honors degree from Cambridge and the eminent position of my father in Aligarh Muslim University affairs. However, things were not easy for one who had come to acquire ideas on philosophy and religion very different from the mindset which prevailed here. Basic books on contemporary philosophy were just not available, and there was hardly any possibility of informed dialogue with my teachers, who had great ability but were unaware of recent developments. I was myself still rather new to the philosophy of Wittgenstein and Wisdom and lacked the powers of smooth and easy communication with colleagues and students. I had even greater difficulty putting down on paper my still nebulous thoughts and ideas.

Two or three years after my joining the Aligarh Muslim University as a lecturer in Philosophy I came in contact with some brilliant fellow teachers in other University departments. Most of these teachers had leftist leanings and they all looked up to Professor Abdul Aleem Siddiqui, known as the '*Red Molvi*' while he was at Lucknow University prior to his joining Aligarh. Aleem Sahab, as he was called at Aligarh, was a close friend of Zakir Sahab who had brought him to Aligarh to head the Department of Arabic and Islamic Studies. (Much later on he became Vice-Chancellor himself) I felt greatly drawn to Aleem Sahab despite the charge in some quarters that he was an atheist. I liked his sharp critical mind and his ability to grasp the substance of various points of view at seminars and discussions and sum up the proceedings in a concise and objective manner.

At about the same time I read the famous work, *The God That Failed*, which is, perhaps, one of the most powerful indictments of the Communist movement. Paradoxically, despite intellectually agreeing with the criticism made by the distinguished contributors (who themselves had once been great champions of a broadly Marxist approach to the human situation) I arrived, quite surprisingly to myself, at a different conclusion. I developed a soft corner for the Communist party, despite my inner and firm commitment to Islamic liberalism, the seeds of which had been sown in my student days at Cambridge. The thrust of my apology was that Communist action should not be equated with the truth of Marxism in the broad sense, and that the eminent ex-Communists who had contributed to the book had been too harsh on the human failings of the successors of Lenin. I still vividly recollect how one day I came perilously close to going to Aleem Sahab to take him into confidence about my rising inclination to joining the Communist party. But this did not happen. Perhaps, my fascination for Nehru, my father's fascination for Gandhiji and my partly unresolved inner perplexities were jointly responsible for my inaction.

In the early and middle fifties Indian universities had a rather small teaching staff with a still smaller proportion of Professorships and Readerships. The result was that many well qualified and hard working teachers felt stagnated in their professional careers. Many in this category felt that the existing three tier cadre of lecturer, reader and professor should be replaced by a two tier system of assistant Professors and full Professors, and that there should be a provision for time bound promotion as in the case of civil services. However,

I noticed that as soon as some aspiring colleague got promoted he started defending the present system. Some of my colleagues who had recently benefited from a University Grants Commission scheme of creating additional higher posts began to discover virtues in the present system they had never talked about earlier. This was, perhaps, my first experience of how one's own interests at a particular point of time determine one's perception of right and wrong, and how easily one may advance reasons (convincing to oneself and also to others) in justification of one's shifting interests.

In the course of my long association with the University I came across several other instances of this natural human tendency or failing. I may refer, in passing, to the controversy regarding the proper role of the Pro Vice-Chancellor in his relationship with the Vice-Chancellor. Some of my colleagues resorted to double standards on this matter at different times when different personalities were on the scene. Again, while some teachers who habitually alleged that the Central Government had a soft corner for appointing Communists, Leftists or 'Progressives' as Vice Chancellors of the AMU, turned actively hostile to a distinguished Vice-Chancellor soon after he took office and dubbed him as a *'masjid ka mulla'*. This appellation, obviously, refers to Saiyed Hamid Sahab.

My affectionate teacher and Head of the Department, Professor Umaruddin, a reputable writer on the ethics of Al-Ghazzali, had put me in charge of the Seminar library. The job of selecting new books dealing with recent developments in Philosophical Analysis and Methodology helped in my intellectual growth, as did formal teaching work. I was not satisfied with my performance, but I enjoyed teaching and learning in the process. I honestly believed that my students thought well of their young and rather unconventional teacher.

I was still struggling to become more productive when Jawaharlal Nehru declared at several public places that fresh blood was needed inside the Congress party. Nehru had always been my hero, and he and father had been together at Cambridge. But due to several reasons father stood rather disillusioned and unhappy with the then Congress leadership and its policies. I, however, thought differently. Ideas began to stir in my mind that in addition to the pursuit of philosophy I should also try to 'serve' my people and country. Little did I, then, realize that such ideas and dreams partook more of conceit and ambition to make my mark on society rather than of pure dis-interested concern for a larger social cause.

At the suggestion of a senior relative and friend and without the explicit permission from father I made bold to meet my 'hero' and request him to consider inducting me in the forthcoming second *Lok Sabha*. And lo! My request met with his immediate approval. He, I came to learn later, chose a few others in the 'fresh blood' category for this purpose. Among the four or five so chosen was Dinesh Singh, who, soon afterwards, became a dear friend to me as long as he lived.

Babu Bhagwan Das, the eminent sage and savant of Benares, one of the earliest recipients of *Bharat Ratna* knew our family well. It occurred to me that I should seek his blessings at my entry into politics. I had already read and admired parts of his voluminous book, *The Essential Unity of All Religions*, and thought I must seek the blessings of an outstanding scholar and patriot in addition to Jawaharlalji. I was gratified and delighted when he said he was recommending my case to Sri Govind Vallabh Pant. I knew that Pantji had become rather estranged from my father due to some differences over Uttar Pradesh politics. And Pantji did remain cool towards the idea of my elevation to the *Lok Sabha* at such an early age. Since, however, Nehru had already included my name in the 'new blood category' my name had a smooth sailing in the long and complex process of the final selection of Congress party candidates for the state and central legislatures. I felt no resentment at the honest opposition to my name in several quarters since I was well aware of my political inexperience.

Nehru's idea of inducting fresh blood into the Congress party was announced more or less at the same time when Col. Basheer Husain Zaidi, former Chief Minister of Rampur State, and member of the first *Lok Sabha*, had succeeded Zakir Sahab as Vice-Chancellor of the Aligarh Muslim University. A man of vision and integrity, Zaidi Sahab was democratic in the best sense and took the university forward on all fronts without attempting to 'run' a cultural institution like a government department. Affectionate towards the students, committed to tolerance and Islamic liberalism, he had deep respect for able and devoted teachers, irrespective of their rank. He followed Zakir Sahab in this respect as in several others.

ENTRY IN PARLIAMENT

My double member constituency covered the entire Aligarh district and one of the two seats was reserved for *Dalits*. However, *Dalits* were eligible for election from both the seats. I was almost unknown to my voters. But as the son of a veteran Gandhian and old freedom fighter I won the sympathy and support of the voters. For six weeks I became an automaton who had to address village meetings and gatherings throughout the sprawling constituency according to the strategy of the local party bosses. I learnt a lot about rural India and the ways of politicians in a short period. The election battle was, however, far from being a cakewalk, mainly because the *Dalit* candidate, B.P.Maurya, was a sharp strategist and mass speaker who had chosen to work systematically on caste lines. If a novice like me eventually carried the day, it was due to my father's unsullied reputation and Nehru's blessings. Incredible as it may sound the total expenditure by family and myself was approximately twelve thousand Rupees. When the result was formally declared at the Collectorate, it was midnight. Congress workers and personal friends loudly cheered me and my eyes became moist with tears of joy and gratitude to them all

In mid 1957 I found myself transplanted, as it were, from the Strachey Hall of Aligarh Muslim University to the Central Hall of Parliament. After the elections were over I found myself moving in territory whose topography was almost unknown to me. I recall my first experience when I was surveying on foot the residential houses for MPs available to me in North Avenue. It was a hot day in May and I felt very thirsty. I just knocked at the first house in the row of MP's flats and asked for a glass of water. Somebody from the family gave it to me. Soon afterwards I learnt that the MP belonged to a supposedly 'untouchable' caste. Very soon we became good friends.

I tried to become an avid learner only to discover, with a sense of disappointment, that the responsibilities and rewards of a political career did not really touch my innermost chords. However, I decided to stick on at least for one full term to avoid any possible embarrassment, consequent upon resigning from my seat in the middle of the term. I did not actively participate in the hard political agenda of the House, nor was there much scope for this work for a backbencher from the ruling party. I concentrated on the work of obtaining redress of the just grievances of my constituents at Aligarh and also others. This was a great education for me in understanding men and matters, if not, the abstruse issues of philosophy. Having to write brief but effective representations and personal letters to ministers and high officials was very good education for me, later on, in picking up the art of simple and clear writing.

I also made effective use of the rich collection of books in the library of Parliament. I also sought contacts and eagerly learnt from several eminent personalities who adorned Parliament at that time. I did this purely to learn from them rather than with any ulterior motive of worldly gain or profit. I made no distinction of political affiliation among the prominent people with whom I entered into candid dialogues. They ranged, among others, from Dr. Radhakrishnan, who was, then, Vice President, Dr. Tarachand, Mahavir Tyagi, Hiren Mukerjee, Humayun Kabir, Akbar Ali Khan, Sushila Nayar, Uma Nehru, Morarji Desai, Raja Mahendra Pratap, to the promising young Atal Bihari Vajpayee. I also came in contact, for the first time, with Rafiq Zakaria Sahab, who was then an important intellectual and political liberal in Maharashtra. But his works on Islamic liberalism were yet to be published. To my great misfortune, however, the passing away of the great Maulana Azad in 1958, not much long after the formation of the *Second Lok Sabha*, deprived me of a golden opportunity to draw inspiration through personal contacts with a giant. After all, inspiration through reading the written word is not quite the same as inspiration through a personal relationship.

I was, however, a regular visitor to the house of Dr. Syed Mahmud in my capacity as a virtual member of the family. He was not a member of the government by that time but he was still very close to the Prime Minister and socially prominent in the Congress circle. Once he was 'at home' in honor of a prominent Arab diplomat, Clovis Maqsood. I happened to be sitting next to the host and the chief guest. An important person meeting the Arab dignitary for the first time innocently assumed the Arab to be a Muslim and started lamenting the prejudiced behavior of the Christian West against the Islamic world. This was a *fau pax*, since the chief guest was an Arab Christian, not a Muslim. I find this anecdote both amusing and instructive.

My wife and I, very early in our stay at Delhi, became frequent visitors to the venerable aunt of Jawaharlal, Uma Nehru. Long back in the mid thirties her daughter, a professional lawyer, had contracted a civil marriage with a Muslim police officer hailing from the princely family of Rampur. In those days both the parties to civil marriage were legally required to declare that they did not profess any religion. When the matter was referred to Gandhiji who was a father figure for the Nehru family he did not oppose the inter-religious marriage but insisted that it be solemnized according to both Hindu and Muslim rites, instead of being a civil marriage. The prospective bride and some family friends, however, refused to accept Gandhiji's advice on the ground that this would not constitute a legal union. A civil marriage was then solemnized followed by traditional Muslim and Hindu rites. Soon after independence Parliament removed the declaration of non-belief in any religion as a condition of a valid civil marriage. Some orthodox sections, both Hindu and Muslim, continue to oppose the idea of civil marriage.

Visit to Afghanistan

As is well known India and Afghanistan have had a very close and intimate relationship until very recent times, while there was a lot of antagonism between Pakistan and Afghanistan due to the Pakhtoonistan issue. The Afghan government used to celebrate every year its independence or national day with great fanfare and several friendly countries sent goodwill teams to participate in friendly sports and cultural events during the ten-day long celebrations. The Ministry of External Affairs sent me as leader of the delegation in 1959. India and Pakistan were still at the top of world Hockey and our team (perhaps a C team) was good enough to win comfortably in a friendly match with the top team of the host country. The Indian manager and captain gladly agreed to my suggestion that although we should clearly win our hosts might be spared a crushing defeat, in view of the nature of the occasion. I was quite clear that this was not match fixing in the bad sense.

The Afghan team was the first to score a goal. I was expecting a quick equalizer, but nothing of the sort happened until half time. I grew worried indeed but could do nothing in the presence of our hosts and other diplomats watching the match. In the second half India equalized, but the winner would not come and time was flying past. At long last just a few minutes before the close of play the Indian team won 2-1, to my tremendous relief. At the first opportunity I queried the manager and the captain why our performance was so poor that we were in risk of losing or just drawing the match. Well, they confessed that initially they took the game easy, as suggested, but when they started exerting themselves in right earnest the extra-rich Afghan '*pillao*' served to the team the previous night came in their way and did the mischief!

There were teams from Russia, China and other countries, but Pakistan was conspicuous by its absence. Pakistan used to accuse India of colluding with Afghanistan on the Pakhtoonistan issue, while the Afghan government had the perception that a friendly India was not giving it full support. The fact of the matter was that India was honestly neutral.

The Afghan hosts graciously offered to arrange for my visit to any desired place in the country, but I was short of time. However, I became very friendly with my Afghan interpreter, an officer from the foreign office of the host country. He happened to be the real sister's son of the legendary King Amanullah, who was deposed as monarch in the late twenties or early thirties. In reply to my question what led to the deposition, the young officer replied that though his illustrious uncle was a dedicated and farsighted reformer he was devoid of patience. This remark made me think that patience and democracy go together and that when the passion for quick results leads to diluting democratic means, disaster is the result.

For ten days I had to participate in grand dinners, garden parties and watch numerous games of hockey, tennis etc. However, I also met with several ministers and diplomats. I became friendly with a Deputy Minister who was about my age. While exchanging views on subjects of common interest I mentioned our high birth rate as a major obstacle in our slow development. The Minister innocently remarked that the Indian government should put into jail all those who resist family planning!

There was, however, another side to the picture in the Afghanistan of those days. I was astonished to learn from high official sources that in 1960 lady stenographers received salaries higher than that of their principal officers. When I expressed my surprise over this anomaly I was told that the Afghan government had launched a plan of rapid female education and the excessively high grade being given to women was part of an incentive plan for the said purpose. The irony of the states of affairs in Afghanistan today is tragic, indeed.

There is a clear distinction between modernization and westernization of ancient societies. The Western educated elite in several Muslim countries has always tended to confuse the two. To be modern is not to dress, eat, live and consume industrial products as the Westerners do, but rather to profess and practice free enquiry, tolerance of dissent, and govern with the consent of the governed. Unfortunately, there has been no effective and sustained movement of liberal humanism within Islam. Muslim rulers and ruling classes have adopted indifference to religion in the wake of materialistic consumerism, while Muslim intellectuals have turned either to Communism or to religious fundamentalism. In the sixties Afghanistan was making steady progress on the path to liberal reform under a constitutional monarchy. Unfortunately, the feudal impatience and unbridled ambition of the then Prime Minister, who was closely related to the Monarch himself, led to the strangulation of democracy. This led to a power struggle and eventually triggered a civil war in which the Afghans became the pawns of a prolonged proxy war between the super powers.

In the beginning of the same year, 1960, I had another educative experience when I attended the plenary session of the Congress at Bangalore. It was our first visit to southern India. My wife and I were both thrilled and happy and came back better educated by the great courtesy and consideration shown to us by the people, by their much higher standards of cleanliness and their freedom from cast, pomp and show.

Two Memorable Visits by Foreign Dignitaries

My father in law, Mohammad Akbar, was one of the three senior officers of the undivided British Indian army promoted to the high rank of Major General by the British on the eve of the transfer of power to Indian and Pakistani hands. My father in law hailed from the Jhelum area of undivided Punjab, and, as an army officer, was assigned to the Pakistan army, under statutory provisions of the *Transfer of Power Act*. He and Generals Cariappa and Rajendra Singh were and remained very close friends. Major General Akbar (not to be confused with his namesake, Major General Akbar Khan, of the Rawalpindi Conspiracy fame) was a liberal humanist at heart and an entirely disciplined and apolitical professional soldier. A patriotic Pakistani as he was, he had numerous Indian friends and was also a great admirer of Gandhi and Nehru. He readily accepted the semi-official Indian invitation to join the *Indorite Reunion* organized around 1959 by the Indian army at Delhi at the instance of General Cariappa.

General Cariappa desired his Pakistani friend to stay with him, but my father in law insisted on staying with us at 77, South Avenue. The top brass of the Indian army and the Government extended warm hospitality to the guest. We also gave a grand lunch, which was attended by several top people in the armed forces and the close Indian friends of the Pakistani General. He also had an exclusive meeting with Jawaharlalji. I was deeply moved by the warmth and depth of the affection and mutual shedding of tears by old comrades turned into 'foreigners' through the vagaries of history.

The other memorable visit was that of President Eisenhower, the first ever visit by an American President to India. My wife and I were most pleasantly surprised to be invited to the Prime Minister's lunch in honor of the President. But more memorable, if also slightly amusing, is the fact that while Hamida was being introduced to the President, Jawaharlalji failed to recollect her first name for a good many seconds during which time the President and Hamida continued to hold each other's hand, and a smile played on the PM's face. But the *fau pax*, if any, had a happy ending as the host finally did recollect her first name and husband's name, both of which were needed for a proper introduction.

JAI PRAKASHJI'S ADDRESS TO A JOINT MEETING OF PARLIAMENT MEMBERS

After Jai Prakashji had given up electoral politics and taken to Sarvoday work he was asked to address a joint meeting of the two Houses in the Central Hall. To the best of my memory the Sarvoday leader had recently returned from a European tour in which he had expounded his ideas of party-less democracy. Though his approach did not find favor with Nehru, Jai Prakashji continued to command great respect in all quarters for his dedication to the country and his integrity. The younger Gandhian wanted the government to lay greater stress on removal or reducing of corruption in the fast growing economy in a developing democratic society. But the government had adopted a relatively pragmatic approach to the issue, even though Nehru himself had remained the model of probity and integrity in the midst of all his tremendous prestige and power as a towering world figure. Indiraji carried this pragmatic approach much too far. This, among other factors, prompted the inner voice of her father's once trusted colleague and a giant of the Indian freedom struggle to put forward the rather confused idea of 'total revolution'. The remedy proved to be worse than the disease. I shall say more on this theme later on.

AKBARBHAI CHAVDA

Akbarbhai Chavda Sahab was a two time Congress member of the *Lok Sabha* from Gujrat. A Muslim by religion, he dressed exactly like Gandhiji, his political mentor and spiritual guide. Akbarbhai lived in the servants' quarters of the houses meant for Members of Parliament. He thought the servant's quarters were decent enough for the simple needs of a Gandhian social worker like him.

Akbar Sahab also told me that it was Gandhi who had encouraged him to take Islam more seriously than he, on his own, was inclined, and to read the Quran in the original. On Akbarbhai's telling Gandhiji that he was rather attracted to the higher version of Hinduism followed by Gandhiji himself, his mentor pointed out that there was no need for anybody, whatever his or her religion, to convert to some other religion. All that was required was the willingness to give up whatever violated one's depth conscience and to accept whatever accorded with it after an honest and 'prayerful' submission to the God within every soul.

Here I must point out that Akbarbhai Sahab was the lone exception among the several hundred members of Parliament to live by choice in humble conditions. The general pattern was entirely different. Just behind the apartments for MP's there were rows of garages and servant quarters, which were available to MPs at a small rental in addition to the normal rent of the apartments. A large number of MPs took the garages/servant's quarters on rent and then sub-let them to whomsoever they desired. Some MP's did the same with even their own apartments.

Some time after Maulana Azad's sudden death in 1958 Nehru circulated a letter among all the members of the Congress Parliamentary Party expressing his sense of having become stale and gone out of steam and being in need of temporary withdrawal from the burden of high office for the greater good of the party and the country. I could not resist calling on the Prime Minister the very next morning to express my profound anguish at the way he felt. At the breakfast table he radiated his characteristic charm but he looked tired and pensive. He just listened to an ardent pupil pleading with the master, as it were, not to take to heart the obstacles created by some in the party. However, after he left Indiraji took me into confidence. With eyes moist with innocent and sincere tears she remarked that some quarters in the party were of the view that Gandhiji had foisted on the party a favorite who had done nothing on his own to be Prime Minister. She further added that she would rather have '*Papu*' resign than function ineffectively. I strongly controverted her stand on the ground that opposition in some quarters should be ignored when the party and the people, as a whole, were solidly behind the leader.

A day or two afterwards an urgent party meeting was held. Every speaker strongly rejected the proposed or contemplated step and suggested steps for rejuvenating the party and working with greater dedication and discipline under the leader. It is noteworthy that most of the speakers were from South India and from the minority groups. Perhaps, the most powerful and eloquent speaker at the occasion was Dewan Chaman Lal, and next to him, Humayun Kabir.

How deep was Nehru's hold on the affections and loyalty of the party is well illustrated by the following. India and Pakistan had agreed to border demarcation or adjustments in the Bengal region.

This involved the transfer of a small enclave (perhaps Beru Bari) to the Pakistan side. The local people had not been consulted, and there was considerable opposition in some circles and speculation in the press about the fate of the forthcoming ratification in Parliament. A party meeting had been fixed shortly before the voting date. Many party members were wondering how the leader would prepare the Members, especially from the eastern region, to subordinate regional interests to the broad national interest. Nehru spoke in great detail about several important matters and concluded his speech without any reference at all to the Bengal issue. I was really shocked at this unexpected omission. Then he suddenly rose and in a postscript speech, as it were, he made a brief reference to the issue asking the members to support the government stand. All the previous hue and cry appeared to have been a storm in a teacup after Nehru's speech. Perhaps, the only occasion on which the party as well as the country refused to follow the great leader was the issue of Krishna Menon's resignation as Defense Minister after the China episode.

Nehru-Tyagi Exchange at Party Meet

Here I record an episode when my beloved mentor, Nehru, lost his composure. He was presiding over a meeting of the Congress Parliamentary Party in the Central Hall packed by tense members from both the Houses. Mahavir Tyagi, a highly respected loyalist of Nehru, had become a vocal critic of Nehru's inability or refusal to correct the Defence Minister's distorted perceptions of the China issue. Probably, the majority view inside the party was that Krishna Menon was harming national interests, but none was prepared openly to charge Menon, due to his closeness to the leader. Tyagiji, who once told me that he loved Nehru as a dog loves his master, however, did confront the leader. Tyagi rose on a point of order or information while the proceedings were on. I do not remember whether Nehru himself or somebody else was on his feet. However, I vividly recall Nehru ordering Mahavir Tyagi to sit down. Tyagiji refused, whereupon, Nehru angrily ordered him to get out of the House. All of us were stunned at this sudden and unexpected denouement. Nehru thundered he was the leader of the Party. Tyagiji retorted he was a member of the Party and he would not leave. Shortly after this angry exchange a number of senior members rushed to Tyagiji requesting that he calm down and that they supported him in this grave situation. Nehru also regained his calm and natural charm and the highly charged air became still. The rest is well known history.

I had always looked up to Mahavir Tyagi Sahab, an old friend and comrade of my father in the freedom struggle, with respect and admiration. He had categorically told his close relatives not to attempt throwing their weight around while he (Tyagiji) was a Union minister. He had on one occasion admonished his son-in-law that he would rather resign from his high office than hear any complaint of misuse of his position or name.

Two experiences relating to the functioning of Nehru in Parliament are worth sharing with my readers. Though devoid of any political significance, they, perhaps, reveal the personality profile of the great man. Since I was never interested in foreign affairs I had not opted to be on the Parliamentary consultative committee on external affairs. This was despite my great closeness to my leader. Once I just happened to bump into Dinesh Singh who was hurrying to attend a meeting of the said committee. He literally dragged me along with him and I found myself attending a meeting of about twenty-five or thirty members, representing different political parties. Members were supposed to exchange views and give advice, if necessary, on foreign affairs to the Minister for External affairs. What actually happened was that with my own eyes I saw the Prime Minister being transformed into a Professor of Economics. He spoke for a good forty minutes or, perhaps even longer on Rostov's new book, *The Stages of Economic Growth*.

The next episode in a similar vein concerns some Parliamentary proceedings in which I had also participated. I had suggested that in order to promote the scientific temper among the Indian people the Ministry of Education might sponsor a scheme for translating into modern Indian languages a few outstanding books on social sciences recently published in the West. To the best of my memory, Nehru heard part of my speech and then left the chamber. That very day or the day next somebody from the PM's staff met me to seek full information about one book I had specifically named. I vividly remember it was Clyde Kluckhom's *Mirror For Man*.

I recall another Parliamentary experience of educative value for others and myself. The late, Prakash Vir Shastri, then member of the *Lok Sabha*, had levelled serious allegations on the floor of the House against several prominent persons, including my own father. I was taken aback as I heard my father's name come up in the rather longish list of corrupt persons and cheats. At least as far as the allegation against father was concerned the Hon'ble member had every facility of ascertaining the facts from a colleague well known to him.

So excited and angry I felt that I got up and declared on the floor of the House that most of the seventeen or so allegations made, including the charge against my father were either baseless or wrong in my personal knowledge. Let an impartial enquiry be held and the guilty be punished, I demanded. I further added that in case my father be found guilty I shall resign my seat even though I was not legally responsible for the misdeeds of others. I asked if the Hon'ble member was also willing to give an undertaking to resign if the enquiry were to reveal that the charge against my father was utterly baseless. I also made this offer in writing, which was delivered, to him.

Well, a high level enquiry was, in fact, set up. After completion of the enquiry I wrote back to the member that since it had conclusively shown the charge against my father to be totally false, was he now willing to resign? However, he did not bother to reply or to tender oral regrets though we naturally brushed against each in the House until the dissolution of the *Second Lok Sabha*. Barring one or two charges, which were partially correct, all other charges also turned out to be the product of fancy or confusion. This episode taught me how people use character assassination as a political weapon. I am not implying that the Hon'ble member concerned was deliberately trying to malign and harm the persons against whom the charges had been leveled. But someone was, perhaps, so motivated.

The weapon of character assassination had already been used against me right when I was contesting in the general elections. Then, however, the weapon was rather crude. Some local newspapers repeatedly brought out that my father was spending huge amounts on purchasing votes for me. It was also alleged that I had tried to elope with the unmarried daughter of a Hindu Deputy Collector residing in my neighborhood. These allegations were 200% false and baseless and yet my opponents had thought it fit to brandish them without any pangs of conscience. This taught me very early never to give credence to rumors without verifying them, and to do unto others, as I would have them do unto me.

Rajendra Singh and Dinesh Singh

The persons whom I met with very frequently were Dinesh Singh and family, and Rajendra Singh, the MP from Chapra, Bihar. My close association with them was a school of political education, which could not have come out of books. I would like to share some educative anecdotes relating to these two friends, neither of whom is alive today. I would also like to relate two or three other experiences, which greatly deepened my insight into the minds of men and contributed to my mental growth.

Rajendra Singh and I were in the same age group and we were neighbors in South Avenue, close to Teen Murti. Rajendra was an avowed atheist and in the course of almost daily long and friendly conversations used to ridicule and repudiate Hindu mythology and also other metaphysical beliefs. I also criticized conventional Islam but at the same time claimed to be a good Muslim. I held that every religious tradition had plural strands or versions and each version ought to be judged on its own merits or demerits instead of passing a blanket judgment, positive or negative, on the religion as a monolithic whole. I told him that a Ram Mohan Roy, a Tagore, or a Gandhi, or a Tarachand were Hindus no less than the most orthodox of *Brahman* priests, just as Sir Syed and Azad were Muslims no less than those who held them to be apostates from Islam. However, Rajendra could never agree and stuck to his stand that neither he was a Hindu nor I a Muslim.

Dinesh Singh too was in my age group and there were no reservations between us. He was a cabinet minister when he related an amusing true story of a 'fundamentalist' Muslim group in Brussels. The group had built a mosque in a posh locality. Soon they found out that there was a swimming pool very close to the mosque and that the ladies in swimming costumes were a source of dire distraction to the pious worshippers. In all seriousness the custodians of the place of worship moved the competent authorities to shift the pool even though it was there prior to the building of the mosque. Dinesh cited this incident to support his thesis that the rise of militant Hindu communalism or fanaticism was a reaction to the attitudes displayed by fanatical or fundamentalist Muslims.

On one occasion when we called on him both he and Rani Sahiba were out but were expected back shortly. A charming Indian lady and a European gentleman were also waiting in the lounge. We were not introduced but we started with a polite hello. By the time Dinesh Singh and Nagu Bahen joined their waiting guests the conversation had turned into a virtual controversy between the Indian lady (a total stranger to me) and myself. The controversy was who, between India and China, had produced a higher culture and civilization. The lady was absolutely sure that India came on top, while I was inclined to bracket the two giants of Asia. We had unwittingly placed our gracious host in a rather delicate situation. However, Dinesh, with the skill of a diplomat and his honest style and commonsense defused, in no time, the air of tension in his drawing room. Dinesh took the line that whichever country might come on top in regard to 'creation of culture or civilization'; India came on top in regard to 'diffusion of culture' due to her greater involvement with Asian and European peoples. I think this was a fair and honest mediation. Later Dinesh informed us that the lady was a 'society intellectual' from Bengal married to a French artist located in Paris. The artist, whatever his artistic or professional status, was rather reserved when it came to drawing room talk on art and culture.

Here I may also mention another interesting meeting in Dinesh's house with a total stranger when the Raja and Rani Sahiba were out. My wife and I were asked by the staff to wait in the lounge where a European lady was also sitting. We began a polite general conversation without the least idea of who she was. Later on Dinesh informed us that she was Svetlana, the daughter of Comrade Stalin, and the widow of Dinesh's uncle, (late) Raja Suresh Singh. A day or two later she escaped to USA.

SOME VALUABLE EXPERIENCES

I may here mention two small incidents that throw light on human psychology. My closeness to my leader was the source of great satisfaction to me. One day I saw Nehru affectionately patting another young MP in the 'fresh blood' category. Immediately a pang of jealousy stirred in my heart at the realization that my status was far from being unique. I learnt how petty human nature could be despite philosophical pretensions. The other small but highly revealing incident concerns Mr. Fateh Singh of Baroda. He was one of the youngest members of the *Lok Sabha*. Soon after his election he was appointed Parliamentary Secretary in the Defense Ministry. The very next day when he took his seat in the House at the beginning of *Question Hour* I heard a senior Congress MP sitting just next to me utter words of abuse against the Prince turned politician. I interpreted this uncharitable remark as sheer destructive jealousy. This was proof that success of others stings those left out. Perhaps, this is raw human nature without the varnish of morality or acquired wisdom.

The late Mridula Sarabhai was at one time the golden girl of the Congress party. As is well known, she had some conscientious objection to the Kashmir policy of the Government involving the indefinite incarceration of Shaikh Abdullah on political charges. I found that the vast majority of politicians and former friends of hers had deserted her like a plague-invested place. However, she went on crusading for the truth, as she saw it, and spent large sums from her private wealth for the cause. Close as I was to my leader I made no secret of my admiration for the moral courage of Mridulaji and her capacity to stand alone. And as the world knows, the Indian government, at long last, veered to her stand rather than she to theirs.

Another ennobling incident relates to S.K.Singh, an old friend of father. Bachhan Babu, as he was called, was a leading lawyer of Aligarh and we once happened to travel in the same railway compartment from Bareilly to Aligarh. Bachhan Babu was a self-proclaimed atheist. I greatly respected him as a senior citizen and family friend. As the train started to cross the railway bridge at *Ramganga* just near Bareilly railway station, the atheist lawyer took out a few coins from his pocket, placed them in the hands of his spouse (who had just recovered after a serious illness) and threw them in the river down below as an offering. I, obviously, noticed his behavior with considerable surprise but said nothing. Soon afterwards Bachhan Babu, *suo moto*, explained to me that while he was a confirmed atheist he had done so purely out of regard for the Hindu sentiments of his spouse. I could not help thinking and remarking that this was tolerance at its best.

Yet another memorable lesson during my days in the *Lok Sabha* was the advice given me by a *Sufi* saint of Delhi, Imam Jafar Sahab, to whom I was introduced by my maternal uncle Maqsood Ullah Jung, a sincere and deeply committed conventional Muslim. I asked the saint about the best and surest route to spiritual development. '*Ninety-nine percent honesty and truthfulness and one percent spiritual technique*', was the saint's categorical and clear reply to my question.

The experience, which, I dare say, taught me the most about human nature and its pitfalls took place when my five-year term in the *Lok Sabha* was drawing to a close and the Congress party had already started the process of selecting candidates for the third Parliament. As already mentioned, rather early in my brush with Parliamentary activities I had come to realize that I was not cut for active politics. But once having tasted the pleasures and gains of being inside the corridors of power I was in two minds. My predicament was all the more because of the insistence of friends that I should continue as well as the fact that the Congress party had re-nominated me for a second term. My chances of success at the polls were also fairly bright, and my leader was also desirous that I continue. The negative factor was that I did not have enough material resources of my own to cover election expenses and I was totally unwilling to depend upon the party or others. I was consumed by the fear that if I depended upon others I might lose my integrity and independence of judgment.

There was yet another conflict. This was the inner tension between my inner promptings concerning my 'true' vocation or natural personality type and the promptings of ambition or worldly glory. I had to go through almost sleepless nights and endless inner dialogues. The vacillation between ambition and integrity and the extended anguished suspense revealed how little I knew of my own inmost self.

It was only after I had found final rest and peace in the conclusion that I was cut for the life of the mind rather than for active politics and that the versatility of genius combining both was beyond me I came to realize how easy it is for the gullible human head or heart to perceive personal ambition as dedication to a cause, convenience as duty, vanity as self-respect, spiritual conceit as absolute faith, self-interest as justice, and a thousand similar false equations. The vulnerability of human judgment and the wisdom of humility dawned on me with a new force, and I felt I had grown in wisdom and self-insight far more in the space of a few weeks than ever before in decades.

SOME INSTRUCTIVE INCIDENTS

A prominent MP from Karnataka was a vegetarian but had no objection to culinary adventures provided his strict orthodox spouse remained blissfully ignorant. I learnt about this at a dinner party at our house. One of our children was ill and our friend's wife went to see the ailing child for a few moments. The intimate friends of my friend tempted the official vegetarian to have a bite, in the meanwhile, of the forbidden fruit. The mature leader was sorely tempted, but he resisted. This was very well, indeed, otherwise his spouse would have caught him red handed.

Another similar case in our personal knowledge is that of a non-vegetarian wife who did not allow her husband, who was a VIP, to sleep in the bedroom if he took any meat dish at some party, unless he first took a purificatory bath after returning home. Such instances afford revealing glimpses into the depth attitudes of Hindu society relating to the secret and subtle power of the female over the male. I dare say Muslim husbands would not behave in the same manner.

I was astonished when a Minister casually told me in the lobby that he had done the needful in response to my letter on a matter that was not at all in my knowledge. I later came to know that a friend who was a former Member of Parliament had forged my signature on a letterhead and passed it on to the Minister. A businessman who was never a Member of Parliament did more or less the same thing. I understand that in both cases the motive was to help somebody in redressing some genuine grievance, rather than any selfish or material gain. However, I was not at all prepared to believe that such things happened in decent society.

Some friends were chatting at some important reception of how bad it looks when worldly ambition makes MP's and junior Ministers indulge in flattery or other forms of obsequious behavior in public towards those in power. By sheer coincidence, the venerable Gobind Vallabh Pant happened to cross the corner where we were chatting. The person who, a moment ago, had agreed with the sentiments being expressed in our little gathering rushed forward to touch the feet of the virtual Deputy Prime Minister. Subtle and vast indeed is the distance between profession and practice.

The Indian National Congress had formally adopted at the Nagpur session the basic policy resolution on cooperative farming.

Nevertheless there was a strong current of opposition to the idea. Nehru, in all sincerity, suggested and encouraged an open debate inside the Parliamentary party. It is in my personal knowledge that many Parliamentarians had serious misgivings on cooperative farming but opted to remain silent, and even to support the Nehru line in favor of cooperative farming, even against their better judgment. Up to a point discreet silence or subordination of one's independent views to the collective wisdom is essential and desirable. In this case, however, the safe limits seem to have been crossed, resulting in opportunistic doublethink.

Here I am reminded of a remark made at more or less the same time by a bright student who had studied Philosophy with me at the Aligarh Muslim University. He had Communist views and was far from being reverent to my idol, Nehru. He said that everybody has a price though the price varies from case to case. Perhaps, this was his way of debunking Nehru. The student, who was also related to me, knew that I, as his old teacher, had never felt offended by any honest difference of opinion. I spontaneously asked him if he held that Marx and Lenin too had had a price. And this silenced the skeptical or cynical young man. I think, it is supremely important for the human family to retain a sense of proportion in all judgments.

Another incident relates to the appointment of a member of the *Jamate Islami* as lecturer in Economics at the Aligarh Muslim University. The selected candidate had a bright academic record but his ideology was on the wrong side of the Congress establishment. I do not remember exactly how the issue came to be raised in the *Lok Sabha*. I justified the selection on the principle of academic freedom though one or more of the candidates concerned were personally known to me and might have expected my support to them. However, I made quite clear to all concerned my honest and strong opposition to the theocratic anti-secular approach of the *Jamate Islami*. Lala Achint Ram, the veteran Congress leader from Punjab, greatly lauded my stand, as did many others.

SOME PERSONAL REGRETS DURING MY TERM IN PARLIAMENT

One evening after we returned to our residence in South Avenue I found that our music system had been tampered with. I assumed, without a moment's doubt, that our eldest son, Jawahar, then about eight or nine, had done the tampering and straight away slapped him on the face. Soon afterwards the truth came out that a neighbor's son had done the mischief and that Jawahar had tried his best to prevent his naughty friend from doing so. I was deeply mortified at my silly logic and rash parental response despite all my pretensions of being a philosopher and a rational person.

At about the same time I asked Jawahar to memorize the Islamic Lord's prayer comprising seven short verses of the Quran. Jawahar was indeed a brilliant child and a topper. However, my expectations bordered on the irrational and I wanted him to reproduce the Arabic verses in one or two attempts, and do so with perfect accuracy. The child faltered and I burst out in disappointment and reproach that he was not sensitive to matters, which were important to a good Muslim home. The poor child broke down at my parental harshness.

One evening we had taken the children out for a ride on the Children's Railway at Kotla Road. When it was time to return our second son, Rajen, about four at the time, started romping about in the complex instead of getting into the car. This was just an innocent prank or defiance of parental authority, but I got exasperated, when he persisted in defying both his parents. I warned the child he will be left behind if he failed to return, but the defiance continued. I started the engine and started slowly moving the car but the child's defiance had turned into a war of nerves. He still did not respond, but his face began to betray a sense of panic. As the car began slowly moving forward he started running towards the vehicle, though he did not cry. At that very moment a passing cyclist got down, seated the child on the front bar and safely brought him to the car. Rajen was now scared out of his wits. At this point I feel deeply pained and wished I had shown greater patience and tact in dealing with a child of whom I was very fond indeed.

On two other occasions I was harsh in my behavior, successively, with our daughter, Geeta, and our youngest son, Nasser. When Geeta was about four, I, in my supposed wisdom, judged she was being over attentive to her clothes and hair, and that at times she behaved in a somewhat coquettish manner. With a stern expression on my face I glared into her terrified innocent eyes to warn that coquetry was out of bounds in her parental home. I have forgotten the exact episode relating to Nasser when he was about five. All I recollect is that I hastily prejudged him in some matter and wanted the child to apologize, as a precondition of his father's love being restored to him. I was going out of station for a few days, and the child must have remained in suspense for quite some time until my return. The bottom line is that I have had to struggle pretty hard, indeed, to achieve a sense of proportion in social relations and in my treatment of loved ones. In other words, I have been slow to grasp the wisdom of humility and to realize the subtle evil of spiritual pride or conceit present in my psychological make-up.

South Avenue, links the rear court of the President's House with Teen Murti House, the then official residence of the Prime Minister, was subject to the monkey menace, at the Presidential House side. Members of Parliament living closer to the Rashtrapati Bhawan side were continually troubled by their simian cousins, who however, avoided going over to the Teen Murti side. The interesting reason for this strange behaviour was that at the Teen Murti end the Prime Minister's instructions to discipline the erring monkeys were strictly followed, while at the other end, under the orders of the President, leniency was meted out to the erring monkeys.

I understand this menace is growing rapidly in different Indian cities. Even in some parts of the South Block complex officers on duty and public visitors have to seek external aid and protection from attacking or aggressive simian intruders. The giant windows of the Rashtrapati Niwas, Shimla, have had to be covered with broad wire gauze, not as a protection against flies or mosquitoes but against monkeys.

CHAPTER 5

ALIGARH ONCE AGAIN: SLOW MATURITY, PART 1

THE HOME COMING

Almost immediately after my term in the *Lok Sabha* ended in early 1962 I rejoined my post as Lecturer at the Aligarh Muslim University. Hardly any change had taken place in the Department during the years I had been away. I came back, firmly determined to produce some good written work as early as possible, in order to overcome a rather gnawing sense of guilt at not having published any book or paper so far.

Before I could settle down to writing work in right earnest the Central Ministry of Education sent me as a member of a two member delegation at the first ever international session of the *Pakistan Philosophy Congress* being held at Peshawar. The other delegate was Professor Sachitananda Murty of Waltair University. I was hardly known in the philosophy circles of India at that time, while Professor Murty had already made his mark. I, therefore, told him at our very first meeting at the Delhi airport that I regarded him as the leader of the team. He just did not agree, and we had to perform jointly the inevitable ceremonial functions connected with a mini international gathering of philosophers. The main architect of the Congress was late Professor M.M.Shareef, my former teacher at the Aligarh Muslim University. The person responsible for my appointment as delegate was Humayun Kabir, then Union Minister of Education and Scientific Research.

I could hardly contribute to the proceedings, as I was too immature to make my presence felt at an international gathering. However, I learnt a lot and came in contact with some established and some very promising younger philosophers. The well-known Professor Dev of Dacca University was the General President. I recall a rather regrettable but amusing experience while I sat next to him at a meal served to the delegates. The non-vegetarian food was abundant and delicious but the menu did not include any fish or vegetables, and the general President of the session was a vegetarian. Professor Dev had no choice but to take this omission in a very philosophical way. However, I felt sorry at the lack of imagination displayed in this matter, though Professor Shareef himself was the picture of grace and courtesy to every delegate.

It was at Peshawar that I met Professor Husain Nasr of Iran who soon became a celebrity in the Islamic world due to his liberal humanist approach to Islam, but who, most unfortunately, was to become a persona non-grata in Iran after the Islamic revolution some years later. On our way back to Delhi Professor Murty and I spent a few hours at the ancient university site at Taxila. The Pakistan government headed by President Ayub had made special efforts to preserve and beautify this world heritage. Whatever the policy of others might have been in Pakistan Ayub himself had a liberal and catholic approach to Islam. He patronized the outstanding liberal Islamist (late) Fazlur Rahman of Oxford fame.

A Sordid Episode at the AMU

Shortly after Ali Yavar Jung took over charge as Vice-Chancellor of the Aligarh Muslim University he was unfortunately subjected to a criminal assault by some totally misguided students while the Court of the university was deliberating on the crucial issue of the quota of seats reserved for internal students of the institution. Zakir Sahab, in his wisdom, had fixed the quota at fifty percent of the total intake, but Badruddin Tyabji, during a short stint as Vice-Chancellor, had raised the quota to seventy-five percent. Many thoughtful Aligarians were of the view that the increased quota for internal students was not in the best interests of the Muslim community on an all India basis, though it was useful and expedient for the local people of Aligarh. Ali Yavar Jung wanted to restore the tried and tested formula of Zakir Sahab. Unfortunately student-politicians got involved in the controversy along with some teachers and local politicians and this led to the most sordid episode of a brutal attack upon the head of an academic institution. However, I always was and still am, certain there was no conspiracy to murder him. Unfortunately some quarters in the then Government of Uttar Pradesh began to think and act on this premise. Incredible as it sounds, three eminent and responsible persons, namely, Basheer Ahmad Sayeed, a distinguished retired judge of the Madras High Court, Professor Abdul Baseer Khan, an eminent Zoologist of the Aligarh Muslim University, and, then, a non-Congress MLA, and Mujtaba Siddiqui, a distinguished retired IAS (Indian Administrative Service) officer and the, then, Registrar of the AMU, along with some students were charge sheeted for conspiracy to murder the VC.

I, along with a few friends and influential people, pleaded with the Prime Minister and other leaders at Delhi to view matters in the proper perspective and advise the Uttar Pradesh government accordingly. I do not wish to go into further details of the complex drama and personal tragedy that gradually enfolded. Suffice to say, that this episode provided me with a deep insight into the labyrinths of the human mind, and the fads and foibles of powerful and responsible persons at the top. I saw them pathetically distort plain facts and become subjectively convinced of the other's guilt without any objective evidence. After irreparable damage had been done the government eventually withdrew the cases. However, the trauma contributed to the death of the Professor of Zoology due to cancer. In his case justice delayed became justice denied, in the literal sense of the maxim.

MY FIRST BOOK: ROOTS AND THE FRUIT

My first book, *Five Approaches to Philosophy*, carried a foreword by Professor I.T.Ramsey of Oxford and was published in 1965. *Five Approaches to Philosophy* was an exploration in Metaphilosophy. After a brief critical exposition of the basic approaches in vogue in Western thought I pointed out the need of adopting a multi-dimensional approach. My philosophical understanding has naturally developed over the years since my first book. Nevertheless, my basic approach remains unchanged. In fact, the more I have read and reflected on different ways of doing philosophy, and the greater has become my familiarity with great philosophers, past and present, the more I have come to appreciate the concepts of 'conceptual illumination and misdirection', developed by John Wisdom, in response to the influence of Wittgenstein.

Philosophical theories or 'isms', therefore, should not be regarded as exclusive alternatives but rather as complementary correctives of each other. The real situation or states of affairs under consideration of the philosopher is always complex. Different features or aspects of the situation assume crucial significance for different philosophers. And this generates different theories. Philosophical controversies also arise when words of the natural language, as used in familiar empirical contexts, are shifted to totally extraordinary non-empirical contexts, thereby generating confusions, puzzles or cognitive vacuity. It was the special contribution of the linguistic analytical philosophers to focus attention on the above issues.

Wittgenstein, and following, him Wisdom and Ryle pointed out that philosophical problems get 'dissolved' through exposing the above confusions, which arise when the same word or expression is used in different contexts. The proper task of philosophy is to point out in specific detail these confusions and their source rather than finding solution to 'deep' problems or enigmas through abstract argumentation or even through the type of philosophical analysis done by Moore or Russell. The dissolution of philosophical problems or disputes, thus, puts to an end the need for taking sides in philosophy or the building of rival theories.

If one studies the history of philosophy in the light of the sociology of knowledge it becomes plain how the point of departure of every great philosopher and the main theme and thrust of his thought arise from the 'spirit of the age' he lives in. Seen from this angle, Moore, Russell and Wittgenstein philosophized in the midst of the problem posed by the sharp contrast between the systematic verifiability and growing agreement in the case of scientific investigation and the opposite position in the case of philosophical enquiry.

Wittgenstein, the chief architect of the new 'Copernican revolution' of the thirties in analytical philosophy at Cambridge was not well versed in classical Western philosophy. He started from the scientific realism of Russell and the common sense philosophy of Moore. It is hardly surprising that the controversies he attempted to analyze and resolve through his own innovative linguistic analysis centered on simple perceptual statements, rather than the classical themes of human destiny or nature of the Divine. The concern of the new movement was with the 'language of perception/sensation' rather than with the 'language of world views' or metaphysics.

The early Wittgenstein had dismissed metaphysics as 'nonsense' and the classical conception of philosophy, as a super-science of ultimate reality, as an illusion of philosophers indulging in speculating on the nature of reality without first studying the nature of language as such. He held that unless a truth-claim going beyond pure logic or Mathematics, could be verified or falsified through perception, at some point or the other, the truth claim was not in the realm of knowledge, whatever else it may be. In short, Wittgenstein continued to accept scientific knowledge as the supreme and exclusive model of 'truth'. Since metaphysical theories were, obviously, not verifiable, in the scientific sense, they stood devalued and dethroned from the seat of authority. But no systematic attempt was made to enquire into the proper function of metaphysical theories or worldviews that have been the core of classical philosophy, both Western and Eastern.

The early linguistic analysts, thus, missed to register the vital function of truth claims which, though not verifiable, nevertheless, wielded immense power of conviction over the human mind and provided significance and direction to the individual and society in life as a whole. In other words, the early analysts did not distinguish 'existential interpretations' from purely emotional responses or judgments of taste. They were so much under the grip of the purely scientific model of verifiable hypotheses and objective truths that they did not bother to explore the nature and depth of what may best be called 'existential convictions'.

This was understandable in the early period of the New Philosophy. But it would not be proper for philosophers to evade analyzing existential convictions on the ground that their 'subjective' truth-claims cannot be objectively confirmed or verified. The evasion or 'fear of metaphysics', if allowed to last indefinitely, may turn into a pathological 'fear of commitment'. A brave new world based on pure positivism might usher in a technological paradise, but this will amount to the death of morality, art and spirituality as such.

Creative thinkers of the European continent have generally scored over their Anglo-American counterparts in making a more balanced and harmonious response to the human situation. There can be no quarrel with the primacy of the scientific method. However, every area of human experience subjected to critical enquiry should have its own appropriate method of enquiry or investigation rather than be subjected to the scientific method in a 'blanket' sense.

In other words, Axiology, or the critical analysis of value judgments, in general, including Ethics, Aesthetics, and Metaphysics etc. must develop its own procedures of validity and truth. The same remarks apply to the Philosophy of History, as well as the critical study of artistic experience, mysticism and mythology. It will naturally take considerable time for a measure of agreement to evolve as to what are the proper criteria of validity of 'existential interpretations'; this agreement or consensus will always fall short of the rigor of the scientific method. Yet, it will partially help to reduce the role of pure fancy or unexamined assumptions by unsuspecting human observers who just cannot avoid interpreting the human situation and the universe as a whole.

No human being could possess universal knowledge or apply the same measure of critical acumen to the entire gamut of human experience. One can only aim at the maximum possible accumulation and integration of knowledge and the pursuit of moral and spiritual values in all humility and authenticity. To my mind, the best course is a joyful surrender to a Cosmic Mystery, by whatever name it may be called. I find liberal spirituality of the East more satisfactory than any theology of any 'chosen religion', or any philosophical 'ism'.

Modern science and technology have ushered in the age of the globalization of the human family. The process started with growing inter-action and inter-dependence in the sphere of trade and industry and the creation of a world market in goods. Now a world market is being created before our very eyes in the 'idea of the good'. In the far corners of the earth facilities are now growing for instant translation from one language to the other and of access to computer-based data banks dealing with every imaginable subject or theme for the purpose of affordable telecommunication. Television and tourism have abolished the natural cultural insularity of far-flung and remote human groups. New possibilities of total power of a few over the many have arisen. It is well to ponder what the human state today demands. Those in power and also those who aspire for power should realize that the ideal is not greater uniformity, imitation or conversion to any ideology, religious or secular, but rather a greater degree of 'informed freedom of choice' for the common man of the human family as a whole.

Working on the drafts and reading the final proofs made me aware, for the first time, of the labor and skill involved in writing. I had never suspected that what I had supposedly grasped or comprehended through intensive reading and sustained thinking was still so opaque when I tried to express these ideas through using ordinary language and avoiding high sounding technical terms. My preference for simple language had grown under the influence of my old teacher, Professor Umaruddin, no less than that of Bertrand Russell and Moore.

I realized with full force that using high sounding expressions, technical words and theories is the easiest way to deceive oneself into believing that one knows or understands sentences or theories, when, in fact, one only plays linguistic games without first clearly defining the rules of the game that is being played. I greatly admired Moore's search for clarity and Russell's talent for simple yet elegant language. But in the light of Wisdom's method of analysis the older analytical method of Moore and Russell no longer seemed satisfactory or valid. However, I could never persuade myself to believe that the search for clarity through linguistic analysis was the only job of philosophy, and that classical philosophy was sheer wasted effort and mere illusion.

My fear of 'reducing' philosophy to only one dimension prolonged the time taken by me to produce even a small book. Moreover, I still had a fear of writing. I would be failing in my duty if I were not to acknowledge my deep gratitude to my father-in-law, Major General Muhammad Akbar, of Pakistan (not to be confused with his namesake involved in the Rawalpindi conspiracy case) who forced me to write, as best as I could, rather than to hanker after perfection in what I wrote.

The retired General living in Karachi was quite justified in egging his son-in-law to commence writing since the General himself (without any pretensions to scholarship) had authored several books in Urdu, well received in Pakistan. Rather sketchy as was my *Five Approaches to Philosophy*, it was the product of a sound methodological approach. I felt gratified when it was generously appreciated in several quarters. Here I must express my gratitude to the distinguished Indian thinker, (late) Professor N.V. Bannerji, who had kindly gone through the draft of my first book and suggested valuable improvements. He always guided and encouraged me in my work.

LIFE AND TEACHING AS A SCHOOL OF LEARNING

Muslim Theology had always formed a compulsory part of the Aligarh Muslim University syllabus at the undergraduate level ever since the foundation of the College by Sir Syed. It was essential to clear the subject, though the marks obtained were not counted for ranking the examinees who graduated. Non-Muslim students, however, had the option to study History of Civilization in lieu of Theology. When the well known Aligarh historian and educationist, Professor Noorul Hasan (later a distinguished Union Minister of Education) was Dean of the Faculty he took the laudable initiative to introduce Applied Ethics or Problems of Morality as a third alternative to Theology. This was an excellent idea, indeed.

In course of time the scope of the paper was enlarged to include Comparative Religion. The Department of Theology staked their claim to teach this paper. However, the members of the Philosophy Department were unanimous that the teaching should not be done by theologians who would find it extremely difficult, if not impossible, to command the requisite degree of critical analysis and detachment necessary for teaching comparative religion or spiritual geography in a non-judgmental spirit. Teaching Applied Ethics to non-Muslim undergraduates gave me great pleasure and intellectual profit all through my long service at the Aligarh Muslim University.

In 1965 India and Pakistan went to war over Kashmir. My two sisters lived in Lahore, Pakistan. When India opened the second front I found myself in a painful dilemma. The logic of the military situation had compelled the Indian government to order the march on Lahore. I shuddered to contemplate the consequences. It was during this emotional upheaval that Reinhold Niebuhr's classic, *Moral Man and Immoral Society*, came to my notice. I read the book with the closest attention possible and my confusions and inner conflict were completely dissipated. Niebuhr's thesis was that morality ought to govern politics, yet he also conceded the distinction between the morality of individual and public life. The two types of morality should not be confused, he said. The use of force was inevitable, but force should be used in a moral manner in an, essentially, immoral world. This makes tragedy the shadow of history and renders impossible the realization of Utopia in society. In other words, the belief or faith in human perfectibility, the postulate of modern Humanism, was an illusion. Man must learn to be humble and patient and contented with imperfect states of affairs without, however, giving up the struggle against evil.

Niebuhr's book illumined for me the complexities of the human situation just as earlier John Wisdom had illumined the dark and unknown conceptual spaces behind the words and expressions of human language. I gradually regained the anchor provided by ethical ideals, minus the illusions of liberal Humanism or liberal Theology. I can never describe in adequate words my spiritual and intellectual debt to Niebuhr.

I had introduced Analytical Philosophy in the Philosophy syllabus shortly after my joining the Department. But before I could do any solid work in the field my fascination for Nehru seduced me from academia to politics. After rejoining the Department I tried to make amends and to focus on the work of Wittgenstein. To the best of my knowledge, Pitcher's *The Philosophy of Wittgenstein*, was the first sympathetic, yet, critical textbook on the later philosophy of Wittgenstein. While I had become quite appreciative of the basic approach and thrust of his writings, thanks to the early influence of John Wisdom during my Cambridge days, I had not been able to make a sustained critical study of Wittgenstein's *Blue and Brown Books* and of his *Philosophical Investigations*. Pitcher became my mentor and guide in this regard and I owe a great intellectual debt to him for the same. Many lucid expositions of the pioneering work of the Austrian genius and father of the new Copernican revolution in philosophy have appeared since Pitcher's early textbook on the subject.

Another source of abiding influence on me, around this time, was a little book on the subject of religious training and indoctrination of children. The name of the writer (perhaps Walter Lee) has been forgotten but not his message. The writer was a Christian existentialist with an Oxford background. The thrust of his teaching was that children should not be indoctrinated but must be given only moral training in the ambience of tender love and truthfulness. Above all, they must see that their parents and teachers practice what they profess. The writer went on to say that the well-meaning efforts of committed believers to catch the child young in regard to creedal matters, hinders rather than helps, the child to acquire authentic faith as an adult. Doctrinal information should follow, not precede adolescence.

Another popular book, which influenced me a lot, was Josuha Liebmann's *Peace of Mind*. This book by a famous Jewish Rabbi on the primacy of the simple goodness of heart and the power of pure love also underlined the crucial importance of self-esteem and self-love in the higher therapeutic sense. The intellectual stimulation provided by the above and similar works moved me to commence writing on Islam, as I had gradually come to understand it over the years of study and honest independent reflection. Our eldest son, Jawahar, had already reached his adolescence and I was keen to share with him the fruits of my quest for truth without demanding that he should accept my own findings. Hence, the title *Quest For Islam*.

QUEST FOR ISLAM

My work *Quest For Islam* contains a fairly comprehensive statement of my beliefs and value system. I still stand by what I had to say when the work was published more than twenty years ago. Naturally, since then an enormous amount of literature has been produced representing different points of view. On the whole, the debate and controversy in the Islamic world now centers on what is termed as 'Islamic Fundamentalism'. New political and economic forces have become operative on a global scale and terrorist methods have become the order of the day. I, however, submit that the validity of my philosophical approach to religion, with special reference to Islam, remains unaffected by the said changes or developments.

My *Quest For Islam* is a philosophical work which points out the intellectual difficulties in the traditional understanding of Islam as well as its, relatively, liberal versions current in my milieu. My philosophical approach lays great stress on the vital distinction between 'existential certainties' of religion, on the one hand, and the certainties of logic or of science, on the other. However, humankind cannot and ought not to live in compartments, but must strive to achieve an integrated worldview or an existential perspective on the mystery of the universe. This, necessarily, involves reconstructing or revising the basic concepts and values of the religion concerned. But this task must not make the believer fall into the trap of conscious or unconscious 'apologetics'. This has been my sincere effort in the *Quest for Islam*.

Iqbal, the eminent philosophical poet of the Indian sub-continent, had already undertaken the task. But, in view of the ever advancing growth of factual knowledge as well as new perspectives on the human situation, arising out of human creativity and the ceaseless quest for value, the task must, necessarily, be undertaken afresh from time to time.

My task proved to be much more demanding than I had imagined, since my store of information on Islamic Studies lagged far behind the level I had been able to reach in philosophical studies. I now began concentrating on Islamic history and Theology and, obviously, the Quran, though I had to be content with English or Urdu translations of the Arabic text. The prolific writings of Montgomery Watt on Islam and Prophet Muhammad were the single largest source of information as well as inspiration in this task. I may single out Watt's *Islam and the Integration of Society* for special mention. I also learnt a lot from the writings of several eminent Western scholars of Islam, such as Gibb, Nicholson, Arberry, Grunebaum, Cantwell Smith, and Anemarie Schimmel *et al*. Among Muslim scholars or creative minds I drew inspiration from Shibli, Amir Ali, Iqbal, Azad, and Muhammad Ali, of Lahore, and I vastly profited from the excellent synoptic contributions by Aziz Ahmad and S.A.A. Rizvi. I often had long intellectual chats with (late) Professor Hamieduddin Khan, who was a scholar of Persian and sincerely committed to his own creative understanding of Islam. The great and still growing *Encyclopedia of Islam* was also like a muse to me in my search for reliable critical information on Islam.

This is the appropriate place to acknowledge my gratitude to a person whom I hold in special regard: (late) Fazlur Rahman, an outstanding civil servant from the erstwhile Nizam's Hyderabad, who became Pro-Vice Chancellor of the AMU at the request of his friend, Ali Yavar Jung, who was Vice-Chancellor for a brief period. To both, but especially to Fazlur Rahman Sahab, I shall remain indebted for his appreciation of my work on Islamic Liberalism. Possessed of a sharp logical mind and a wide-ranging grasp of the liberal arts, including classical Urdu and Persian poetry, Fazal Sahab was not merely a literary humanist but a person of extraordinary moral integrity and renunciation of worldly ambition. He had suggested several improvements in the drafts of my *Quest for Islam*.

I found that in several Muslim quarters there prevailed an air of distrust and defensive resistance against the findings of contemporary Western scholarship on Islam no less than against the earlier work done by missionary scholars. I just could not equate the work done by noted Western scholars (many of whom were agnostics keeping an equal distance from historical faiths including their own mother religion) with the work of committed Christian believers or missionaries. Even among several eminent Christian believers there were honest and impartial scholars who had open minds. The existentialist approach to Christianity clearly reflected how modern Christian theologians and creative thinkers had broken away from the rationalistic pretensions and illusions of the missionary thinking that prevailed a century ago. I also found that the impartiality of *Shia* scholars was suspect in *Sunni* quarters. I would like to share my experience relating to the defensive resistance of my circle to Western and *Shia* scholarship.

In the course of my reading I found Grunebaum had quoted several passages from the writings of Ghazzali (d. 1111) about the proper conduct of Muslims towards unbelievers. Likewise, S.A.A. Rizvi had quoted several similar passages from the writings of the 17th century Indian *Sufi*, Shaikh Ahmad of Sarhind. The contents of these excerpts were plainly not acceptable to modern sensibilities and they betrayed the limitations of these two great figures of classical Islam. When I raised the issue with some friends and colleagues they vigorously expressed their doubts about the accuracy of the translations of the Arabic/Persian texts or the concealment of the full text/context of the excerpts.

Since I myself had no doubt whatsoever on this score we agreed jointly to consult the original sources. This academic exercise became unduly prolonged since the editions of the original work used by Grunebaum and Rizvi, respectively, were different from the editions found in the AMU library. However, a lengthy search confirmed the accuracy and honesty of the modern writers concerned. This is not to say that subjectivity or prejudice is non-existent in Western academic circles. Indeed, a lot of genuine plain ignorance about Islam or Muslims is very common in different quarters, including our own people.

INTERNATIONAL ISLAMIC CONFERENCE, KUALA LUMPUR:

My work, *Quest For Islam*, was under way when it fell to my lot in 1969 to participate in the international Islamic Conference at Kuala Lumpur. I was one of the five official delegates sent by the Indian government. The eminent elder statesman, Ali Zaheer, was the leader of the team. This was my first, and to date, only visit to the Eastern region of Asia. My ten-day stay brought me in contact with Malaysian and Indonesian Muslims and their version of Islamic modernism or liberalism, and several interesting and significant facets of Islamic issues and themes came to my notice. I shall mention one or two.

I would like to share with the reader a few non-academic highlights of the Conference. I and all other delegates from India were given to understand that we were full delegates. However, at the inaugural plenary session the leader of the Indian delegation was not invited by the Chairman to convey his country's greetings to the host country and other delegates, as had been done in the case of other delegations. We then realized that the organizers of the conference, namely, the Malaysian Government had given the Indian team the status of observer, not full participant. This had been done, presumably at the instance of Pakistan on the ground that India was a secular state, and not an Islamic country. Our leader, Ali Zaheer Sahab, immediately took up the matter with the steering committee and informed them that the Indian delegation was not prepared to sit as dumb observers, without active participation.

Indonesia too was a secular state, and the leader of their delegation had thought it fit to point this out at the plenary session. He had gone on to add that as his country had an overwhelming Muslim population his government was happy to be associated with other Muslim countries at the Islamic Seminar. In the case of India, as well, what counted was the immense size of the Muslim population in Mother India. Despite stiff opposition from Pakistan the Indian stand prevailed.

The other highlight was the dramatic appearance of Yasser Arafat at the Conference. Though he had acquired the status of an Arab patriot the mantle of terrorism was still on his shoulders and he had not been invited to participate in the conference. However, he barged into the imposing conference hall as an Olympic god, and the Malaysian guards and security dared not question him. Later on his entry was regularized, as it were. I never had the pleasure of an introduction to him but I saw him at very close quarters.

Two other interesting things are worth mentioning. When I participated in a large congregational Friday payer in the magnificent modern mosque in Kuala Lumpur I noticed that a large number of devotees had no caps or other covering on their head. In India and Pakistan this permissive approach is conspicuous by its absence, and those who do not cover their heads while praying are often hooted out or literally forced to conform to custom. Modern hotels served pork without any restriction. Floorshows were also regularly held even though Malaysia, unlike Indonesia, was an Islamic, not a secular, state. One was free to choose the version of Islam according to one's inner lights without any fear of being penalized by any Inquisition. The Malaysian and Indonesian Muslims had a social and cultural identity quite distinct from the Muslims of India or West Asia. The women were not required to use any *shawl* or extra garment over their bosoms and they were not segregated from men at wedding functions. Indeed, the bride and groom sat together at the main wedding ceremony.

Much more surprising to me was the fact that the University hostels were co-residential. When I expressed my surprise in view of Malaysia being an Islamic state I was told that the educated Malaysian people stood for modern liberal Islam and for gender equality. Indonesia had gone a step further since it was a declared secular state even though the population was preponderantly Muslim. Such experiences further confirmed my principled de-linking of politics with religion together with the Gandhian stress on the ethical approach to politics. The emphasis on morality was a legacy common to the higher version of every religion.

My participation in the Islamic conference led to a life long association with a fellow delegate, (late) Maulana Abul Irfan, of the famous Nadwa Seminary, Lucknow. A scholar of Muslim religious thought and a person of integrity and moral courage, the Maulana later on defended me, several years later, against the charge of apostasy leveled by a Seminar participant at Tirupati. The seminar was meant to be a dialogue between the *Ulema* and modern Muslim intellectuals. It had been organized through the initiative of the well-known Indian philosopher, Sachitananda Murty, who was then Vice-Chancellor of Tirupati University. The participant had held that my expressed views on Islamic liberalism amounted to atheism. The Maulana observed that my honest perplexities contained a greater and deeper faith than the conventional talk of the formal believer. I felt greatly strengthened and elevated by his moral support and nobility of character.

Some Memorable Academic Gatherings

Another memorable conclave is the fortnight long national seminar convened by Nihar Ranjan Ray, renowned intellectual and first Director of the *Indian Institute of Advanced Study*, Shimla. The theme of the seminar was *Modernity and Contemporary Indian Literature*. Young as I was in this galaxy of seasoned and established intellectuals and writers, the Director had asked me to analyze the concept of modernity in the inaugural paper.

I was rather nervous when I began, but the final outcome was a tremendous relief to me. The great effort I had to make to justify the honor done me by the Director immensely helped in clearing my own ideas and to express them in simple language. I attempted to analyse modernity in terms of a set of basic concepts and values/attitudes, which I enumerated in short but suggestive paragraphs. Modernity, I submitted, was neutral to religious faith and it did not imply that the scientific temper opposed cultivating spirituality as a dimension of the good life. I was literally overwhelmed by the generous appreciation of my paper by the great stalwarts present, including the world-renowned scholar and elder statesman, Suniti Kumar Chatterjee.

This is the right place to recount three other academic occasions of considerable educative value for me. The first was the golden session of the *Indian Philosophy Congress* held at Delhi around 1976. The organizing committee had very kindly asked me to present my paper as part of the proceedings of the inaugural session. I regarded this as a great honor done to a person who was not yet a Professor. I worked very hard on my paper on *Knowledge and Truth* and went on revising and polishing it, but failed to send it in time to the person concerned. I, however, read out the paper as scheduled. The thrust of the paper was that the classical attempt to define the nature or essence of truth and knowledge sprang from the misleading assumption that every noun refers to an object, entity or essence. My intensive effort to do a good job greatly helped in clarifying my ideas on truth and authenticity.

My participation in a truly all India Seminar on the *Concept of Tolerance in Indian Culture* was also an education for me. *The Indian Council for Philosophical Research* had organized the seminar at Madras University around 1990. A large number of delegates from the length and breadth of the land were present. Several Marxist philosophers aggressively tried to dismiss the usually held view that Indian culture has always been characterized by religious tolerance. They gave linguistic as well as historical evidence. The approach of the organizers and some other philosophers was just the opposite. I had anticipated the possibility of this controversy and my presentation was of considerable help in reaching a consensus. My main point was that tolerance has several dimensions and traditional Indian culture lacked in social tolerance, but allowed full freedom of belief, even to the point of indifference.

The third occasion was the session of the *Afro-Asian Philosophy Conference* held at Delhi around 1991. The speech of the distinguished Egyptian philosopher who was one of the founding sponsors and office bearers of the organization impressed me greatly. When we met at lunch I enquired from him into the social and political state of Egypt. My specific question was what would be the verdict of the nation if free and fair general elections were held to elect a democratic government? The philosopher candidly answered that Islamic fundamentalists would come to power and attempt to destroy democracy in the Western sense of free elections and plural political parties. Under these conditions, he held, the preservation of democracy required a measure of restrictions on the democratic process itself for the time being. This was a bitter pill that had to be swallowed by true lovers of democracy for its effective preservation. My conversation with the Egyptian philosopher was a piece of education and a new insight for me.

Some Islamist quarters sharply criticize the 'unIslamic satanic governments' in Egypt, Algeria, and Turkey etc., which suppress popular Islamic parties at the polls through rigging or military force. It is alleged that this policy is the negation of true democracy since the corrupt camp followers of Western democracy know that free and fair elections would bring to power, not the liberal secular Muslims, but the Islamic parties as such. This argument appears valid at face value, but is highly delusive and misleading when carefully analyzed. The Islamist parties openly reject the basic concept of universal adult franchise without any discrimination of race, religion and gender in favor of a vague and undefined Islamic democracy based on the Quran and the *Sunnah*. Yet, the Islamic parties want to capture power through the Western democratic process based on the concept of human equality and fundamental human rights, without any discrimination of religion. In other words, the declared adversaries of liberal democracy are out to use the democratic process to scuttle democracy itself in the name of 'Islamic democracy' that, avowedly, makes a distinction between Muslims and non-Muslim 'protected citizens' (*dhimmi*s) of an Islamic state, thus discriminating against pure humanist equality of status and opportunity. The above latent contradiction in the stand of the Islamist parties, however, could be removed (for argument's sake) if they could assure the convening of a constituent Assembly, democratically elected, for framing an Islamic constitution that does not abridge the basic concept of human rights and that affirms the equal right of all citizens to modify the constitution without any fear of loss of life, security and status. This condition, however, will never be acceptable to the Islamist parties, as it will negate the very *raison de'tre* of their movement for the Islamization of modern secular democracy in Muslim countries, and eventually in the world at large.

Much earlier the Gandhi birth centenary had been celebrated by the Aligarh Muslim University in 1969. Among other things the University decided to publish an anthology of Gandhiji's writings. The work of selection of material was entrusted to me and Dr. Alvi of the Education Department. The labor of preparing a good hundred-page anthology was a valuable education for me, as this required an extensive survey of the writings of the father of the nation. Though not creative or philosophical work it helped to clarify my ideas on several points.

Moreover, the inaugural speech of the chief guest, Professor Ramachandran, was a great event. In the course of a truly illuminating and deeply moving speech on Gandhi the eminent scholar from south India made a quite general observation which has left behind a deep impression upon me. He said that nobody could, possibly, understand the full meaning and depth of humanistic love, at its best, until one becomes a grandparent. I had then accepted this observation merely at the intellectual level. But it was only after twenty years or so, when I had myself become a grandfather that the full psychological implications of this pregnant observation started to dawn on me at a deeper emotional and spiritual level.

Learning from the National Emergency, 1975

Soon after the Allahabad High Court declared Indiraji's election to the *Lok Sabha* from Rai Bareilly null and void on the ground of corrupt electoral practices she clamped a national emergency pending the final verdict on her appeal to the Supreme Court. My honest spontaneous reaction was that she should have resigned during the interim period pending the final decision and I communicated in writing my honest view to her.

The first ten months of the emergency led to positive results, but eventually the good started turning into evil just as fresh food starts to rot and eventually becomes toxic. We used to meet Indiraji and also Sanjay fairly often and did our best to inform them of grass root realities, but they preferred to rely on their own sources of information. A stage came when some close friends warned us that if we kept up our friendly efforts to remove the inaccuracies in her official inputs she might just drop us from her circle of friends as she had done in several known cases. Well, this did not happen, but she went on with her own plans of action without heeding what we used to say.

The twenty-month long emergency is full of lessons for all times. To condemn its imposition as well as to defend it is equally futile and simplistic. It was imposed as a desperate response to Jai Prakashji's call for total revolution. In the name of Gandhi he exhorted all services, civil as well as the police and military, to refuse to carry out the illegal orders of the duly constituted democratic government on the ground that it had become incorrigibly corrupt and immoral. It was the honest and the correct perception of the Prime Minister that this stand of a united opposition amounted to a grave threat to the internal security of the state. On the other hand, it was the honest and correct charge of the opposition that the government was guilty of totally callous indifference to removing the various evils that had crept into the system at the grass roots. If JP's protest and challenge was born of total desperation the government's stand was also unpardonable.

The emergency promised to deliver goods, to begin with. But as usually happens the gains were temporary and after eight or ten months its corrective function evaporated into thin air and the evils of a 'dictatorship of a kitchen cabinet' began to offset the advantages of quick decisions or speedy implementation. I tried to persuade some likeminded honest friends to join me in making a last effort to apprize

Aligarh Once Again: Slow Maturity Part 1

Indiraji of the harm being done to the party and the state due to the style of functioning of Sanjay Gandhi and other connected matters. But with one notable exception nobody favored my proposal. The exception was my very good friend, (late) Peareylal, of District Aligarh. An MLA from a rural constituency, he was one of the noblest souls I have come across in my entire life. Barely literate, he had a very sharp and balanced mind and was a highly evolved and an integrated personality whose memory I shall ever cherish. The general fear was that the exercise proposed by me would prove utterly futile since Indiraji, as a mother, would never be willing to hear anything disparaging to her son.

As suddenly as the Prime Minister had clamped the emergency she lifted it and announced general elections. My genuine regard and loyalty to Indiraji prompted me to offer her my sincere and disinterested services to the Congress party though I had ceased to be an active member ever since my renouncing of electoral politics in 1962. It was a very critical phase of the Congress and there was wide spread dissatisfaction against it. However, Indiraji and Sanjay were not at all interested in my offer, which in any case, was a very unwise step for me from the worldly angle. I was, then, at the height of my academic attainments and had just been appointed Professor at the Aligarh Muslim University, a position that I had coveted above all else.

I would like to close this reference to the emergency period by mentioning the case of the (late) Akbar Ali Khan of Hyderabad, a veteran Congressman of un-impeachable integrity. Indiraji had appointed him Governor of Uttar Pradesh. While the emergency was on he was transferred to Orissa. After a few months he resigned as Governor of Orissa and the President at the advice of the Prime Minister readily accepted his resignation. The reasons behind all this are in my personal knowledge. In the first case the Governor had invited his old friend, Jai Prakashji, to a private lunch when the campaign against the Congress government was in full swing. In the second case the Chief Minister of Orissa had become displeased with the Governor's Gandhian stress on the ethical approach to politics and administration, though the Governor never interfered with the actual working of the Chief

Minister's office. The Chief Minister expressed her displeasure to the Prime Minister and this prompted the veteran Congressman to retire and return to his native Hyderabad well before his term was to end. It is noteworthy that Akbar Sahab never joined those who turned against the 'mother and the son' in their hour of defeat, but rather stood up as an honest and impartial statesman who spoke the truth without fear or favor. With no scores to settle, no axe to grind and no ladder to climb, his was the voice of sweet reason and moderation. This is the role of Governor as envisaged in the constitution.

There is another instance in my personal knowledge when a Governor was transferred in a rather questionable manner. For reasons best known to her Indiraji had become over-critical and allergic to the, then, Chief Minister of Jammu & Kashmir, Farooq Abdullah Sahab. As a family friend, I was very close to her without having anything to do with politics. It occurred to me that in the prevailing circumstances Professor A.A.Suroor would be the best person to give her sound and impartial advice because of his intimate knowledge of Kashmir affairs and personal contacts with both the Chief Minister and the Governor, who was none else than the famous B.K.Nehru. I requested Indiraji to give an appointment to Suroor Sahab and this was promptly done. However, quite contrary to her usual style of meeting others, all the talking was done by her and the burden of her monologue was that there had to be a new Chief Minister. The Governor was totally unwilling to take to take this step, and offered to resign. However, he was prevailed upon directly or indirectly by the Centre to accept a transfer to Gujrat.

Something similar happened to my good friend, Dr. U.N.Singh when he was Vice-Chancellor of Allahabad University. As a person of high ideals and integrity he strove for the ethical and administrative betterment of the university. This led to appropriate disciplinary action against some erring students and employees of the University. The disgruntled elements directly approached the Chancellor, who, most unfortunately, got personally involved in the dispute. The Chancellor overruled written orders of the Vice-Chancellor issued from his office in accordance with the statutes. A serious crisis was created and a writ petition was filed before the Allahabad High Court challenging the validity of the action taken by the Chancellor. The High Court referred the matter back to the Chancellor for reconsideration. The Chancellor remained adamant and the matter came up once again before the court. The learned judges ruled that the Chancellor ought not to have cancelled the order issued by the competent authority, but having done so, the Chancellor's order shall prevail. As a man of principle and honor, U.N.Singh resigned. The Central and State governments made no effort to intervene and his resignation was promptly accepted by the Governor of Uttar Pradesh as if it were a golden gift. When I came to know of this sordid drama it was too late for me to do anything constructive in the matter. However, I thought it was my duty to express my strong moral disapproval in a letter to Indiraji, who was Prime Minister. I ended my letter with the request that she should consider taking more interest in the affairs of the Allahabad University, once the pride of India.

A New Phase of Intellectual Growth

Sometime later in the normal course of my academic work I had to supervise a student doing research on the philosophy of Karl Jaspers. The student was bright and hard working. My desire to render the best possible guidance I was capable of became a means of my own intellectual growth. Jasper's conception that philosophy must be an amalgam of analytical clarification of basic concepts, illumination of the authentic self and the building of metaphysical 'ciphers' shaped my own ideas on the basic distinction between Physics and Metaphysics and the nature, function and justification of worldviews or perspectives as plural 'existential interpretation of the universe. His profound analysis of the basic features of the human situation shows tragedy to be its essential ingredient. One of the forms of tragedy, according to Jaspers, is that no human being can escape from being misunderstood by other human beings. This insight is very penetrating and has far ranging implications for philosophy and society.

A fresh stage of intellectual development began when I found I was becoming rather disenchanted and disillusioned with the historical unfolding of the idea or ideal of Socialism. From my early post-graduate student days I, under the influence of Nehru, H.G.Wells and Bernard Shaw, had remained under the spell of Fabian Socialism. This early attraction got strengthened and confirmed in the Cambridge period. Nehru's version of a mixed economy with the state in charge of its 'commanding heights', and the private sector for consumer goods appeared to be the optimally balanced and fruitful synthesis of the 19th century thesis of capitalism and its 20th century anti-thesis of Soviet Socialism. It seemed to me that it was the best of all possible economies since it avoided the defects and limitations found in both pure capitalist and pure socialist economies. Though I admired Western democracy the fierce competition, perhaps, inseparably connected with the free market economy, was morally repugnant to me.

The principal ground of my preference for the socialist model was the theoretical belief that it would eliminate the soul killing competition and the various aberrations of the profit motive. However, this sincere belief got shattered by the passage of time. I first came across some sober and compelling critiques of Soviet society and Russian character in a number of serious and objectively written works. *The God That Failed* had greatly provoked and disturbed me, but (as mentioned earlier) my socialist conviction had not changed. Now another book by an Oxford scholar led me to question the theoretical assumption that competition is a demon. But my final disillusionment with textbook Socialism came when I read Malcom Muggeridge's autobiography, *A Chronicle of Wasted Years* in two volumes. I gradually had to reject my previous rather unexamined assumption that a socialist society 'breeds' responsible and co-operative individuals, while the free market economy selfish and corrupt. Human society is exceedingly complex and numerous variables operate and determine the concrete course of events. I began to appreciate the deep wisdom of the liberal humanist tradition when it is impregnated by ever-growing sociological and historical inputs.

At this point I am reminded of my dear cousin and friend, Mustafa Rasheed Shervani. About four years elder to me he possessed a first rate mind though he was far from being a scholar. His untimely death when he was fifty-nine came as a crushing blow to his numerous friends and admirers. As an industrialist member of the Congress party and member of the Rajya Sabha he always tried to convince me that my socialist approach would never work satisfactorily or deliver goods in actual practice. He had made it a point to visit Russia and on his return he became even more convinced than before that the profit motive and the need for competition were indispensable for a healthy economy. All his practical wisdom made little dent upon my theoretical mindset and fascination for the Nehru vision. But Rasheed (who was always *Achhey Bhai* for me) died in the early eighties and he did not live to see the change in my thinking. I now realize the intuitive wisdom of his approach. I respectfully submit that the collapse of the Soviet Union and the sweeping changes in the entire Communist world should also make us all think afresh on the foundational issues involved.

As I matured and reflected on the history of the human family I grew increasingly conscious of the recurring pattern of historical change. Cultural cycles are no less a fact than the impact of material or technological factors. The theme of the philosophy of history became my focus of intellectual interest, next only to Meta-philosophy. Classical metaphysical concerns almost withered away in my intellectual pursuits. It was in this period that I wrote a long paper titled *The Wisdom of History*. It was published in the journal, *Man and Development* in the issue of June 1983. Writing this paper helped me clarify the notions of historical causation, explanation and evidence. I also put forward my own independent views relating to purpose in history.

Psychoanalysis and personality Psychology had been my area of special interest even earlier than philosophy of history. I had admired the writings of Karen Horney and Erich Fromm from my Cambridge days. I found Fromm's *Fear of Freedom* and Horney's *Neurosis and Human Growth* especially illuminating. Much later I began to appreciate the existentialist approaches of Albert Camus and Simone Dubois. I had no difficulty with their atheism precisely because they had no quarrel with the theism of others. The agreement to differ was the grand part of the existentialist passion for freedom and authenticity.

Moreover, the existentialist approach to religion was quite free from the pretensions of the so-called rationalistic approach to religion.

My commitment to Islam and deep interest in comparative Mysticism continued along with my view that linguistic analysis was the proper method of doing philosophy. In other words and in short, I appreciated John Wisdom, Ramsey and Jaspers. Albert Camus came into my life after I had done my main work. My integrated approach to philosophy and religion is fully reflected in my *Quest For Islam*. I hold that my approach is not a patchwork synthesis but is a holistic response to the mystery of existence.

I had always been interested in spirituality without dogma. The writings of Guru Mahesh Yogi were somewhat familiar to me. Under encouragement from my talented nephew, Mansoor, a prominent cardiologist of Lucknow, I started practicing *Transcendental Meditation* (TM) on a regular basis. I supplemented it with critical studies on related subjects and came to the conclusion that TM was definitely fruitful, but not a panacea by itself. It had to be supplemented by other tools such as existential reflection on the human situation, self-analysis, and, above all, sheer hard systematic work connected with one's vocation or profession. Inner peace and optimum productivity did not automatically follow or flow from meditation alone. In other words, TM was not a magical formula at all as some are ever ready to believe.

Another stage in my intellectual development came about due to the literary influence of my long friendship with the Aligarh economist, Professor Aulad Ahmad Siddiqui. Due to various reasons I had had very little to do with English or Urdu literature until quite late in life. My friend taught me the proper place of great novels and of poetry in the good life. He advised me to go through great European classics, such as *Brothers Kamarazov, Jean Christopher, Le Miserables, and Magic Mountain* etc. I soon came to realize the immense power of great literature to plumb the depths of the human psyche and illuminate the human situation, to the envy of philosophers, psychologists and historians. I also started enjoying and learning from great biographies or memoirs. But my meager knowledge of Persian stood in the way of my appreciating the great treasures of Persian *Sufi* poetry. English translations helped only marginally.

Our 'Umra' Visit to Saudi Arabia:

My *'Umra'* visit to Saudi Arabia in 1982, accompanied by my spouse, Hamida, and our daughter, Geeta Anjum, was a turning point in my life. After reaching Jeddah I resolved that for the entire duration of our stay in the Holy Land I shall regularly perform all the five obligatory Islamic prayers. I had then no idea that my resolve would flower into the practice of daily meditation and prayer thrice a day ever afterwards to date. This discipline is based on the Islamic pattern but in an extremely flexible manner with regard to timings and format.

A small portion of the immense oval court of the *Kaba* is called 'the place of Abraham'. This place contains a block of stone bearing what is believed to be the impression of the feet of Abraham, the common father of the Jews, Arabs and Christians. In another area is the source of the perennial spring *'Zam Zam'*. Close by are the two jutting rocks, *Safa* and *Marva* between which the wife of the Great Patriarch had run to and fro in search of water. The Quran refers to the ancient beliefs or myths, but mentions no details. I submit, it is improper to claim that numerous stories and legends of popular Islam are integral parts of the essential Islam.

My most memorable experience during the pilgrimage took place on my first visit to the *Kaba*. As I sat down to meditate after offering my very first prayer tears began pouring and would not stop. They were tears of humility, gratitude and the yearning for self-purification and for Divine forgiveness and seeking of blessings from the Lord of the worlds for a lowly miserable creature sitting in the precincts of the *Kaba* hallowed by its association with Abraham and Muhammad. The flow of tears may well have continued for five minutes or so. But I remained in a state of effortless meditation, peace and bliss for not less than half an hour or even more.

A totally different type of experience occurred when we tried to reach the cave of *Hira*, not very far from the *Kaba*. Prophet Muhammad used to frequent this cave located on the hilltop and meditate for long hours. It was here that he had received the first revelation that had shaken him and he had rushed back to his house and was comforted by his spouse. It was the considered policy of the Saudi custodians of the sacred places to discourage pilgrims from reaching the cave. The route to the cave was purposefully kept in a state that inhibited visitors from seeking access to it. We tried to do so but had to abandon the attempt half way because of fading light. On our way back we came across a solitary Egyptian pilgrim who was also trying to reach the cave but had to give up. The Saudi stand is that giving importance to visiting sites connected with Prophet Muhammad encourages polytheistic sentiments and dilutes the pure and strict Islamic monotheism. We could not disagree more with this line of thinking but were helpless in the matter. So was the Egyptian.

While traveling by car from Mecca to Medina, a distance of approximately two hundred miles we saw several rock formations and stone impressions, on the roadside, strikingly similar to the 'feet of Abraham'. This observation, however, does not prove anything at all. Later on when we were in the USA we were to see the pre-historic stone caves in Texas. Our nephew, Shafiq, an engineer permanently settled in Houston, especially took us to see these living underground rocks that were still growing and assuming all sorts of geometrical and natural architectural shapes and configurations such as houses, animals, birds and what not. We were told that similar stone caves exist in Petra and one or two other places on the globe. On our way from Arabia to the USA we broke journey for a day at Cairo to see the ancient Pyramids. It was certainly worthwhile catching even a fleeting glimpse into the achievements of the Egyptian wing of the human family. However, the poverty of contemporary Egypt filled us with sadness specially after having just seen the affluence in Saudi Arabia. But Saudi Arabia was culturally starving due to restrictions placed by the puritanical Saudi rulers.

VISIT TO THE USA

From Arabia we proceeded to Cairo and thence to the United States. Our visit to the *Library of Congress* is an unforgettable experience. Its impact on me was far more than that of the Senate and Congress buildings. The elegance and beauty of the main Reading room of the Library are without parallel in the entire world. The choice of Italian marble paneling from floor to high ceiling is, indeed, breath taking and the serene atmosphere of the place completely overshadowed, for me, the charm of the rest of the Capitol Hill complex.

Another place, which left me gaping in sheer wonder, was the Beverly Hills area of Los Angeles. The houses did not have lawns and gardens attached to them; rather the entire area was one mega-garden where enchanting cottages and pavilions sprouted like flowers. Still more impressive was the new industrial area or complex in California where instead of smoke, grime and grease associated with industrial areas we came across pastel colored elegant offices and production sites.

The main campus of the famed Harvard University, however, came as a disappointment to me as one who had spent two full years at the banks of Cam with the daffodils of Wordsworth dancing in the green meadows and woods of Cambridge. The main limitation of Harvard is due to the surprising fact that the Harvard campus does not run parallel to the course of the river. The MIT is better located in this regard. The disappointment at Harvard, however, was more than compensated by the thrill at visiting Brown University and the famous sites in New England and Rhode Island region where the Pilgrim Fathers had established the first secular state in the world. I also saw a computer in action for the first time.

STAY WITH RAVEEND AT NORWICH

On our way back home from the USA we broke journey to stay with my brother, Raveend, a medical practitioner at Norwich in North

England. Raveend was actively associated with the local Islamic Centre. About five hundred English men and women had recently embraced Islam and an unused church had been bought and converted into a mosque under the auspices of some Islamic trust under the management of English Muslims. Regular congregational prayers were held there and Raveend was frequently present at the services.

Raveend introduced me to some of his English Muslim brothers after congregational prayers one Friday. I was shocked to learn that many English Muslims had thought it fit to break away from those members of their families who had refused to embrace Islam for whatever reason. Further questioning the new converts revealed that they had done so on the belief that Islam did not approve of close and intimate relations of Muslims with non-Muslims. Raveend later on informed me that he had done all he possibly could to disabuse the minds of the English converts of this false and distorted notion of Islam, but unfortunately they enjoyed being more Catholic than the Pope.

Since Raveend had introduced me as an Islamic philosopher from the famous Aligarh Muslim University I also ventured to talk to some of the young English Muslims to remove their wrong ideas and to encourage them to cherish their family ties, irrespective of religious differences. I was shocked still more when some of the more articulate English Muslims came up with Quranic quotations or sayings of the Prophet in support of the distorted and pernicious view that believers should not befriend unbelievers. It became obvious to me that this was how their English Islamic mentors who had initiated them into the faith had interpreted Islam. I tried to convince the young English Muslims that every religion or faith could and did have plural interpretations, and that I was afraid their Islamic mentors had erred in interpreting the concerned Quranic texts or sayings of the Prophet on the subject of proper relations between believers in different faiths. But, obviously, the matter was not so simple and we parted on a friendly note that they would ponder over the issues raised by me as a born Muslim and also as an Islamic thinker.

Aligarh Once Again: Slow Maturity Part 1

Another episode relating to the leader of the English Muslim community was still more shocking and sad. The leader, a graduate of Oxford University, whose Islamic name was Abdul Qadir, took to seriously encouraging his Muslim flock to resort to bigamy as a method of increasing the population of Muslims. The English Shaikh tried his best to steer the newly converted Muslims to the viewpoint that it was an Islamic duty to follow the Prophet of Islam in every matter, including polygamy. Here again Raveend tried his best to oppose this line of thinking, but several English Muslim converts, unfortunately, succumbed to this strange and fantastic logic in the name of Islam. However, when this almost incredible exhortation gradually led to disrupted families and broken homes, as was inevitable, a revolt broke out against the Shaikh who was forced to flee to Spain and to abandon his dream of glorifying Islam through quickly multiplying the faithful.

After ten weeks of a rewarding pilgrimage and study tour we returned home. I began to see more clearly than ever before that religious faith or creed has rather little effect upon the inner character of the believer, since individuals behave more under the influence of ethnic genes and their distinctive cultural environment than according to their formal religious or ethical teachings. In other words, I began to see more clearly that goodness of heart is more important than professing any particular creed or 'the' one true religion, namely one's own. Equally clearly, I saw that no country in the world cared more for the physically or mentally handicapped members of society than the USA.

CHAPTER 6

ALIGARH ONCE AGAIN, PART 2

MY ASSOCIATION WITH THE KHUDA BAKHSH LIBRARY, PATNA:

Returning home I resumed my familiar life style and work. Shortly after I returned I was invited to deliver the *Khuda Bakhsh Memorial* lecture at Patna by the Director, Khuda Bakhsh Oriental Library, Dr. A.R.Bedar. My first lecture was followed by several others. In these lectures, which have been published, I attempted a more detailed exploration of the economic, political and social contents of liberal Islam, as I had presented it in my *Quest for Islam*. In this way Bedar Sahab provided the stimulus for my creative work at this stage. I can never thank him enough for this. Bedar Sahab had also transformed the Khuda Bakhsh Oriental Library into a vibrant center for research in Islamic Studies.

Shortly before retiring in 1988 as Professor of Philosophy my small book, titled *Authenticity and Islamic Liberalism* was published. Like my Patna lectures this book also carried forward the basic themes of the *Quest*. But there was no repetition. By 1985 my work on Philosophy and religion was almost over. But it was plain that hardly any serious discussion or debate occurred in Muslim circles, though the noted Catholic scholar, Christian Troll and a few other non-Muslim circles took serious note of my work. I was told by a reliable source that prominent conservative quarters were greatly displeased with my approach, but they decided that the best defense of their version of Islam would be to ignore my work and let it die a natural slow death in the darkness of oblivion. I felt sad but was not demoralized. I knew how the Muslim establishment had ignored the Islamic vision of Sir Syed, despite lionizing him as the savior of Muslims in modern India.

I was and am honestly convinced that in the modern age of experimental science different religions can flourish only in their respective liberal humanist, rather than in their ancient or medieval, versions. However, the Muslim establishment remains in full control of the commanding heights of the culture of the establishment. The *Ulema* honestly believe that the liberal intellectuals are not qualified to reinterpret Islamic concepts and values without having mastered Arabic and also traditional Islamic learning. This, I submit, is only a half-truth, at the very best. The other half of the full truth is that in the modern age the *Ulema* too would have to re-earn their old right to interpret traditional values after they honestly master the thought and value system of modernity. And they are nowhere near this happy position. Indeed, they have not even embarked upon this journey. But the matter is crucially urgent. Modern Muslims all over the world must be awakened from their dogmatic slumber. This was the dream of Sir Syed that Indian Muslims should learn science and modern tools of research together with adequate knowledge of traditional learning.

FRIENDS AS MY TEACHERS

All through my life 'intellectual gossip' with close friends has been my hobby. I have learnt a lot through such dialogues though I may have, unknowingly, bored them at times. I must express my gratitude to them all. I would specially mention Professor Hamieduddin Khan, scholar of Persian, Professor Mohibbul Hasan, the eminent historian, Professor Zafar Ahmad Siddiqui, Professor Anwar Ansari, Professor S.A.Akbarabadi, Professor Masoodul Hasan, Principal Jamil Siddiqui of the Muslim University City School, Dr. Kamauddin Siddiqui of the Education Department, Mr. Ali Ashraf, veteran freedom fighter and journalist, Mr. Farrukh Jalali, who specializes in Aligarh Studies, Professor M.H.Razvi of the Maulana Azad Library, Professor R.R.Sherwani, and Professor G.K.Gahrana, the veteran political scientist and social activist. I deeply regret I missed opportunities to benefit from the conversational wit and wisdom of the legendary Rasheed Ahmad Siddiqui.

In a unique category of friends I must mention (late) Haji Hasan Abidi of Jalali, Ghulam Warris of Dharampur, a perfect gentleman of the old landed aristocratic hue, and dear Ishtiaq Alvi of Kakori, who has authored well received books in Urdu on *Shikar* and jungle life. I have a special corner in my heart for Naushad Husain, friend and colleague, who, as a research student, used to oblige me often by taking down lengthy pieces of my philosophical dictation. (Late) Professor Jamil Qadri was another young colleague in the early phase of my academic career, and was of great help in academic and practical matters.

I acknowledge what I learnt from Nawab Ali Yavar Jung, perhaps the most polished and charming figure, after Nehru that I have come across in my life, and Nawab Ahmad Said Khan of Chattari. I am bracketing them as they shared a remarkable common trait of character. They never spoke ill of anybody behind his or her back. They named the person, if his action or actions merited impartial praise. If, however, they judged some action of others as blameworthy, they both made it a point not to name the person or persons, but merely made an indirect reference without giving away their identity. The hearer could make his or her own guess. In this way both engaged in an honest and transparent dialogue with others without compromising the sanctity of their personal relationships or friendships. Both the eminent personalities, thus, practiced courtesy to all without any hypocrisy.

LEARNING THROUGH UNIVERSITY ADMINISTRATION

This is the place to refer to my ventures in university administration from which I had tried to keep myself aloof on the principle that it interferes with purely academic work. However, I could not say no to the then Vice-Chancellor, Professor Abdul Aleem, when he insisted upon my joining his team as Provost of the *Non-Resident Student's Centre*. I completed one full term of two years and tried to give my best to my *alma mater*, but gratefully declined any further extension. The second occasion arose in entirely different conditions when I was Head of the Department of Philosophy, Dean of the Faculty of Arts and an ex officio member of the Executive Council of the University. On this occasion I voluntarily offered my services as honorary Proctor of the University. This is how it came about.

Due to a combination of circumstances prevailing in the AMU and the country as a whole there had been a long delay in the selection and appointment of a new Vice-Chancellor after Professor A.M. Khusro had completed his term. At long last Saiyed Hamid Sahab was appointed but he informed the authorities that he would take charge after three months or so in view of his prior commitments as Chairman of the Subordinate Services Commission. The university statutes required the senior most professor of the university to function as acting Vice-Chancellor during this period. Consequently, Professor M.Shafi, the eminent geographer, functioned as Acting Vice-Chancellor, and Professor Masoodul Hasan was Dean of the Arts Faculty.

Out of sheer disgust and helplessness to arrest the sharp decline in academic and administrative matters in the Faculty the Dean of the Faculty suddenly resigned. I learnt of his resignation from The Registrar who came to my office and asked me to take over charge as Dean with immediate effect. He further wanted me to preside over the meeting of the Faculty, which had been scheduled to be held that very day. The Registrar met me just two hours before the meeting was due. The Registrar appeared to be quite certain that there would be no difficulty or hitch in my stepping into the office of Dean and that it was a purely routine matter. But that was not my idea of how university administration ought to be run, and how a brother Professor should respond to the resignation of his senior colleague.

I promptly got in touch with Professor Masoodul Hasan, a close friend and highly esteemed colleague. Expressing my pain at the course of events I and other friends tried our level best to persuade him to reconsider his resignation. But he was firm as a rock. I had the least desire to step into his shoes as I shared his pain and disillusionment with the state of affairs in Indian Universities as a whole. However, if I had declined to be Dean the next senior most Professor would have become Dean in a routine manner and things would have remained as they were. I, therefore, thought it best to take into confidence all the senior Professors who were prospective Deans with a view to exerting moral pressure upon the higher authorities of the University to mend matters. No Professor was willing to accept the position of Dean without full assurance that he will get full backing from the acting Vice-Chancellor and that he will not succumb to political or other pressures. After a delay of two months or so I gave my consent to function as Dean.

Things went well for some time. Shortly afterwards, however, things became so difficult for the acting Vice-Chancellor, that able and honest as he was, he collapsed under the strain and was advised complete rest by doctors. He took leave and Professor Qamar Farooqui, as the next in order of seniority took charge as acting Vice-Chancellor. There was some respite. But he was on the very verge of superannuation and was rather uncertain of the future. The law and order situation in the campus was shocking and student indiscipline was at its peak. There was a general apprehension that annual examinations will have to be postponed and students will have to suffer from the loss of one academic year. None among the senior teachers was willing to take the risk of managing the AMU in that period of turmoil. Professor Farooqui, therefore, convened an emergency meeting of the local members of the Executive Council (EC) to decide the best course of action in a grave situation.

As ex-officio member of the Executive Council I was present in the above crucial meeting. It seemed to me that gloom and depression were in the air and there seemed to be little chance of improving the situation. On a sudden impulse I offered my services to my *alma mater* as an honorary Proctor for a short period. I said that complete resignation or the giving up of all effort was to accept defeat even before the fight, while honest efforts might, conceivably, lead to success. And lo! The Executive Council unanimously accepted my strange offer. Nobody present, including myself, could have imagined that this would be the outcome of this emergency meeting.

The next four or five months saw the transformation of a rather retiring teacher into an active, determined and bold administrator. My first and most crucial task was to build a team of sincere associates in the proctorial team. I appealed to personal friends as well as other teachers of known integrity and sincerity. Almost every one whom I approached for help generously responded to my call for vigorously tackling student indiscipline and petty crimes in the campus. But I must make special mention of Athar Parvez of the Department of Urdu and S.K.Singh of the University Polytechnic.

An immediate improvement took place. The new proctorial team took immediate steps to expel a number of students who, unfortunately, had fallen on anti-social ways, but all this was done in a spirit of kindness and concern for the good of themselves and the *alma mater*. Professor Farooqui fully backed the efforts of the proctorial team, which functioned as one man, and most teachers and administrative staff were also helpful. An immediate improvement took place. However, the imminent superannuation of Professor Farooqui meant that the next senior most Professor will step in his place as acting Vice-Chancellor, and none among the senior Professors was willing to accept this seat of thorns.

I literally begged Professor J.N.Prasad, of the Medical College to save the university from closure and he kindly agreed after much persuasion. Professor Farooqui handed over charge to Prasad Sahab. For about a fortnight I found myself in the very embarrassing role of an extra-constitutional authority in the affairs of the Aligarh Muslim University. On one occasion Professor Prasad resigned in disgust and I had to rush to his house to beg that he should not desert us in the midst of a crisis. I would have collapsed under the strain if Prime Minister Indira Gandhi had not come to my rescue. My wife and I requested her in person that she may kindly 'direct' the Vice-Chancellor designate to take over charge of the Aligarh Muslim University with immediate effect. This she kindly did and the third day following my request Saiyed Hamid Sahab took over charge. This was a new and happy dawn for the University.

The new Vice-Chancellor had a glorious start and despite several challenges and difficulties in the way the annual examinations were held as per schedule. I was Dean of the Arts Faculty and Professor Irfan Habib headed the Social Science Faculty. However, fresh difficulties arose or were created by those elements, which could not see eye to eye with the remarkably honest and apolitical approach of the Vice-Chancellor who was a deeply committed Muslim. Paradoxically, the loud protagonists of Islam began to dub him a '*Mullah*' while the Communist or Leftist elements in the Campus became his supporters.

The noted historian, Irfan Habib, whose father had been my teacher and a great family friend, led the left elements. I had a soft corner for Irfan, despite my honest disagreement with his Communist Party (M) brand of politics. The Vice-Chancellor also held the historian in high regard though he was, obviously, none too happy with the political and religious views of the Marxist scholar. Unfortunately, the idea that an active Communist had no place in the AMU community carried some prominent senior teachers and Muslim opinion makers away. Slogans appeared on the campus walls that the 'Russian dog' must go. Irfan Sahab was also physically attacked more than once. I and some other University liberals boldly took the stand that Muslim society, in general, and the University, in particular, as a place of free enquiry and research, must tolerate honest dissent, political as well as religious or ideological. I recall my friendly 'advice' (in a humorous vein, of course) to those sections that would not have shed tears if the AMU could possibly have got rid of the atheist professor, that calling names was not Islamic. If, however, they had to call the atheist professor a dog, they should have called the economic historian a 'Chinese', not 'Russian', dog. To call a distinguished ideologue of the CPM a 'Russian' dog reflected the hollowness of the fanatics who wanted to cleanse the Muslim University by hounding out the 'Russian' dog.

The University had to pass through a long period of internal strife leading to the *'gherao'* of the Vice-Chancellor and local members of the Executive Council and also to police firing resulting in the death of one student. The Vice-Chancellor was heartbroken and felt shattered and was keen to quit. Once again, my personal appeal to Indiraji helped to rescue the University from further political interference from various quarters, including some active and influential Congressmen themselves. After giving a patient hearing, at my request, to Sayid Hamid Sahab and myself she issued necessary instructions on the hotline to the Cabinet Secretary to ensure the Centre's complete backing and cooperation with the Vice-Chancellor. The derailed Aligarh Muslim University was soon put back on rails. The Aligarh Muslim University, with minor ups and downs, ran smoothly under Saiyed Hamid Sahab, and later, under his very distinguished successor, Hashim Ali Sahab. My superannuation almost coincided with that of the latter. He graciously offered me an extension of service; but I gratefully declined.

This is the place to mention a very welcome and thoughtful initiative taken by Saiyad Hamid Sahab: the revival, after almost a century, of Sir Syed's famous Urdu journal, *Tehzibul Akhlaq*. The Vice Chancellor was the Chief Editor. Every issue contained a reprint of some original article penned by Sir Syed. But on principle Hamid Sahab excluded such articles as contained Sir Syed's interpretation of Islamic doctrines and beliefs. Hamid Sahab thought it prudent to avoid any controversy on religious matters and a free and candid debate on Sir Syed's Islamic vision. Hashim Ali Sahab, on the other hand, was very much alive to this need of the hour, and deeply appreciated my own humble efforts in this direction when some friends and I launched the *New Aligarh Movement* and published a collection of Sir Syed's writings on Islam. I have yet to come across a prominent committed Muslim more intellectually honest and candid than Hashim Sahab with the exception of my father.

Saiyed Hamid Sahab, a deeply religious and ethically oriented person (rather suspicious of aggressively secular or leftist politicians) was also allergic to the pose of religion without honest commitment and was bent upon removing indiscipline, corruption and laxity in academic and administrative matters. Now, a good many of the loud protagonists of Islamic values and champions of Muslim interests started resisting and opposing his reform measures. On the other hand, a good many of the secular leftist and communist quarters heartily cooperated with the new Vice-Chancellor. This was yet another confirmation of my oft-repeated refrain that loud members of the party of Allah/God/Sri Ram can be highly immoral and unprincipled, while atheists and antagonists of God can be highly moral and principled supporters of the right cause.

It is very common in India for vested interests in India to misuse and exploit religious sentiments for their own material gains. Some employees of the Maulana Azad Library, AMU, tried to malign the Head Librarian on the false and malicious charge that he obstructed them from offering the obligatory Islamic prayers whose timings fell between office hours. The plain fact was that the Librarian tried to stop some unscrupulous and lazy employees from shirking professional duties through unduly prolonging the time they took in preparing and performing the obligatory prayers. The Librarian himself was a sincerely religious liberal Muslim, but he was dubbed as a communist, or as a *Shia* dissident. Something contrary to the above happened in the Department of Persian when the guardian of a post-graduate girl student complained to me when I was the Dean of the Faculty of Arts. The complaint was that his daughter wanted to wear the veil in the class lectures, but that some students, teachers and university employees of a Muslim institution were putting pressure on the girl to give up the veil. While confessing that I myself did not approve of the veil (though I greatly value sexual modesty and chastity) I assured the anxious guardian that his ward should not be obstructed from following her own concept of female modesty. I am firmly convinced that social attitudes and religious convictions just cannot be ordered or forced upon individuals and societies.

THE CASE OF THE HINDU STUDENT WHO FREELY CONVERTED TO ISLAM

When I was Dean of the Faculty of Arts a research student in the Department of Hindi came to me for help in a very personal matter. He had been placed in the first division in all examinations right up to the MA level and was getting a University Grants Commission research fellowship. But his nerves had almost broken down as a result of his inner religious perplexity and conflict. Born into a lower middle *Vaish* family in eastern Uttar Pradesh, he had converted to Islam soon after passing the High School examination in the first division. This was under the influence of a well-read Muslim divine in east Uttar Pradesh, but it was his free decision. He kept on his study of Islam in addition to his academic studies in which he excelled. His initial Muslim mentor was a *Sunni* theologian, but as he continued his study of Islam he began to be drawn to *Shia* Islam. But a second conversion from the *Sunni* to the *Shia* version was repugnant to the young man. Moreover, in the course of time even the *Shia* doctrines had ceased to satisfy him intellectually. He found himself in the wilderness of agnosticism and, at times, of total atheism. He had lost his sleep and inner peace, and was totally unable to concentrate on his research. His fellowship was about to expire, and as a married man he had a family to support.

I advised the research scholar not to worry about the past happenings or even the expectations or reactions of his present Muslim or Hindu associates, but to search his inner depths, without any fear or favor, and to follow the voice of his conscience. I told him that religious conversion should never be done in a hurry or at a young and immature age. It was futile crying over spilt milk. What he needed now was the courage to be authentic and inwardly free without caring for public opinion. Since, however, first things should come first, he should, for the time being, defer his inner search for truth and concentrate all his energy on completing and submitting his Ph.D. thesis in good time.

Well, the student did respond and he made a remarkably swift recovery. In due course he was awarded his doctorate and was also appointed as a Lecturer at a good university. At our last meeting several years ago he informed me that he had found inner peace and full satisfaction in Islam. I did not probe any further into the details of his Islamic faith.

While I feel very happy at the above role I played as a teacher I have feelings of deep regret at my behavior in two or three academic matters. A student in my Department was very bright and promising but his religious and political views differed sharply from mine. I never penalized the student in any way. But I now feel that I did not or could not sufficiently encourage and appreciate the student and extend to him the loving empathy a teacher should ideally and unconditionally have for the student.

The second case of regret concerns a student whose political activism brought him into some trouble with the authorities. It was in my personal knowledge that he was not to blame in a particular case. Yet, I failed to give him moral support and sympathy in his hour of need and was heartless enough to point out that his troubles were the inevitable consequence of his wrong and foolish line of thinking. I was more indignant that the student concerned had not paid any heed to my 'counsels of wisdom' than I was sorry at his distress. In other words, my fund of sympathy and concern for the particular student was not what it should have been.

The third lapse concerns my role as an examiner of a doctoral thesis. I was asked to give my consent to evaluate a Ph.D. thesis on a subject with which I was not sufficiently familiar. My original reaction was to decline the offer. But I fell under the temptation that I could first study the subject and then evaluate the thesis, and that this would be a good means of my own intellectual growth. Unfortunately, procrastination got the better of me, and the matter dragged on and on. Reminders from the Registrar concerned fell on deaf ears. Eventually I was asked to return the thesis unexamined. Ashamed to do so or to confess the real reason I set upon the task of evaluation without the intensive initial study I had planned. My performance was bound to be inadequate. I still suffer from a sense of academic guilt at the entire episode, which ended in my reluctantly recommending the award of a doctorate. However, I can say with full honesty that I had no ulterior motive when I accepted the assignment.

In the late sixties or early seventies some friends and I, notably the Oxford educated Arabist, Professor Maqbool Ahmad (who passed away a few years back) formed an informal discussion group named 'Islamics'. About a dozen or more teachers and research students used to discuss Islamic themes. The main purpose was to enable teachers and students to exchange their honest views or ideas in the spirit of free enquiry without any fear or external constraint. A number of meetings were held and proved moderately fruitful. In order to make the exchange of ideas more meaningful and also beneficial to a wider circle I suggested that the initial speaker should prepare a brief written note for presentation. This proved disastrous for the life of the discussion group. A good friend who had agreed to initiate a discussion on some theme excused himself on the ground that putting his thoughts in writing might expose him to the risk of the charge of heresy or heterodoxy. In retrospect I think I should have been satisfied with oral discussions. But at that time I allowed the infant group to fade away.

The disillusionment and frustration, which resulted from the above experience, however, did not dampen my spirits and my eagerness for informal friendly dialogue with intelligent and honest believers, irrespective of their belief systems. Sincere dialogues aimed at better understanding of different points of view rather than converting others to one's own viewpoint help in bringing to the surface one's own angularities or hidden contradictions. I continued informal and friendly dialogue with *Shia* and *Sunni* friends and disregarded the conventional wisdom of polite silence when talking with all out-groups.

When I was the Head of the Department of Philosophy the Board of Studies formally sponsored a comprehensive research scheme for promoting the study of Muslim Philosophy in a modern comparative and critical spirit. The scheme was submitted through official channels for inclusion in the University Grants Commission (UGC)

Development plan. Unfortunately, the scheme did not materialize due to the apathy of Syed Hamid Sahab. It would be wonderful if it could be revived since the idea of reconstructing religious thought in Islam (first mooted by Iqbal in modern times) is the need of Muslims and the entire world.

CLOSING STAGE OF MY INTELLECTUAL GROWTH:

Towards the close of my retirement in 1988 some close friends and I founded a voluntary association, 'The New Aligarh Movement' for promoting Islamic liberalism and creatively developing its concepts and values. The noted Urdu scholar and doyen of Aligarh intellectuals, Professor A.A. Suroor, consented to be the President. The Society held a number of seminars and published an anthology on Sir Syed's Islamic vision. Working for the Society has been a labor of love for me. Hashim Ali Sahab was Vice-Chancellor when he released the said Anthology. He greatly appreciated and encouraged us. He himself was an outstanding Islamic liberal and a man of great vision and integrity. He settled down in the US after his retirement and published a very readable volume, *The Essence of Islam*. The work gives extensive quotations from the Quran.

How tortuous and thorny is the journey before us was vividly brought home to me when I presented, rather offered to present the book to a retired Professor of the Aligarh Muslim University. He spontaneously remarked that he did not care to read Sir Syed who was a heretic and disbelieved in the revealed status of the Quran. The fact is that Sir Syed had only denied the fanciful popular mythology relating to the mode of Divine revelation, but not the basic faith in revelation as such. Sir Syed had the clarity and courage to point out the difference between the primary faith in Divine revelation and the secondary mythology that had grown around the nuclear faith. Sir Syed wanted to 'demythologize' Islam as some great Western or Hindu thinkers have tried to do with respect to Christianity and Hinduism respectively.

Founding of the New Servants of India Society

The *New Servants of India Society* (NSOIS) was the second society some friends and I founded. This society organized several seminars, the most important and noteworthy of which was the seminar on *Techniques of Organized Moral Pressure* at the Nehru Museum, New Delhi. The objective was to develop the Gandhian concept of *satyagraha* in contemporary Indian conditions. The writing of the background paper proved a challenging and fruitful task for me. Professor Amrik Singh, one of the rare breed of Vice-Chancellors who have resigned their high office when the state encroached upon academic autonomy or failed to stand by established principles and conventions, played a leading role in making the seminar a success.

The Society also undertook redress of public grievances, and promoted communal harmony. It also produced reports on moral education for students, and an objective analysis of the Bhagalpur communal riot in 1989. My preparation for drafting the report led me to study a number of famous reports on communal disturbances and outbreaks of violence in different parts of the country over the past decades. These reports were the work of high-powered statutory commissions manned by outstanding individuals. They were a great source of insight and education to me. Most outstanding among these reports was the *Madon Report* submitted by an eminent judge of the Bombay High Court.

The Madon Report is a truly monumental piece of patient objective research and constructive suggestions for preventing communal violence and promoting lasting harmony between different communities and castes. It describes without fear or favor the actual conduct of politicians, civil servants, policemen, and the armed forces from the highest to the lowest ranks. The recommendations for curing the social evil in question can hardly be improved any further.

The NSOIS drew attention to the speedy implementation of electoral reforms. I and my colleagues realized that politicians, as a class (including those indulging in high talk about morals and honesty), were more interested in maligning others or building false images rather than in serious and honest schemes for eliminating or reducing corrupt political practices.

My participation in the *International Philosophy Congress* at Brighton, United Kingdom in 1988, as one of the official delegates from India, was a great experience for me. But the direct academic gain could not, possibly, have been much because of the mega size of the conference. In the tremendous rush of paper reading and guest lectures hardly any leisurely dialogue; the lifeblood of conceptual growth: was possible. This was, precisely, why I had been rather shy of participating even in the annual sessions of the Indian Philosophy Congress. I, however, always enjoyed participating in national and regional seminars and learning from others. In this way I came in friendly contact and learnt from several well known Indian thinkers, such as Rajendra Prasad, Devaraja, Daya Krishna, Sachitananda Murty, K.J. Shah, Margaret Chatterjee, Roop Rekha Verma and others. Memories of my association with K.J.Shah, Rajendra Prasad and Daya Krishna are especially dear to me. The moral courage Roop Rekhaji showed during her fairly long term, as acting Vice-Chancellor of Lucknow University deserves to be written as an inspirational story for our intellectuals as well as politicians. It is a sad commentary on our political system that she was not appointed Vice-Chancellor.

THE CARDINAL EVIL OF INTOLERANCE

Life has taught me that next to being untruthful, intolerance is the greatest evil and curse of the human family. Unfortunately, we have little realization of the subtle ways intolerance has of creeping into our ideological arteries and poisoning the quality of life. Here I shall venture to mention some glaring instances of intolerance I have come across in my Muslim circle.

During the national emergency clamped by the central government in the mid seventies the Saharanpur District authorities sounded the distinguished Islamic scholar and venerable head of the Deoband

Islamic Seminary, Qari Tayab, if he was willing to issue a public statement (if he honestly believed it to be true) that the Quranic text does not specifically prohibit contraception, though some *muftis* or *Ulema* oppose family planning. This was the exact truth and the government thought that such a statement by the eminent divine would go a long way to encourage family planning by such Muslims who might have some conscientious objection due to ignorance of the factual position. The learned divine agreed to do so. No sooner this was done many Muslim quarters at Aligarh planned a black flag demonstration against the impending visit of the great theologian to the Aligarh Juma Masjid. This happened in my personal knowledge, as his son, Azam, then a young lecturer at the Aligarh Muslim University lived in our family house as a paying guest. I immediately extended my moral support to him and his venerable father for whom our entire family had great regard. The threat fizzled out, as I had foreseen, and Qari Sahab addressed a public meeting at the Juma Masjid of the city without any ugly obstruction.

The second incident concerns the publication of my Khuda Bakhsh lectures. When the Khuda Bakhsh Library in Patna published my lectures, the eminent Director, a liberal Muslim himself, was constrained to delete some portions from the text, much against my wishes and his own desire to publish the full text. The hue and cry raised in Pakistan several years ago against (late) Fazlur Rahman for some honest and scholarly observations in his admirable book on Islam resulted in his expulsion, as it were, from his own country. Tolerance of dissent and plural interpretations of scriptures is, indeed, the most crucial need of Muslim society.

Here is an instance of intolerance, which I find very sad. A bright Muslim engineer, long settled in the USA, has developed extremely puritanical and rigid views on the prohibition of music, photography, sculpture etc. in Islam. While on a visit to his parents in India he thought it fit and his Islamic duty to remove (even without asking or informing his parents) some decorative metallic objects from the table or shelves in the parent's house, because he could not bear to see his parents violating the *shariah*.

My brother, Raveend, once invited a Muslim family visiting Norwich to lunch at his house after Juma prayers. The subject of interest happened to crop up during the conversation before the food was served. Raveend expressed his view that Islam permits interest on bank deposits. The guests held ultra-orthodox views and said that this amounted to watering down of the strict prohibition of interest by the Quran and *shariah*. Incredible as it sounds, they left the house without eating any morsel of food at 'the house of a heretic'. Raveend and the entire family felt stunned at the behavior of their guests but were utterly helpless to do anything in the matter.

Another instance related by Raveend also borders on the incredible. Raveend had a minor surgery done in Norwich on his toe by a surgeon assisted by a female nurse. Shortly after the surgery he attended some Islamic meet in the United Kingdom. Raveend casually mentioned the surgery to a brother Muslim delegate who (quite unknown to Raveend) believed that Islam ordained complete segregation of the sexes. The delegate spontaneously remarked that Raveend had fallen in his estimation because he was guilty of a 'rape of the toe' when the female nurse touched him.

Here I may well mention, by way of glaring contrast, an example of British tolerance, as related by Raveend himself. A Libyan Muslim, married to an English woman, was on very friendly terms with an English neighbor in Norwich. While the two friends had gone for a walk in the town the Englishman, in a friendly manner and in all good faith, happened to remark that he could not understand the Muslim doctrine that the Holy Prophet was perfect and infallible when he, at fifty, had married a minor girl of seven or eight. This remark so infuriated the Libyan Muslim that he landed a powerful punch on the temple of his British friend. And the Englishman died on the spot. A court case of manslaughter was the natural result. With the lone exception of the accused all others involved in the legal proceedings were Englishmen. The court held that the crime was not murder but of irrational rage against a 'perceived insult' to the Prophet of Islam.

I think this is the right place to draw the reader's attention to another pernicious attitude to life in general – living in compartments instead of living an integrated life according to one's honest beliefs and values. Illustrations of this attitude are galore – a devout religious believer (no matter of what religion or sect) who throws toxic waste in a river, or peddles narcotics, or adulterates food and drugs, or a vocal champion of democracy who does booth capturing for his party or candidate, or a Professor of Zoology who teaches Darwin's theory of organic evolution in the class room, but indoctrinates his children and others in the home that Darwin was the Devil's agent, or a legislator who vociferously supports a bill on the minimum age of consent but does not oppose child marriage if contracted by a religious figure. Living in compartments also occurs whenever we use double standards of right and wrong, good and bad, while judging in-groups and out-groups. Integrated thinking is consistent and clear and flows from moral courage to face the truth without illusions, unconscious distortions or emotive reactions.

Here are some other instances of living in compartments. These case are in my personal knowledge, and the persons involved are, otherwise, good and honest persons. 'A' believes that Hitler was a good and strong personality who is falsely accused of the genocide of the Jews; 'B' holds that the Quran does not permit the owner of female slaves to have sex relations with them without marrying them; 'C' holds that the Quranic texts that prescribe unequal shares to sons and daughters in inherited property, or prescribe that the evidence of two women equals that of one man, or permit the male, but not the female to give unilateral divorce do not amount to any gender discrimination; 'D' holds that a married woman feels psychologically more hurt by her husband's taking to a mistress than by his bigamy.

I respectfully submit that the above beliefs are false, but the persons holding them, perhaps, feel that to question the above beliefs would remove the ground under their feet, making them fall into a bottomless abyss of uncertainty and the total collapse of faith. That is why they remain in a state of denial and prefer to live 'in compartments' rather than strive to reach an 'integrated outlook' on life.

I shall give yet another striking case of the life of denial. This instance is also in my personal knowledge. A young girl of a decent family fell in love with an eligible young man, but the guardian of the girl was too old fashioned to permit a 'love marriage' to take place in the family. She fixed her marriage elsewhere and insisted upon her own choice. The desperate lovers approached my wife and myself and implored us to help them in making the family elder see reason. After fully satisfying ourselves that the lovers were serious and mature and promised to be a good match we met the lady concerned and requested her to respect the sentiments of the young people. Incredible as it sounds, she burst out against us, charged us with maligning the honor of the family, and quite literally ordered us out of the house, saying that our family association had come to an end. We were flabbergasted and stunned, and I still keep wondering what gave us the strength to keep our cool despite the grave humiliation we had to face. Without any rancor or bitterness we quietly left the place. However, after the lapse of a few months the lady relented and agreed to the marriage of the lovers. We were present at the occasion, though it was plain to all that she was not inwardly happy at the idea that a 'love marriage' was taking place in the family.

Chapter 7

Himalayan Retreat: Discovery of Self

Solan is situated at a height of 5,000 feet and is the gateway to the famous Himalayan city, Shimla. Solan enjoys an excellent moderate climate. Ever since my youth I had loved mountains. After my retirement from the Aligarh Muslim University I started living for six months in the year in my wife's cottage at Solan. My main work had already been done, but I was hopeful my reading and writing would go on. Fortunately, Solan has a public library, which, at one time, had the largest collection of books in the entire state.

Our cottage in Solan happens to be very close to the *samadhi* of the founder of the Dev Samaj, which, along with the Arya Samaj reform movement, was born in Punjab in the last quarter of 19th century. While the *Arya Samaj* became a powerful religious, social and political force in north India and a serious rival to the much older and cosmopolitan *Brahmo Samaj* of Bengal, the *Dev Samaj* has remained a, relatively, marginal movement that stands for a purely rational and ethical approach to religion. The founder of the *Dev Samaj*, known as *Dev Atma* to the initiated, hailed from Uttar Pradesh and was, initially, a committed *Brahmo*. For various reasons he became disillusioned with Keshab Chandra Sen who was then the top leader and guide of the *Brahmo Samaj*. Thereafter Dev Atma founded the *Dev Samaj* in Lahore in the closing years of the 19th century.

The *Dev Samaj* upholds the supremacy of reason and the scientific method and rigorously rejects miracles, petitionary prayer, Hindu and all other mythologies, the caste system, authority and infallibility of the Vedas or other scriptures, all organized religions, even the concept of a Personal Creator-God. Even more radical than the Arya Samaj and the Brahmo Samaj, the Dev Samaj affirms Evolutionary Naturalism and the all sufficiency of reason and pure morality for the welfare and salvation of the human family. One of the earliest stalwarts of the movement, Dr. Kanal, and later, his able son, the younger Kanal (who had a degree from London university and who taught Philosophy for long at Delhi University) have given considerable intellectual respectability to this rigorous rationalist movement within the all embracing Hindu religious tradition. By the very nature of the case Dev Samaj (like its ancient prototype, Jainism) can, perhaps, never become a powerful mass movement. The emotional satisfaction, sense of security and consolation, which flow from a theistic perspective, is missing. Moreover, the Samaj does not appear to be as permissive and catholic in its official creed as is traditional Hinduism ranging from primitive 'mythologism' to *Theistic Bhakti* to Vedantic Monism. The Samaj, however, remains a living movement and runs several schools and colleges in Punjab. Every year in June a large number of its active members congregate at the *Founder's samadhi*. A magnificent auditorium has recently been constructed adjoining the *samadhi*.

I cannot thank God enough that I have found deep peace and satisfaction reading and writing in Solan. On a few occasions I have spoken in public. Once I had to speak on the contribution of Dr. Zakir Husain to national integration. The function had been organized by the Urdu Centre at Solan. Great as was my personal knowledge of and also admiration for the famous son of India I suddenly realized that I had never studied his biography or his works. It was then that I read the remarkably warm and objective biography of Zakir Sahab written by Muhammad Mujeeb of *Jamia Millia*. I have just discovered the penetrating and balanced writings of Sudhir Kakar on psychoanalytical subjects. His writings introduced me to the great work of Joseph Campbell on Comparative Mythology. The fascinating and baffling world of mythology has deepened my sense of mystery when contemplating the depth and range of human response to the mystery of the universe. But this has not weakened the validity and value of the mature spirituality which is the crowning glory of the great religions.

Himalayan Retreat: Discovery Of Self

I have enjoyed getting acquainted with the works of the American psychiatrist and writer, Scott Peck. His profound analysis of humanistic love is a further development of Eric Fromm's views presented in *The Art of Loving*. Peck's gradual movement from secular Humanism to spiritual or Christocentric Humanism could, possibly, serve as a model way for other spiritually minded Humanists to relate themselves to their own respective religious tradition. Indeed, Peck's universal compassion and tolerance and his permissive, rather than dogmatic, faith in Christian doctrines makes me think that spreading this spirit of tolerance is the true vocation and function of the liberated sage or saint in any religion.

I have also immensely enjoyed reading B.K.Nehru's monumental autobiography *Nice Boys Come Second*. I am eagerly looking forward to meeting him in his cottage at Kasauli. It was here that I met Khushwant Singh Sahab, several years ago, soon after reading his classic, *A History of the Sikhs*. A warm friendship has grown with two bright members of the younger generation in Solan; the ophthalmologist, Dr. Sanjay Grover, and the research scientist, Dr. Luqman Khan. Sanjay's first novel, *Nine Days to Nirvana*, dealing with philosophical themes has recently come out and I trust it would be well received. Luqman teaches at the *Horticulture University*, Solan. We spend hours together in fruitful intellectual chats. Here I may as well mention Padma Sri Miss S. Das Gupta, who passed away recently. In her late eighties she continued to be a fighter against all forms of social injustice and violation of ethical principles. She had a passion for caring for dogs.

I have always been blessed with good friends, irrespective of caste, colour or creed. But, due to accident rather than design there were hardly any Sikhs in my intimate circle. Our shifting to Solan removed this unwanted lacunae in our social life through bringing us in close touch with some fine Sikh families settled at Solan. Here I must specially mention (late) General and Mrs. Gobinder Singh, very old friends of my parents in law. Hamida had lost touch with them ever since our marriage and our departure for Cambridge. At our very first meeting with the General in Solan in the early seventies he insisted that we shift to his cottage. At that time we had no house in Solan and used to stay in the Municipal Rest House. We just had to obey the General's affectionate order to Hamida to shift immediately to his place, and from that day onwards we almost always stayed with him until our own little cottage was built in the early eighties. The General and his wife Vimmy passed away a few years back.

The General introduced us to his old friend and next-door neighbor, (late) Prithi Singh, belonging to the old princely state of Bharatpur. We soon became close friends. A perfect gentleman and a Cambridge graduate, Prithi Singh, as a young diplomat posted in United Kingdom soon after Independence, had worked very closely with Jawaharlalji during his several official visits to the United Kingdom. Later, Prithi Sahab served as Indian ambassador in several countries. A superb conversationalist, his repertoire of jokes and anecdotes was inexhaustible. Prithi Sahab was also intellectually honest and candid. He once surprised me by telling that, despite his sympathy for the Congress party, he voted for the BJP candidate for the Himachal Assembly election because the candidate was honest and had personally met with him, while the Congress candidate was dishonest and had not bothered to canvas support. Prithi Sahab also thought that with the passage of time the BJP would outgrow the present mindset of narrow Hindutwa and evolve into a conservative Indian Party, and that an effective two party system would be good for Indian democracy.

In Solan I read several books on Sikh history. I also wrote a longish article on *Mughal-Sikh relations*. The thrust of my paper, which was read at the *Khuda Bakhsh Oriental Library*, Patna was that the conflict between the Mughals and the Sikhs was essentially, political rather than religious. My antecedent veneration for Guru Nanak was further heightened. So was my faith in liberal Humanism. The unique blend of Hindu and Islamic concepts and values constituting the soul of Sikh teachings further deepened my awareness of the immense cultural impact of Islam on India. I found it to be deeper and greater than I had hitherto thought to be the case. This realization, in turn, deepened for me the poignancy and tragedy of the partition of the great Indian family.

Himalayan Retreat: Discovery Of Self

The partition of the country has remained for me the greatest setback and retreat of value for the protagonists of liberal Humanism. It is futile to cry over spilt milk. But it became my passion to try, in a spirit of humility and impartiality, to fix the degrees of responsibility on the great makers of Indian history who brought about partition. The more I read the greater grew my emotional fixation on events, which could not be undone or reversed. However, I realized there was great scope for finding new ways and means of promoting understanding and harmony in the divided Indian family. Having already done my bit to present the human face of Islam and now enjoying warm friendship from a growing circle of Hindu and Sikh friends in Himachal I became interested in the idea of presenting the human face of Hinduism. My thoughts naturally turned to the Gita, which I had long admired and venerated under early family influence and the later influence of Radhakrishnan and other Hindu liberals.

I decided to base my modest work exclusively on Radhakrishnan's translation and commentary on the Gita, but to interpret the great poem, shorn of its mythology and purely local elements, in the light of my own authentic conceptual framework. My object was the critical appreciation of Gita's basic metaphysical vision and value system and, most importantly, its spirit of tolerance. Perhaps, among all the great world scriptures, the Bhagwad Gita takes the most unequivocal stand that the disinterested performance of one's duty leads to salvation, irrespective of the creed one may profess. Maulana Azad had stood for the 'essential unity' of all religions. I was, therefore, happy when the *Azad Educational Foundation* accepted my *Essay on the Bhagwad Gita* for publication. The monograph was published in the late nineties by the *Maulana Azad Foundation* and carried a foreword by the eminent Indian administrator and ambassador, Abid Husain Sahab. But the Foundation did not price the monograph, which is not available for sale to the public. I understand it is the policy of the Foundation to send complimentary copies to selected persons of eminence. However, the Foundation has not yet disclosed to me who these eminent persons are. I do hope and trust the work will not go down the drain due to some reason or other.

Two recent books on Applied Psychology also struck me for their insights and practical utility. They are *Emotional Intelligence* by Daniel Goleman, and *Feeling Good* by David Burns. I decided to prepare a summarized version of the two taken together and add some thoughts of my own on the cultivation of spirituality without dogma. A typed monograph is now being circulated among family members and close friends.

The handbook deals with two main themes. The first relates to the damage done by different types or forms of negative thinking and how to overcome it through concrete 'cognitive analysis'. Secondly, it discusses the concepts of 'emotional intelligence', and 'meta-awareness'. Writing this handbook has brought into focus once again four crucial truths. First, there are plural paths to mental and spiritual development and peace of mind. Second, the appeal and efficacy of the different paths differs for every individual. Third, no path by itself or in isolation (be it psychoanalysis, cognitive analysis, drug therapy, religious surrender, *Yoga*, Transcendental Meditation, Reiki, *Zen* or *Sufism*) will provide optimum rewards. Fourth, there is no shortcut to lasting peace of mind that *'passeth all understanding'*. The most effective strategy is to combine different approaches, keeping in mind the personality type and the specific situation of the individual.

A new experience I had in Solan had a great educative value for me. I had come to hold, on the basis of my actual experience over the years, that paradoxical as it seemed, atheists and agnostics generally possess greater strength of character and social or civic sense than visibly religious or pious characters. My explanation of this rather unexpected phenomenon was that the atheist stood in a permanent need to prove that he was a decent human being, despite his poverty of faith, while the conventional theist had no such inner compulsion. But I had a totally contrary experience at Solan where a prominent Communist or leftist threw integrity and impartiality to the winds out of blind partisan support to a friend in a land dispute with a neighbor. On the other hand, a prominent RSS figure went out of the way to see that fair play and justice were meted out to the victim without bothering about his religious or political affiliations. This experience has confirmed and deepened still further my long conviction that character counts more than ideology in the scale of values. If I were asked to choose, for the purpose of friendship, between a so called secularist (who had double standards) and a so called communalist (who was consistently honest and sincere), I would prefer the latter as a friend, quite unmindful of any honest religious or political disagreements with him or her.

I came to realize that a good Hindu friend of mine whom I greatly admired for his integrity and honesty had distanced himself from me without any apparent or discernible ground. Rather reluctantly he confided that it was all due to the Ayodhya issue resulting in the demolition of the *Babri Masjid*. He said he wanted to avoid any possible controversy with a highly respected Muslim friend. I knew that my friend was entirely free from hypocrisy and guile and intellectually honest, though his vision was rather limited because of the circumstances of his background and education. His candid approach did not put me off and I tried my best to convince him that good friends should agree to differ rather than distance themselves for the sake of avoiding social friction or a clash of opinions. However to my great regret the alienation did not stop and our friendship turned into a cool nodding relationship.

A year or two elapsed and then equally suddenly my friend on his own came back to me with the confession that he had come to see that the *Mandir-Masjid* issue was, essentially, political rather than religious. He now felt that politicians had exploited the faith of simple people for political gains. Nothing could have made me happier than this turn of events in our sincere relationship.

A Sikh friend having a liberal religious and theological outlook honestly believes that Sikhs would lose their sense of group identity and get absorbed into either the Hindu or the Muslim fold, were they to give up their distinctive headwear and beards. This was his response to my friendly observation that the essence of any religion lay in its basic thought and value system, and that, like modern reform movements in other religions, liberal Sikhs should also focus basic spiritual values enshrined in the Sikh scriptures rather than on headwear, or keeping the beard. In the course of the friendly conversation it occurred to me that like all other religious or ethnic groups half of the Sikh population comprises women, and that their Sikh identity does not get lost despite their dress and appearance being exactly like that of other *Panjabi* women. I had fancied my friend would not be able to refute an argument that seemed irrefutable and conclusive. However, back came the immediate retort that a Sikh woman did not have any identity apart from her father or the husband. No sooner my friend made this remark the wife angrily and emphatically protested against male chauvinism. And we all broke into hearty laughter.

This is, perhaps, the right place to record two other incidents, though they happened outside Solan. A Sikh friend of mine was my host in Delhi. At that point of time I was a regular smoker. One morning my host casually asked me whether he could smoke a cigarette of mine. I was rather surprised at this request, but answered that it was up to him to decide, as he had never smoked in my presence or to my knowledge. Well, he decided he would. But when he lifted a cigarette from my pack his hands were trembling and there was a clear nervous look on his face. Before lighting the cigarette he bolted the door. He had hardly puffed once or twice when the door bell began to ring, as if there was a conspiracy somewhere to catch a poor smoking Sardar red handed, and my dear friend was really thrown into a panic situation. He immediately dumped the cigarette before he gathered enough courage to unbolt the door.

I dare say the above episode impressed upon me with a peculiar force the truth of my rational conviction that food and drink regulations constituted a marginal content of the basic value system governing the individual and society. The basic ethical principles or norms of virtuous conduct were quite other than food restrictions or regulations. In other words, whether the meat one eats is '*halal*' or '*jhatka*' is not an ethical or a serious religious issue, but only a matter of social conditioning. It appeared to me that had I, as a Muslim, decided on taking alcohol, for the first time, in the house of a Sikh friend I might have panicked in the same way my Sikh friend did in regard to smoking, which, for me, was a perfectly innocent and morally and religiously permitted activity.

The other incident happened at Allahabad and relates to a remarkable lady doctor. At ninety, Dr. Samanth still retains her natural sharpness of mind, energy and dedication to her profession. A picture of humility, she has a record of selfless service to the *Kamla Nehru Hospital*, Allahabad. She claims to be an atheist, and it is her atheism in action I want to write about.

I have met her several times in the house of my dear cousins, Mehboob Bhai and his wife, Rashida, who is known in the family as Rasho. They are more or less permanent hosts to Dr. Samanth at Allahabad. Mehboob Bhai (affectionately called MZ in the family circle) is a true humanist and is totally free from all cant, prejudice and hypocrisy. He has the gift of entering into the heart and mind of others and seeing things as they appear to them before daring to pass any judgment on them. And this is something rare, indeed.

Once I was staying with MZ and Dr. Samanth was also there. At about ten in the night there was a phone message for Dr. Samanth that a patient of hers was in labor. The hosts wanted to make suitable arrangements for transporting the ninety year old doctor to and back from the hospital, but she was concerned only with reaching the patient at the earliest, totally unmindful of any other consideration. And this she did.

Next morning when I met the doctor at breakfast I asked her about the patient and also the time she managed to return. With a smile all over her serene face, charmingly young for all her ninety years, the doctor blurted out 'false alarm'. I could only admire all the more the selfless compassion of a professed atheist. After a moment she reflectively added, 'you see, I don't believe in God, but I believe in Nature'.

CHAPTER 8
THE INNER CALL: CONTENTED SELF

As is well known, the traditional Islamic view has it that the believer must perform *Hajj* at least once in one's lifetime, provided he has the financial means to do so. It is further held that if one does '*Umra*' by doing seven rounds of the *Kaba* during the *non-Hajj* season the full *Hajj* becomes absolutely obligatory for him or her. As my wife and I had already done the *Umra* long back in 1982 several near and dear ones were eager that I, as a good Muslim, should perform the full *Hajj*. Among my sisters, Atu Apa (Begum Akhtar Hasan) and Alima Apa (Begum Abdul Rahman) were specially concerned with my spiritual welfare. However, deeply touched and moved as I was by my sisters' loving concern for me this had little effect upon me. My father too had not performed *Hajj*, and several very pious believers and elevated saints had also not done *Hajj*. So I was not worried that by not doing *Hajj* I would remain a second class or fallen Muslim.

I often used to examine my inner attitude to *Hajj*. I concluded that though I was certainly eager to visit the holy places of Islam, specially the resting place of the Prophet in Medina, I was not at all moved by the background Abrahamic story that he, in obedience to God's command, had left his wife, Hajira (who was in an advanced state of pregnancy) all alone in the wilderness of the Arabian desert, at a place now known as Mecca and that after a lapse of several years he joined her, reclaimed his son, Ismail, but shortly afterwards, again in obedience to God, proceeded to sacrifice his son at nearby Mina, though the Almighty Lord spared his son. This story left me rather indifferent to the value of unquestioning blind obedience to an external sovereign Authority. Moreover, I had heard several stories of Muslims

The Vision of an Unknown Indian Muslim: Part 1

who had done the *Hajj* several times but piety had never touched them. However, I never rejected outright the desire and the advice of my near and dear ones that I should taste the blessings of *Hajj*. In fact, at times I found myself toying with the idea that I should, indeed, do the *Hajj* and see what happens to me at the spiritual level. This idea was strengthened a lot when I happened to read a very insightful and sensitively written book, *The Heart of the Quran*, by a Scottish scholar mystic, Lex Hixon, after he had embraced Islam. Reading about his experience of *Hajj* moved me deeply, but I could not make up my mind at the time. This was around 2003. Thereafter I had a strange experience at the close of 2004 when I was in my seventy sixth year that is worth sharing with my readers.

My general health has been fairly good all through and my relatives and friends often compliment me that I looked much younger than my years. However, I did suffer occasionally from mild vertigo and mild quickening of my heartbeat. These slightly uncomfortable moments were very fleeting and I never took them seriously. But one day in Solan the duration of the vertigo and my level of discomfort was such that a good friend and also Hamida insisted upon a medical checkup. I, therefore, went to Delhi where our daughter, Geeta, was professor of Neurology at GB Pant Hospital. After all the tests were over the consultant casually informed me that I was OK, but that at a later stage I might need a pacemaker. He also added that in the course of one of the tests my heart had stopped beating for just over nine seconds. I had absolutely no idea that this had happened to me though I did pass through a short and strange spell of total stillness and passive peace. The consultant's remark made me think that perhaps I had passed through the state of mind called '*shunya*' in Buddhist parlance. This self-assessment did not make me feel alarmed but it rather filled me with a strange excitement and inner joy. And believe me, this condition persists to date.

Geeta did not share my feelings of elation, but she did not controvert with her father. I returned to Solan and resumed my normal activities. This included occasional silent recitation of randomly selected portions from the Quran. As I opened my copy of the Quran

The Inner Call: Contented Self

the first time after returning to Solan I came upon the *Sura* entitled '*Hajj*'. As I concluded reading and even while I was in the process of reading I found arising in my mind the idea that I ought to perform the *Hajj* at the earliest. I did not disclose my condition to Hamida. The idea persisted though I could not arrive at any firm decision. Shortly afterwards I had to go to Delhi again on some work. There I shared my inner feeling with my aunt (Begum Halim Jung) whom I have long respected as an intelligent and warm-hearted family elder. No sooner did she hear me she declared that I must not entertain any second thoughts but immediately start preparing for my journey. She added that I was very lucky to have been 'called'. It was then that I took the decision to go.

From the very beginning I was absolutely clear that I should not put any direct or indirect pressure upon Hamida to accompany me. I knew her line of thinking and respected her inner reluctance to face the extremely trying conditions of the *Hajj* pilgrimage. I gratefully remembered that it was she who had taken the initiative to perform *Umra* back in 1982. She felt inhibited to undertake the health risks involved in *Hajj* at this stage of our life. On returning to Solan I took her into confidence and lovingly assured her that she should feel absolutely free to decide her own course of action. Later she told me that my unilateral decision had placed her in a rather embarrassing position in the family circle and this was correct. However, I do feel what I did was the right thing for me. She did not go, but our daughter-in-law, Naazneen and our grand daughter, Imrana, accompanied me to the holy land in mid January 2005.

What really moved me to proceed for *Hajj* was a deep desire to be touched, if possible, by Divine grace at the sanctum sanctoras of Islam at Mecca and to taste the spiritual ecstasy of being physically present at the spot in Medina where lie the mortal remains of the human being who (according to the Quran) was sent as '*a mercy to the worlds*'.

The sheer physical and mental strain of long hours of waiting at the Jeddah airport, the very uncomfortable and tedious bus journey from Jeddah to Mecca and the continual movement in the midst of a virtual sea of surging humanity all took their toll on my health and I fell ill on the third day in the plain of Mina; the headquarters of the *Hajj* congregation for five days. However, this did not dampen my spirits or disturb my inner peace of mind.

Even at the start of our journey I knew that I did not much care for the external rites and rituals of *Hajj* such as the kissing of the black stone, the animal sacrifice, the stoning of the three devils, the shaving of the head hair etc. The only rite I looked forward to was the long stay at the plains of *Arafat* and *Mudalfa* (specially the former) devoted to prayer, meditation and introspection. The Islamic tradition also gives pride of place and central importance to the spiritual exercise at *Arafat*. My younger brother Ajmal, a true *Sufi*, who after his retirement from service has practically settled down in Medina had briefed me on this vital point. However, my illness (painful cough and fever) started shortly before leaving for *Arafat* and my schedule of spiritual activity could not be put into practice. I did not complain or despair of Divine grace. And next day at Mecca, quite unexpectedly, I dare say I did taste Divine grace.

The first major rite of *Hajj* is the doing of the seven rounds (*tawaaf*) of the *Kaba* immediately followed by the seven straight marches (*sayee*) between the hillocks of *Safa* and *Marva*. The rest of the rites are performed in Mina. After their completion the pilgrim performs the second *tawaaf* of the *Kaba* and the *sayee*. And he performs the third and farewell *tawaaf* before leaving Mecca for home. It was in the second *tawaaf* that I experienced a deep sense of spiritual fulfillment and inner peace. The first inaugural *tawaaf* as well as the last did not touch any inner chord of my soul and in my subjective perception both were sheer physical exercises devoid of any spiritual dimension. However, the second *tawaaf* (which I did sitting in a wheel chair) was my 'peak spiritual experience' in the language of modern psychology of religion. I was very reluctant to use a wheel chair but I gave in to the advice and strong desire of Naazneen that I use a chair in view of my rather poor physical condition.

The porter placed the wheel chair on the escalator leading to the roof top level of the *Kaba* mosque, which is a double-storied multiple arched gallery encircling the oblong bowl that contains the original square structure fully covered by full length black curtains. The moment I reached the rooftop and the full *Kaba* complex became visible my spirits seemed to be touched by some inner current of overflowing energy and peace at the same time. I just let myself go and started to praise the Lord and surrender myself to Him to be molded as He wished. I recited the *Sura Fatiha*, short Quranic suras and verses and some of the 'beautiful names' of Allah that I knew by heart. I effortlessly recalled such Arabic religious expressions and symbols that had a special appeal for me and my entire being was suffused with deep inner joy, peace and a sense of surrender to a mysterious Being or some Mystery beyond all comprehension. This 'peak condition' lasted for half an hour or so though there were 'ups and downs' or 'highs and lows' in the level and intensity of this remarkable experience. My eyes were moist with tears, which sometimes rolled down my cheeks.

The vast *Kaba* complex was aglow with special electric light coming from very highly placed multiple high wattage lamps, which turned night into day without creating any glare for the eye. This special light enveloped the oval courtyard down below as well as the roof level and the high minarets creating an ambience of sheer beauty. Looking below one could see a never ending circular movement of tens of thousands of white robed pilgrims circumambulating the *Kaba* as if a billion human moths were ardently but orderly moving in an endless attempt to catch a glimpse of some intensely loved but elusive and mysterious sight. The total effect upon me of the illuminated minarets and arches above and the glowing courtyard of the *Kaba* below, every inch of ground space filled with tens of thousands of believers moving in concentric circles evoked in my mind the image of living human electrons revolving round the Divine Nucleus of total existence. The core spirit of the expressions I now use was actually compresent in my 'peak experience', though trying to describe or capture it conceptually, as I have tried to do above, has been hard labor for me. In other words, my total experience was a complex of aesthetic delight, spiritual insight and total inner satisfaction and peace.

From the rooftop were also visible several high-rise modern secular buildings, also well illuminated, standing side by side with the tall slim minarets of the main mosque. These secular buildings were government offices, a royal palace and a few luxury hotels. This co-presence of the sacred and the secular artifacts sounded a rather jarring note for me, to begin with. But very soon the idea occurred to me that this was a reminder or symbol of the complexity of modern life and the impact of science and technology on religion and spirituality.

I did the traditional seven rounds of the *Kaba* and thereafter the seven marches between the hillocks of *Safa* and *Marva* adjacent to the main shrine. The proclaimed purpose of the second rite is to perpetuate the memory of Bibi Hajira's trial and suffering at the time of the birth of her son soon after Prophet Abraham had left her alone in the wilderness. Uncomfortable as I have always felt with the above story or legend I was clear in my mind that the *Hajj* was the least appropriate occasion for entertaining or resolving such perplexities. I, therefore, tried to become a silent witness to whatever response may arise in my mind from the depths of my heart and head at this solemn occasion. This is the Buddhist approach of '*vipasna*', which has great appeal for me.

Safa and *Marva* are less than a furlong apart, and now stand connected by a level path, which is marble topped. It is approximately forty feet wide divided into two up and down lanes of twenty feet each. Wheel chairs are permitted to move in the middle portion. I did the march sitting in my wheel chair. I was very peaceful and relaxed after my peak experience while doing the rounds of *Kaba*. Now gradually from the conceptual vacuity I had tried to induce in myself some ideas began to take shape. One idea was that even if the legend concerned lacks credibility, the fact remains that the female half of the human family, for no fault of theirs, silently suffers at the hands of the dominant male half. Why can't this particular *Hajj* rite be regarded as a symbol of solidarity and sympathy with the feminine half of humanity? With this idea emerging my discomfort and perplexity vanished. And I began to regard every step forward as an orchestrated movement to

The Inner Call: Contented Self

generate and strengthen the resolve to strive to the utmost to promote gender equality and social justice in the wider sense. Incidentally, the Arabic word for this rite is *'sayee'* whose literal meaning is 'striving' or 'effort'. This is how this particular rite also became for me a source of spiritual gain and inspiration, despite my honest disability to accept the concerned legend as a historical fact. However, my feelings of elation and the inner spiritual satisfaction this time did not match the quality of my earlier 'peak' experience while doing the rounds of the *Kaba*.

The full ritual for that day was now over and my porter wheeled me back to the place for disembarkation. Just before doing so he helped me to a drink of the water ever bubbling from the famed perennial *Zam Zam* spring. This was the spring that, according to the Arab myth or legend, had miraculously come to the rescue of Bibi Hajira in her lonely moments of agony at the birth of her son. I profusely thanked my porter. I was feeling so inwardly happy, so profoundly at peace with myself, and the entire world that I could not help giving him a very generous gift of money over and above the agreed fare for his valuable service. Shortly afterwards Naazneen and Imrana who had completed the rituals on their own in the normal way joined me where I was waiting for them. I thanked them also for their advice to take the wheel chair. I very much doubt if without following their insistent and loving advice I could have tasted the spiritual ecstasy described above. They fully shared my happiness and they too were deeply satisfied with how things had worked out for them. We then returned to our headquarters at Mina where, according to ancient ritual, the pilgrim stays for one more night before returning to Mecca. After doing the final farewell *Umra* at Mecca the pilgrim departs for home.

Before I describe how I fared while doing the last rite in Mecca I may describe how I fared while I performed the ritual of stoning the three devils. I did not at all concern myself with the historicity of the story, but dwelt on the wisdom and beauty of the symbolism as interpreted in *Sufi* thought. *Sufis* interpret Satan as the base or evil element or elements that co-exist with the noble or the virtuous in the human constitution. The *Sufi* holds that every time one pebble is thrown at the pillar (now enlarged into a wall) the pilgrim solemnly expunges a specific evil or vice from his inner being as an act of inner purification and resolve to shun the specific evil henceforth. I laid special emphasis on getting rid of my life-long weakness of the evil of procrastination. From the *Sufi* viewpoint all the rites and rituals of *Hajj* are symbolic acts of purification and spiritual regeneration. The circumambulation of the *Kaba* symbolizes the resolve to accept the Creator or basic spiritual and ethical values as the centre of one's total being and behaving. The long introspection and meditation in the silent awe inspiring wilderness of *Arafat* and *Mudalfa*, under the open cloudless Arabian sky, is the timeless silent language of the human spirit longing for union with the Divine. The stoning of the devils symbolizes self-cleansing and self-fortification rather than blaming others for one's own faults or suffering. However, the ritual of animal sacrifice, to my mind, cannot be subsumed under a similar spiritual symbolism, if one accepts the sanctity of all life as such. Perhaps, it provides an additional occasion of social bonding and thanksgiving through collective dining in the then Arab society.

As regards the last farewell *Umra* at Mecca I was very satisfied doing this last rite in the normal way and remained very relaxed and peaceful throughout the strenuous exercise involved. Before finally leaving the *Kaba* complex I sat down at a, relatively, quiet place from where I could clearly gaze at the sanctum sanctorus and started to meditate according to my personally preferred style. After a few minutes I felt somebody gently poking a finger of disapproval on my back. Without breaking my meditation and with my eyes closed I signaled with my hand that I may not be disturbed. The person concerned (probably belonging to the staff of the Saudi moral police) left me undisturbed after this. Later on I related this incident to my brother, Ajmal, who told me that his own experience with the moral police was not so mild, since the Saudi approach to religion disapproves of the mystical dimension of the Islamic tradition. Devotion even to the Holy Prophet and the cultivation of mystical states and spiritual development are looked upon as heretical innovations and distortions of true Islam.

The Inner Call: Contented Self

After performing *Hajj* we left for Medina. We had rooms booked in a hotel in the grand extended and beautifully renovated *Haram* complex. This is, indeed, a magnificent contribution of the Saudi government to the historic city of the Prophet. Naazneen and Imrana stayed in the hotel that was very convenient for them for the purpose of offering prayers inside the main Prophet's mosque. However, in view of my continuing mild indisposition I moved to Ajmal's very comfortable house in a very decent residential colony. Ajmal and his wife, Shakira, who is my first cousin, lovingly looked after me and I greatly improved though my full recovery took place only after returning home. Ajmal, as a true *Sufi*, radiates universal goodwill and tolerance and bears no bitterness or anger towards even those who reject the *Sufi* approach. Shakira is deeply committed and devoted to *Sufi* ideas and is well versed in the traditional approach to Islam tempered by a dash of informed liberalism, thanks to the influence of a famous *Sufi* scholar of Hyderabad, the late Qadeer Piya.

According to popular belief or sentiment offering forty obligatory Islamic prayers inside the Prophet's mosque ensures that the believer will get the reward of heaven. Naazneen and Imrana, quite naturally and understandably, were very keen to do so. I am most happy, indeed that they achieved this target, which requires strict punctuality and involves considerable physical strain. As Ajmal's residence was approximately five kilometers away from the mosque I was not in a position to aim at the popular target of offering forty prayers. Moreover, my approach was rather in tune with the striking saying of the famous woman saint of Islam, Bibi Rabia Basri (d. 801 A.H.) that she would rather have hell-fire doused and paradise burnt so that believers may neither be afraid of hell, nor crave for heaven but only seek the pleasure of Allah. My principal desire and objective in Medina was to have the privilege of getting as physically and spiritually close, as possible, to the resting place of the Holy Prophet, and seek release from the deafening roar of the gushing rapids of ideas, images, memories and feelings and enter into the interior silence of the spirit. I have been always attracted to this objective. The purgation of all ideas, beliefs, feelings and attitudes and the attainment of interior silence is the gate that opens out into the realm of the sacred presence of the 'Lord of the worlds'. The mystics of all religions, regions and ages have taught and practiced this therapy for purifying the soul and this is an essential pre-condition for the inflow of Divine grace and blessings. This therapy of the heart works quite independently of one's theological beliefs. Consequently, every religious tradition has its own unique mystical dimension. There is hardly any need to seek this dimension in religions other than one's own. However, no harm is done if the seeker of inner peace and Divine grace desires to drink the nectar of spirituality from some vessel or cup used by any other sister religious tradition. The nectar is common though the cups may differ. I, for one, as a born Muslim, am quite satisfied and happy with the cup of Islam, though I am rather unhappy with the variety of cups that bear the label of Islam. All the world religions stand in the same predicament.

What could be a better place for supplicating for Divine grace and blessings than maximum physical and spiritual nearness to the resting place where lie the mortal remains of the human being who, according to the Quran, the *'Lord of the worlds'* sent as a *'blessing for the worlds'*. In all humility may I express my personal sentiment that the tomb of the Prophet should be made freely accessible (barring the *Hajj* season) to every human being (Muslim or non-Muslim) who out of genuine respect and admiration for Muhammad, the man, wishes to savor of the spiritual ambience of the shrine.

As is well known to Muslims, the Prophet, after his death, was laid to rest inside his own living room. Later his close companion, Abu Bakr, was buried just next to him. Still later, another close companion, Omar, was buried next to Abu Bakr. Thereafter the room was sealed forever. There was no dome or protective wall or grill that now exist. Nobody is now allowed to even touch the outer grill which encloses the inner grill or wall that encloses the original living room of the very simple, humble and compassionate human being who used to weep and beg his Creator for mercy and forgiveness for his sins and who never made even the slightest claim that he was all wise and infallible, and could perform miracles that came to be attributed to him.

The Inner Call: Contented Self

I wish not only all formal Muslims but all humans could have had access to the resting place of the person sent by the Creator as *'a mercy for the worlds'*. However, all I could do was to form a mental picture of the shrine's topography and fix it in my memory, and then select a niche for the purpose of meditation no matter where I might be physically. This I managed to do despite the hustle and bustle of the *Hajj*.

The *Hajj* experience has affected me profoundly at the level of human relationships and inner attitudes, but my basic outlook or philosophy of life, and my value system remain what they were prior to *Hajj*. I am still unable to equate myth or legend with history. I happily identify myself as a Muslim and I feel hurt if somebody dubs me an atheist, communist, heretic, hypocrite, and so on. However, my hurt does not partake of bitterness or hostility. I enjoy being a Muslim, but I have no ambition or desire to save the souls of non-Muslims by working towards their formal conversion to Islam.

Hamida fully shares my approach to Islam and gives first priority to spiritual values and moral integrity and ethical action rather than theological creeds. However, as a woman her honest perception is that historical Islam has not been just and fair in the matter of gender equality. Our daughter, Geeta, also thinks on similar lines. Both feel uncomfortable with some Quranic texts on the subject. I have to concede that accepting some texts in the literal sense does create dissonance in me as well. But such difficulties can be resolved if we make a principled distinction between the intrinsic values the Quran inculcates and the prescriptive rules and instrumental regulations it contains in view of the specific conditions or traditions of Arab society at a particular stage of its evolution. With a good Islamic conscience I can say that the rules may well be modified in altered circumstances, not as a matter of expediency, but as a matter of principle.

In this context I would like to refer to the problem of numbers at *Hajj*. Millions of pilgrims now congregate to perform the *Hajj* rituals in the space of a period of five days. The prescribed ritual of long meditation, introspection and spiritual prayer separately performed in the forenoon and early evening by every individual at the plain of *Arafat* and, subsequently, at the nearby plain of *Mudalfa* after sunset, under the open star-studded Arabian sky, to my mind, has the most universal and timeless appeal among all the rites of *Hajj*. Since this rite is performed on an individual basis no congestion, jostling and pushing around mars the serenity and beauty of the rite. But the rite of *tawaaf* at Mecca and, particularly, the ritual of the stoning of the three devils at Mina are performed in tremendous rush and disarray. Serious injuries, stampedes, separation of group members from each other, thefts and, worst of all deaths, take place almost at every *Hajj*. This apart, the sheer congestion and confusion caused by numbers cannot but have an extremely adverse effect upon the spiritual quality of the total experience. The supreme purpose of the *Hajj*: the fostering of the brotherhood of the faithful cutting across race and region, the awakening and education of the human conscience, drawing inspiration for a life of compassion and collective endeavor for promoting spiritual and moral values can hardly be realized in a mega rush of external and mechanically performed rituals in the midst of human waves piling one on the other. This was my frame of mind when I returned home.

Hamida and I found ourselves at the same wavelength. She eagerly pointed out to me that while reading the Quran she came upon the Quranic verse (2:197), which says that Allah has prescribed months (in the plural) for performing *Hajj*. Her intuitive response to this verse was that fixing separate five-day slots for *Hajj* in an extended *Hajj* period would solve, at one stroke, the ever-growing problem of mega numbers at *Hajj*. I found her observation to be correct when I checked the text. Now I also think that hers is a bright idea and administrative experts could work out its modalities, once the religious leadership comes to accept 'creative fidelity' to the Islamic faith as a higher virtue than blind conformity to tradition.

In fact the Saudi government has already effected substantial improvements in some matters. For instance, pilgrims now need not themselves perform animal sacrifice as a *Hajj* rite; they can obtain

The Inner Call: Contented Self

cash receipts from the concerned counter and the *Hajj* administration does the rest. The latest improvement is that the three separate pillars representing the devil (*shaitan*) have been extended to become three separate walls that are, naturally, much more convenient targets for the safe and speedy performance of the old rite. Here it would not be out of place respectfully to remind ourselves that until very recently our ultra-orthodox religious leaders had vigorously refused to use microphones in the mosque, and even rejected the provision of modern flush toilets for pilgrims who had to spend full five days in Mina. These changes were highly controversial, to begin with, but are now lauded by the world Muslim community.

I deem myself extremely lucky and thank God for being enabled to do *Hajj*. However, I am still far from holding that God or the Prophet had called me as a special favor, or that merely having done *Hajj* has elevated my spiritual status. However, to witness the tremendous power of religious faith of millions who throng to Mecca and Medina from the four corners of the earth, serenely indifferent to the discomforts and rigors of the pilgrimage and at great financial sacrifice is by itself a source of inspiration and a great lesson in the education of the higher emotions. But Muslims should not forget that other great religions also afford the same spectacle of heroic self-abnegation at the altar of their own sacred places. Paths of the spiritual journey may differ but the destination is one by whatever name it may be called.

I now close the story of my intellectual and spiritual growth. Much remains untold, since I have not mentioned the social psychological and emotional factors of my personality that must have influenced my intellectual and spiritual development. However, intellectual honesty requires that I briefly mention one very personal facet of my emotional life with which I have ever grappled right through as a frail and vulnerable human being that I am.

At the rather young age of twenty-one I was convinced I was in love with my maternal cousin, Hamida, a girl of sixteen who became my dear wife two years later, shortly before I left for Cambridge. By

God's grace our union has stood the test of time, spanning more than fifty years and it has been a reasonably happy and successful marriage. Many close friends and family members regard us as an 'ideal couple'. Yet, I, for my part, have never been totally free from self-questioning whether my love has been 'true' love, or rather a form of narcissistic desire to be cared for and 'adored' by the 'perceived beloved'. The probe into this personal perplexity has engaged me continually just like the issue of pain and evil and unmerited human suffering.

Occasional and quite understandable differences with Hamida in the normal course of living together often resulted in depression and low self-esteem. Did I really love her, or was my perceived love a mirage or delusion? Of the reality of spontaneous and instinctive maternal love I had no doubt. I also believed that higher romantic love spoken of by Shelley, Keats, Browning, Havelock Ellis, and Eric Fromm, *et al* was also a reality in some cases. But was my proclaimed love for my spouse a romantic illusion of my adolescence, rather than the mature love of a responsible adult?

I continually dwelt on the theme of the source and significance of love in this higher sense. Perhaps, maternal love, sexual love and the mystical love for God all well up from the depths of the soul or psyche as a perennial Divine grace to some though not all creation. Love frees the lover form all fear, doubt, or expectation of return. Love is ceaseless compassion and unconditional giving. The mother gives tender protection to the infant and child, the spouse total sharing in the joys and sorrows of life's journey, the mystic undying loyalty to his own 'Idea of the Holy' and acts appropriately. Love carries the lover into the arms of the heart of the Divine Presence. How the lover conceives or conceptualizes the Divine is of no moment so long as the lover is lost in wonder and humility, freely giving his all without any expectation of return.

The evening of my life has imparted a rose tint to my lifelong anguish caused by my personal perplexity whether I have loved and have been loved in the higher sense of the term. I have learnt, pretty late in life, the pitfalls and illusions of suffering humanity and the insufficiency of human effort alone without sustenance and succor from some Source, beyond conceptualization or comprehension.

At long last I have learnt my own limitations and the higher wisdom of humility and of surrender to the sense of Divine mystery beyond all theories and creeds. I know that the little flame of life in 'my' body will shortly burn out and the body will turn into dust or ashes. What lies beyond? Light or darkness, ever more? I have opted for light. But is this any conclusive proof?

Logic, science, theology do not clinch the issue. Faith does, but this function it does only for the individual. But even faith does not illumine the vastness and complexity of the ultimate mystery – the mystery of creation, death, possible resurrection and accountability. However, the unavoidable opaqueness of faith does not deprive it of its inner beauty as well as utility. In such matters the transparency of detail is hardly important. What is crucial is not transparency of concept, but rather authenticity of faith. In the present context what is crucial is not a definite answer to the enigma of immortality of the soul, but the individual's inner commitment that he, as the bearer of a Divine spark or flame, will endeavor to spread sweetness and light all around and his hope that his own little lamp, whether it shines after death or gets extinguished, the Divine Light shall shine, ever more, in new ways, directions and dimensions.

I close this rather sketchy account of my intellectual and spiritual growth on an English translation of an Urdu couplet from Ghalib. The translation is my own.

"What credit mine when I gave my life for Thee,
After all, it was never mine but Thine trust in me."

Part 2

My Image of India

Quotable

"History is the best medicine for a sick mind, for in history you have a record of the infinite variety of human experience plainly set out for all to see, and in that record you can find for yourself and your country both examples and warnings: fine things to take as models, base things, rotten through and through to avoid."
- Titus Livius. Roman historian (d. 17).

"Standing as I do in view of God and Eternity, I realize that patriotism is not enough, I must have no hatred or bitterness toward anyone."
- Last words of Edith Cavell; British nurse executed during World War I (1915) for helping Allied soldiers to escape.

Chapter 9
India in Medieval Times

The Perennial Human Situation: Its Dynamic

The human family consists of different racial/ethnic groups, each having its own distinct language and culture. Every distinct human group believes in its own superiority, and strives to appropriate the maximum share in the available resources of the environment. This, inevitably, results in a struggle for power among different groups, contiguous to each other and also within each group. Aggression and defence are the two sides of the coin of world history, which is punctuated by victory for one and defeat or setback for the other.

The antagonists perceive this struggle for power as a struggle between the forces of good and the forces of evil. In reality, the fight is between individuals or groups, either on the offensive or defensive, as the case may be. Different groups reach the peak of their inner energy and vitality at different periods of world history. Both sides have their own material interests as well as some cherished ideas and ideals. But the protagonists tend to emphasize the importance of saving the latter. The group whose ideas and interests happen to coincide and to harmonize with 'the spirit of the age', in the Hegelian sense, generally wins in the unfolding drama of world history.

The winners in the battle of arms have an initial advantage over the losers in the ever-continuing battle of ideas and ideals. But sometimes the winners themselves are won over by those they vanquish in battles or wars. This is the paradox of finite existence. To give a few instances of this paradox, the ancient Indo-Aryans both won and lost to the older Indus valley culture. Eminent scientific scholars of Comparative culture and mythology, with no political or religious axe to grind, have shown how subtle changes and shifts in the Aryan 'Pantheon' before and after their interaction with the original Indus civilization.

Much later the medieval desert Arabs both won and lost to Greek and Iranian cultures in West Asia and to Sanskrit culture in India. When the freshly Islamized Arabs embarked upon their world shaking 'political expansion' in West Asia and later in India their only cultural asset was the Quran and pre-Islamic Arabic poetry. They quickly learnt the concept of 'cipher', Astronomy, Medicine, Yoga, Vedanta, storytelling, animal fables from Indian sources, and logic, ethics, metaphysics, science, and medicine from Greek sources, and Theology and Casuistry from Jewish sources. Freely acknowledging their debt to their mentors, they creatively added to the sum total of world culture. Some early Western quarters previously underestimated Arab creativity in culture, but present Western scholars have overcome this rather jaundiced view.

In another rapid historical denouement the pagan Mongols and Turkish tribes literally decimated the Islamized Arabs and Iranians in West Asia, but they got absorbed into the vast matrix of Islamic civilization. The 'barbarians' of yesterday turned into rulers and emperors of vast empires. Inter-action between contending groups goes on in war as well as in peace. Psychological wounds begin to heal with the passage of decades and centuries since fresh ideas and ideals emerge in a mixed cultural space. Change and continuity usually coalesce to preserve the elements of permanent value in the heritage of both victor and loser in the battle of arms. This has happened again and again in Indian history. Medieval Indian culture is, thus, the fruit of Hindu-Muslim or Sanskrit-Persian cultural dialogue in an over-arching Islamic space. It is as much the warp and woof of Indian history as the culture of the ancient Indo-Aryans themselves.

Inter-action between the contending groups goes on in war as well as in times of peace. Psychological wounds inflicted by wars begin to heal as time moves on and fresh ideas and ideals begin to surface in the ongoing story of the human family. At times the losers in the war become the winners in the realm of culture. This happened when the Islamised Arabs and Persians completely lost in the 13th century to pagan Mongols, but the latter were culturally absorbed in Islam. At other times both winners and losers in war gain at the cultural level due to extended peaceful inter-action following the armed conflict. This has happened again and again in Indian history.

The nuclear core of Indo-Aryan culture has stood the test of ages and is still evolving. It had evolved when *Vedic Brahmanism* had creatively responded, through adaptation and assimilation, to the internal challenge of Buddhism and Jainism. This was the contribution of the Shankaracharya's movement in the 8th and 9th centuries. It evolved again under the impact of Islam in the medieval era, in the forms of *Bhakti* and Sikhism. The culture and civilization which evolved in medieval India, after the advent of the Muslims, evolved, still again, under the impact of the West, in the form of the modern Indian Renaissance and Gandhian spirituality after undergoing an inner creative development.

A free united federal India, very probably, could have been yet another stage in the evolution of her rich composite culture. But this did not happen. The partition, on religious lines, of the country in 1947 was a mutation, as it were, under the stress of a prolonged multi-lateral failure of vision and will of the concerned parties. The Indian leaders (at times, adamant Hindus, at other times, adamant Muslims) as well as imperial Britain (victorious in war against Hitler but shattered in peace) all blundered, in haste, under a perceived threat of total anarchy if the issue of partition were not settled immediately.

The Story of the Indian Family

For my present purpose I shall begin the story of India after Muhammad Ghori (d. 1206) established the Delhi *Sultanate* that lasted till Babar overthrew it in 1526. The earlier exploits of Mahmud of Ghazna (d. 1030) on Indian soil were in the nature of raids to capture the famed wealth and craftsmen of India rather than for territorial expansion or propagation of Islam. The still earlier Arab conquest of Sind in early 8th century was imperial occupation, not a phenomenon of hit, loot and run. But it did not involve any mass immigration of Arabs into Sind. In the case of Ghori and Babar, however, both settled down in India, which became permanent home for their progeny and numerous Muslims of central Asian extraction. Amir Khusro (d. 1325), famous poet and statesman of the Delhi *Sultanate* and ardent disciple of the great *Sufi* saint, Nizamuddin Auliya of Delhi, took pride in his Indian identity rather than in the origin of his ancestors from Arabia or Turkey and was devoted to Indian music and literature.

The house of Babar ruled effectively for two hundred years and steered India to the zenith of glory during the reign of the Great Mughals. After the death of Aurangzeb in 1707 Mughal power quickly declined. Nadir Shah (d. 1747) of Persia and Ahmad Shah Abdali (d. 1774) of Afghanistan attacked India and on their way back home ransacked the wealth of the residents of Delhi, Lahore and other places quite irrespective of the religion of their victims. It is, therefore, a totally distorted and perverse approach to lump Turkish Sultans, Mughal kings and Afghan or Pathan adventurers as foreign invaders and despoilers of the sacred soil and wealth of India. In fact, with the dawn of the 13th century India took a new turn in its forward march as a great civilization in the comity of nations.

From the 13th century onwards the Muslim population steadily increased in India. The continuing trickle of immigrants from Central Asia never stopped. But the main factor was the ever-swelling tide of peaceful conversion of the socially backward segments of India in their natural search for higher status and greater dignity than was possible for them in the extremely rigid and hierarchical Hindu caste system. A similar process had occurred six centuries earlier in West Asia. Though the Muslims acquired political power at the point of the sword, the spread of Islam was an extended peaceful process. Likewise, though the British colonization of India took place at the point of the gun her modernization was initiated and sustained by economic factors and cultural dialogue.

The overwhelming majority (approximately 90%) of the Indian Muslims have sprung from the farmers and artisans among the erstwhile Hindu population. The natural growth of their progeny, over the centuries, gradually made Muslims the majority group in the northern and eastern regions of India. A slow and peaceful process, this conversion of the, relatively, deprived and culturally backward Hindu sections was due, primarily, to the perceived promise of greater social equality and vertical mobility under a new Islamic dispensation. Islam was seen as the harbinger of the brotherhood and equality of all Muslims in a deeply caste ridden society. Many centuries earlier the weaker segments in India had viewed Buddhism and Jainism in a like manner.

It is patently wrong to think that in medieval India Hindus and Muslims were two macro groups living in a state of perpetual confrontation. In fact each macro-group was greatly differentiated into numerous sub-groups which did not think and behave alike. Power was shared by a thin upper crust of each macro group. The lower sections of each macro group lived the life of honest toil, enjoyed the consolations of their respective religious faiths, shared the common joys and sorrows of life, were loyal to the ruler, irrespective of his religion or race, and hoped for their ultimate salvation through the path of duty and spiritual discipline.

A thin upper crust or elite among the Muslims and the Hindus constituted the ruling class. Their social and cultural life cut across the religious divide. Likewise, the Indian masses comprising the lower caste Hindus and the neo-Muslim converts had a common folk culture and were co-partners in an integrated feudal agricultural economy. Their language and social customs were, however, subject to regional variations inevitable in a large and populous country like India.

Medieval Indian society was a fresh incarnation of some vital and deeply embedded features of ancient India. The prince waged wars of conquest and wielded power, the nobles and warriors fought for their prince and shared in his wealth and glory, the creative elite enriched culture and were venerated by both prince and the common man, the traders ran the economy and amassed wealth, the artisans engaged in manufacture of simple goods and the farmers in agriculture, and the rest supported the entire structure with their sweat and tears. Each group comprised both Hindus and Muslims. Each group honestly believed (in different ways) that a Supreme Power controlled history according to a plan not fully transparent to man. Whatever happened was just and served some higher purpose. This was the inner world of medieval India. By the time the medieval era came to a close a synthesis of *Bhakti* and *Sufi* outlooks and a composite folk culture had already evolved and was reflected in the emerging regional languages, architecture, painting, music, dress, entertainments, amusements, proverbs, folk-lore and folk religions of India.

What follows in this and the next chapter is meant to give meaningful glimpses into the political, social, economic and cultural features of the undivided Indian family from medieval times right till the partition of 1947. A proper insight into our past is indispensable for understanding our present and rationally planning our future.

THE SHIFTS OF POWER

The story of India is a chapter of the long and unfinished drama of the human struggle for power. In this unending struggle for ascendance new races or ethnic groups, rise from relative obscurity and cultural backwardness and succeed in dominating other more cultured and better established groups of the human family. That Babar was a Muslim does not mean that his attack was an Islamic onslaught against

Hinduism. After all, Babar had fought against several Muslim rulers in Central Asia before turning his attention to India. One Muslim ruler fought against another Muslim in Central Asia in the medieval period, and one Hindu ruler against another Hindu in ancient India. Likewise, Greek fought against Greek no less than he fought against the Iranian or Roman in the ancient period. The same is the case today in the Arab world and also among others.

According to the *Hindu Dharmashastras*, every king is duty bound to enlarge his dominion and fighting is the highest duty of the warrior caste. The raja fought both to enlarge and to defend his territory, but the '*praja*' pursued the prescribed life goals in the normal manner, unmindful of who won or lost in the struggle for power. This social ethic was also applied to Muslim warriors. The Hindu populace did not grudge Muslim rule, provided the ruler did not interfere in '*dharma*'. The legitimacy of the ruler was not dependent upon his race or religion; it flowed from victory in battle.[1]

The falsity of interpreting the struggle for power in medieval India as a confrontation between Islam and Hinduism becomes all the more glaring after the advent of Babar. The antagonists, clearly, were a mixed lot on either side of the fence. Thus, Babar fought against the combined armies of Ibrahim Lodi and Rana Sanga; Humayun struggled against Sher Shah. The power of the Mughals flowed from a firm and lasting alliance between them and the Rajputs, and their adversaries were Muslim princes no less than Hindu. Muslims manned the entire artillery of Shivaji. Both Hindus and Muslims were despoiled of their wealth when Shivaji attacked and looted the prosperous Mughal port of Surat. The same holds good of Nadir Shah and Ahmad Shah Abdali, as already mentioned.

Shivaji's opposition to the Mughal emperor was certainly not directed against Islam or the Muslims. Given the restless energy, daring, and ambition he possessed, Shivaji would have defied any central authority, Muslim or Hindu. Shivaji's father, a 'mansabdar' under the Sultan of Bijapur, was rather unhappy at his brave son's defiant conduct.

The Vision of an Unknown Indian Muslim: Part 2

The son, after a brief interlude at Aurangzeb's court, rebelled against the Mughal emperor and established himself as an independent ruler in the Pune region. He avoided regular battle against the imperial army and opted for guerilla tactics, which ruined the Mughal exchequer. As a king Shivaji was well disposed to his Muslim subjects and his artillery was manned by Muslims. The struggle between the decaying Mughal power and the Marathas, Jats, Sikhs, Rohilla Pathans etc. was, likewise, a struggle for power rather than a religious confrontation.

In the southern region Tipu Sultan (d. 1799) emerged as the hero, both of Muslims and Hindus of Mysore. The Nizam retained the loyalty of all his mixed subjects in Hyderabad. However, Mysore and Hyderabad always remained political antagonists. Coming to more recent times, the great princely states, Gwalior, Indore, Baroda, Jaipur, Patiala, and Kapurthala, etc. (all ruled by Hindu or Sikh kings) gave liberal patronage to Muslims who rose to the highest positions in the state.

As prudent statesmen the Muslim Sultans and emperors did not mix religion with politics. They adopted a policy of non-discrimination between their subjects the overwhelming majority of whom were Hindus. A section of the *Ulema* were not happy at this state of affairs. They held that in an Islamic state the Sultan was bound by the law of the *shariah*, which according to them, prescribed harsh treatment against non-believers. The friendly relations, which obtained between the Muslims and non-Muslims and the power and position enjoyed by Hindu nobles and top administrators irked the narrow-minded section of the *Ulema*. The expression of these views in the writings of some contemporary divines has misled some scholars into thinking that this was the general view and the actual practice. But this was far from being the case.

Muslim divines such as Qazi Mughisuddin of Delhi (during the time of Alauddin Khilji), Mir Hamdani of pre-Mughal Kashmir, Abdul Qadir Badauni (during the reign of Akbar), Shaikh Ahmad Sarhandi (during the reign of Jehangir) all proclaimed in their writings that the *shariah* precluded non-Muslims in an Islamic state from enjoying equal rights with the Muslim citizens. However, Muslim rulers just ignored this stand and opted for a 'functional' secular approach in state matters. Hence, quotations from Muslim religious writings do not tell the actual story, but only reveal the mindset of the *Ulema*. It must also be remembered that the *Ulema* themselves held different views.[2]

The Hindu segment of the population, generally speaking, accorded full legitimacy to the Muslim ruler and gave him due loyalty. According to the *Dharmashastras*, every ruler was duty bound to enlarge his dominion and to strive to become the world ruler (*chakravarti*). Territorial expansion was the highest duty of the king, provided he ruled justly according to the shastras. The raja fought, but the '*praja*' pursued the prescribed ends of life (*purusharthas*) without being much bothered about the identity of the raja. His legitimacy depended, more than any other factor of race or religion, upon victory in battle. Battles did not escalate into extended wars involving the participation of the populace.

Victory or defeat in battle meant only a change of rulers, within the system prescribed by the *Dharmashastras*, not any enslavement of the people. The erstwhile subjects of the defeated ruler did not feel called upon by duty to oppose or overthrow their new ruler. This martial and socio-political ethic was also extended, later on, to the Muslim kings and warriors.

The Hindu populace had come to look upon the Central Asian Muslim rulers who had adopted India as their home as a new warrior caste, which had become an integral part of an already mixed population. The Muslims also considered themselves in this way. Intermarriage between Muslims and Hindus was almost unthinkable. But so was inter-caste marriage within the Hindu fold itself, apart from a limited permission in some cases. The significant point is that as time rolled on the lower castes and weaker sections, in substantial numbers, among the Hindu population, started to gravitate towards Islam. Islamic social egalitarianism promised them a degree of vertical mobility that was denied them in the extremely hierarchical Hindu social system.

Despite the idea of the fraternity of Islam and the equality of all Muslims racial gradations soon became operative. The socially inferior caste groups among the Hindus embraced Islam, as they must have been attracted by its democratic complexion and the promise of vertical mobility in the social hierarchy. But they must have been somewhat disappointed as the Muslims themselves were not free from the evil of racial pride and pretensions of superiority. The Muslims of Turkish, Persian or Afghan extraction did not enter into matrimonial alliances with Muslims of Indian origin.

The Hindu populace enjoyed freedom of religious belief and practice, and there was no interference in their personal laws and social customs. However, there were restrictions on the building of new temples at public places. The Hindu princes who accepted the suzerainty of the central power were accorded high honor and status. They retained their thrones and exercised vast powers under the feudal system. There was one common civil and criminal law, which leaned upon the *shariah* but was, by no means, solely dictated by it. The Muslim sovereigns did not interfere with the personal and family law of Hindus relating to marriage, divorce, adoption and inheritance.[3]

The Sultans who ruled in the independent provincial kingdoms of Kashmir, Bengal, and Golkunda etc. before their incorporation into the Mughal empire were also tolerant and just towards all their subjects. Zaynul Abidin (d. 1470) of Kashmir, the most illustrious ruler of the region, was universally loved. He patronised Sanskrit no less than Persian, the Sant no less than the *Sufi*. Husayn Shah (d. 1519) of Bengal played a similar role in the eastern region. His example was later on followed by Sher Shah (d. 1545); whose administrative reforms were carried on and completed by Akbar. To this day Sher Shah remains the hero of Hindus and Muslims alike.

In the southern region the Bahmani sultan, Tajuddin Feroze (d. 1472) gave preference to people from the south (*Dakhnees*) in state employment, irrespective of religion. Mahmud Gawan (d. 1481), the illustrious Prime Minister of the Bahmani kingdom and an outstanding statesman, was noted for his liberal and functionally secular approach in the affairs of state. The Bahmani kingdom and the Vijaynagar Empire were natural rivals. After the breakup, in 1518, of the Bahmani state into the five *sultanates* of Golkunda, Bijapur, Bidar, Berar, and Ahmadnagar the Muslim sultans continually quarreled among themselves. They formed alliances with Vijaynagar to promote their own political interests without any consideration of religion. The sultan of Bijapur sought the help of Vijaynagar against the sultan of Ahmadnagar. The rulers of Vijaynagar played one Muslim ruler against the other until the eventual defeat of Vijaynagar in 1565. During the protracted period of shifting alliances Vijaynagar rulers helped the Muslim kingdom of Bijapur against the other Muslim kingdom of Ahmadnagar. Rulers changed roles and sides according to political, not religious, considerations. Muslim rulers did the same and fully rewarded all those who served imperial interests. Ibrahim Qutub Shah (d. 1580) of Golkunda greatly patronised Telugu culture, endowed Hindu temples and even discontinued the '*jizya*.'

Though the Islamic orthodoxy held that the '*shariah*' ought to govern every aspect of human life the Muslim rulers followed what might best be called a policy of 'functional secularism', that is, a pragmatic separation of religion and politics without bothering about Muslim theological niceties. The '*shariah*' held that consequent upon military conquest by the Muslims the occupied portions of India had become the 'land of Islam' (*Dar ul Islam*). The '*shariah*' permitted non-Muslim subjects of the Muslim states to practice their religion, seek wealth and live in peace and honor, but denied them complete equality of status and of opportunity in the modern sense, The *shariah* had evolved through reflection on the corpus of the Quran and the reported sayings and doings of Prophet Muhammad and his principal early companions. Though the *shariah* extolled religious tolerance and fairplay towards the non-believers it categorised the subjects of a Muslim state into Muslims and '*dhimmis*' (protected people). The latter did not enjoy equal rights and privileges with the Muslims.

The Vision of an Unknown Indian Muslim: Part 2

THE ROLES OF AKBAR AND AURANGZEB

Illiterate as Akbar was, the emperor had a remarkably keen and sharp mind, an insatiable intellectual curiosity, and an intuitive and abiding concern for natural justice. Interested in spirituality rather than religiosity, the essence of the Islamic faith rather than the letter of the *shariah*, mutual understanding between religions rather than polemics, religious tolerance in his kingdom rather than conversion of all to a single point of view, he sought guidance from the informed and enlightened of all religions and views. Yet, he remained his own master.

Religious authorities, however, were never wielders of effective political power, though they certainly wielded considerable influence. Moreover, even among the religious authorities there was no unanimity of views in regard to the details of the *shariah*. The *Sufi* saints, in particular, had their own interpretations, which were hotly disputed by the orthodox *Ulema*. While some jurists held that the *shariah* prescribes social distance between the Muslims and the non-Muslims the *Sufis* preached and practised universal brotherhood, rather than merely the brotherhood of Muslims. The sultans got on much better with the *Sufis* than with the *Ulema*. Though the Muslim rulers did not accept, in theory or practice many recommendations the *Ulema* made the rulers never presumed to reform the '*shariah*'. Akbar is the only Muslim sovereign who ventured to reform Islam according to his own lights, rather than being content with a mere working secularism.

Akbar attempted to bring about complete emotional integration and equality of status and opportunity between Muslims and Hindus. Akbar's abolition of the '*jizya*' in 1564 (eight years after his accession to the throne) was a very significant psychological innovation in this direction. From one angle, non-Muslims had not much reason to feel discriminated against on the score of '*jizya*', as they were exempt from paying the '*zakat*'. This is the Islamic wealth tax calculated at two and a half per cent on the spare wealth of Muslims. This tax was not levied on non-Muslims. Now the '*zakat*' could be much more than the *jizya*, which, in any case, was not levied upon *Brahmans*. However, at the psychological and political level the abolition of *jizya* was very significant. Perhaps, the orthodox Muslim opposition to the move would have been far less if Akbar had not indulged in the talk of *'Deen-e-Ilahi'*. The over enthusiasm of some courtiers for reasons, perhaps more temporal than spiritual, conspired to confirm the charge or the impression that Akbar was not just liberalising Islam but founding a new religion.

The issue of *'Deen-e-Ilahi'* has become totally obfuscated due to various factors. The *Ulema* accuse Akbar of heresy and apostasy and founding a new religion. Some accuse him of dishonest prostitution of religion for political purposes and appeasing his Hindu subjects, some charge the emperor with an appetite for acquiring a divine status. Some view him as an inveterate antagonist of Islam and the Muslims. Some hold him to be a paragon of virtue, compassion and reason.

Akbar's position appears to be a borderline case between,

(a) liberalizing or restructuring (in a pragmatic commonsense fashion) Islamic concepts and values, and;

(b) founding a new religious tradition on syncretistic lines.

It is significant that the emperor did not demote or disfavor those among his closest loyalists (both Muslim and Hindu) who remained quite skeptical of or indifferent to the royal cult. Most probably, Akbar regarded himself as a Muslim and wanted others also to identify the Emperor as a liberal Muslim. Aurangzeb, on the other hand, is demonized by a large section of non-Muslim circles. Objective historical research done in recent years has exposed the fallacy of both the extreme views.

Aurangzeb continued to enjoy the loyalty and active support of his subjects, as a whole, till the very end of his long reign. His declared policy and practice was to employ honest and efficient persons, irrespective of religion or caste. The percentage of high-ranking 'mansabdars' under Aurangzeb was higher than in the time of Akbar. Aurangzeb's Maratha and Deccan policies were governed by political and economic considerations, rather than religious. His fight against his father and brothers for securing the throne was also a vigorous search for power rather than an exercise in Islamic piety, though his conviction in the supremacy of the *shariah* was all-powerful and honest. However, he misjudged both the political and the spiritual terrain before him. If Dara was poetic and speculative, Aurangzeb was puritanical and legalistic; if Dara came under the spell of the Upanishads, Aurangzeb came under the spell of orthodoxy, if Dara stood for the essential unity of all religions, Aurangzeb stood for the exclusive salvation of Muslims. Aurangzeb, however, was not a tyrant destroying temples, persecuting non-believers and forcibly converting non-Muslims to Islam. Aurangzeb's real failure lay in the limitations of his religious vision and political strategy.

Soon after capturing power from his father and defeating his brothers in the war of succession the emperor abolished the very old practice of levying a pilgrim tax on millions of Hindus who took a dip in the holy rivers or participated in the traditional fairs. This meant an enormous loss of revenue but Aurangzeb took this step as the said tax did not conform to the *shariah*. Several years later the '*jizya*' was re-imposed on the ground that it was in line with the *shariah* though it had been abolished long back by Akbar.

Now Akbar, as a liberal Muslim and creative administrative genius did not feel bound by the *shariah* in introducing a measure calculated to bring about complete equality and a sense of unity among the Indian people. Judged from the modern concept of human rights and complete constitutional equality of all citizens (without any distinction of race, religion, or gender) of a sovereign state, the concept of '*jizya*' is, patently, discriminatory. Akbar had intuitively grasped the wisdom of the yet unborn humanist idea of complete equality. But Aurangzeb was honestly committed to the idea that a good Muslim ruler must follow the *shariah* in letter and spirit. And, indeed, from the angle of the *shariah*, the '*jizya*' was not imposed upon the non-Muslims as a penalty but as a substitute for the Islamic wealth tax (*zakat*) levied exclusively upon the believers. The *shariah* even exempted non-Muslims from '*jizya*' under certain conditions.

Indeed, in medieval times (when the principle of separation of church and state and equal rights of all citizens had not arisen) '*jizya*' was designed to ensure a permissive and tolerant plural society comprising believers as well as non-believers whose life, property, honor and other rights stood guaranteed as 'protected' non-Muslim citizens (*dhimmis*). There can be little doubt that this state of affairs was far better for the non-believers than being wiped out altogether or having to endure forcible conversion. There can also be little doubt that the modern idea of complete equality of all citizens of a state, irrespective of religion or gender, is a higher ideal than the traditional Islamic idea involving a distinction between full and second-class citizens of a state.

When Aurangzeb decided to re-impose the '*jizya*' he, indeed, tried to put back the clock of history. While this shows the limitations of his worldview, it hardly follows that he was anti-Hindu or even a Muslim fanatic in the derogatory sense. Hostile critics refer to the '*jizya*' matter, but conveniently overlook Aurangzeb's abolition of the pilgrim tax that fell upon Hindus. Throughout his long reign Aurangzeb desperately struggled to boost an economy crippled by protracted offensive wars against the Deccan sultans and security operations against the Marathas. He was, thus, subjected to the sociological phenomenon of 'over-stretch'.

The Emperor thought it fit to raise the excise and customs duties, but (presumably under some provision in the *shariah*) allowed concessions to Muslim manufacturers and traders. This measure considerably reduced net revenue because a large number of Hindu traders hit upon the strategy of entering into fake partnerships with Muslims to attract the concessional rates. The economic crisis was further worsened by the sharp increase in the reign of Aurangzeb in the number of '*mansabdari*' units of revenue. This revenue was diverted, under the '*mansabdari*' system, to the coffers of the '*mansabdars*' at the cost of the state.

Aurangzeb's administrative problems got further compounded due to his unwise decision to direct, in person, the anti-insurgency operations against Shivaji in the distant Pune region. The Emperor's long absence from the capital considerably lowered efficiency and honesty in the public dealings of officers. Intrigue and callous self-interest, and deviation from Aurangzeb's high standards of justice, rather than the Emperor's animus against the Sikh gurus, resulted in the atrocities against the minor sons of Guru Govind Singh. The Mughal-Sikh confrontation in general was also, basically, political as it was occasioned by the internecine rivalries and conflicts of Hill Rajas among themselves and with Nepal rulers. Being the suzerain power the Mughals got involved because of treaty obligations.

To sum up, the re-imposition of the '*jizya*', discriminatory tax structure for excise and customs duty, discouragement of music and other art forms, annexation of the *Shia* kingdoms of Golkunda and Bijapur, were not acts of hostility against the Hindus or the *Shias*. While Aurangzeb did demolish a few temples, he endowed several more in different parts of the country. Modern research has shown that his motives in both cases were political or administrative, not religious. The same remarks apply to the emperor's dealings with the Sikhs and the Marathas.

The real dark side or malaise of the medieval period was the unmerited sufferings of the common man due to the continuing misdeeds of corrupt and callous local officers or the governors and the irresponsible sections of the nobility, despite the benevolence of the rulers. Access to the just monarch, who was, in theory, the father figure to all his subjects was not at all a practicable proposition for the harassed subjects. This was, however, the common fate of both Hindu and Muslim.

The shadow of the governor, the district official, the local aristocrat ever stood between the common man and his benevolent monarch. Even if the belief that Jehangir had a bell installed at the palace gate to be rung by the aggrieved supplicant not be a mere benign myth, this arrangement could have helped out only the residents of the imperial capital or nearby places.

The sovereign was, indeed, the father figure for all his subjects, irrespective of religion or caste. But it is pretty certain that life for the vast majority was not idyllic. Disputes over land, money, position and power must have bred, then as now and always, tension, intrigue, revenge and crime. The crucial question is what happened when redress was not available through the traditional institutional structures due to the failure of the village panchayat, the *kotwal* or the *qazi* in the due performance of their duty. There were no newspapers, no democratic machinery for redress of grievances apart from help from feudal or religious quarters having a voice in the corridors of power. And it is here that the Muslim segment of the population must have stood at a natural advantage. Muslims must have felt a relatively greater sense of security and confidence in a system presided over by a monarch with whom they could pray together before the Supreme Creator.

This is not to say that Hindus felt alienated from the power structure since they were definitely an integral part of the system. However, it is quite probable that they did not feel they were influential in administrative and ruling circles to the same extent as their Muslim brothers. Even today in a democratic setup those who vote for the party in power are more likely to have a greater sense of participation in power than those who are in the opposition. In any case, the Hindu nobility and the upper classes and castes among the vast Hindu population lived fulfilled and honored lives. What is even more clear and undisputed is that kindness and cordiality prevailed among Hindus and Muslims in medieval India since the simple goodness of heart knows no barriers of religion, caste or creed.

SOCIAL AND ECONOMIC CONDITIONS

The social customs of Hindus and Muslims in medieval India show a remarkable similarity despite a sharp divides on the issue of idol worship and caste stratification. Social customs were governed, primarily, by class and region rather than by religion. Conversion from Hinduism to Islam modified the theology of the converted but their life attitudes and behavior, with a few exceptional matters, remained unaltered. This is a general human pattern occurring again and again in different societies. Thus, when the Germanic races took to the Christian religion in the early Middle Ages, they retained their ethnic flavor as was done by the Latins who had embraced Christianity some centuries earlier. Likewise, when the Iranians shifted their allegiance from Zoroastrianism to Islam they retained their distinctive life attitudes, which still differentiate them from their Arab coreligionists, quite apart from purely doctrinal *Shia-Sunni* differences. The environment in the broad sense profoundly influences human attitudes and behaviour. The central and West Asian Muslims who settled down in their new Indian environment were gradually Indianized in several respects. Both continuity and change are the inalienable features or coordinates of human society.

The Indians who got converted to Islam adopted a so called Muslim name, repudiated the caste system and idol worship, took to obligatory Islamic prayers, fasting in the month of *Ramazan*, burying instead of burning their dead, and felt free to partake of flesh foods, if so inclined, but to abstain totally from intoxicants. Some basic changes also took place in their personal laws relating to marriage, divorce and inheritance. But at the deeper psychological and spiritual levels the old beliefs, attitudes and responses lingered on as they still do.

The Indian Muslim way of life pertaining to marriage customs and ceremonies, dowry, abhorrence of divorce and remarriage of women, festivities at birth and death, the complex web of family and clan relationships: the obligations of the daughter-in-law, the higher status of the elder brother, special affection for the maternal uncle, the veneration of holy men and shrines, belief in evil spirits, and so on, are quite distinct from that of other Muslim societies. The Indian converts to Islam retained more or less intact their native Hindu customs, in varying degrees, in different regions of the land. In Bengal even after mass conversion the pattern of prohibited degrees in marriage, leaned towards the original Hindu pattern.[4]

Social life in medieval India ran on class and caste, rather than on religious lines. Thus, the upper caste Hindus and Muslims lived and dressed alike, were given to pomp and ostentatious living, sycophancy, horse riding, hunting, fencing, music and dance, wine drinking, gambling, associating with courtesans and so on. The upper classes, especially Muslims, lived extravagantly, above their means, and remained in permanent debt to professional Hindu moneylenders. The rich sought medical help from famous physicians without any discrimination of religion, just as they sought the blessings of holy men or visited tombs and shrines. They enjoyed the same jokes, stories, folk tales (apart from a few purely religious themes). They appreciated the same music, had the same ideal of feminine grace and beauty, they bore loyalty to the same ruler or sovereign, they sometimes rebelled and formed alliances to promote group interests, irrespective of religion, and won or lost power or fortune. They did not inter-marry, but this did not obstruct the forming of sincere and lasting friendships or political alliances. Likewise, the lower classes and the rural folk lived in their own social, cultural and occupational space, which was common for the Hindu and Muslim alike. Seasonal festivals and fairs, epidemics, drought, shortage of funds at marriage times, harassment by petty officers and so on, were the main parameters of this common world.

During the entire medieval period social gradation cut across the distinction between Hindu and Muslim. Poor Muslims were in the employment of affluent Hindus, and vice versa. Muslim rulers and landlords were loved, admired or feared by the Hindus and vice versa. Friends and foes, creditors and debtors, princes and courtiers, clients and courtesans were not selected and did not function on lines of religion or caste. Business partnerships were common between Hindus and Muslims. The common man, be he Hindu or Muslim, had the same grievances against the *'patwari'*, the *kotwal*, the *'sahukar'*, the aristocrat, the artisan, the highway robber or burglar, the dancing girl or prostitute, all of whom could be either Hindu or Muslim.

The restrictions upon inter-dining and inter-marriage notwithstanding, close and sincere friendships were the rule rather than the exception among all sections of the Indian people. Mutual respect and loyalty to one's allies, be they Muslim or Hindu, was the cementing force of society for hundreds of years in medieval India. It is a total distortion of historical reality to attribute the long period of Muslim rule to the cowardice of the Hindu population in the face of Muslim tyranny. Muslim autocratic rule lasted for several centuries due to Hindu doctrinal tolerance (flowing from the Hindu concept of *'Isht Devata'*), and the legitimacy of rule by the military victor, no matter what his religion. The concept of legitimacy flowed from the yet more basic *'swadharma'* of the *Schatrya* caste and of the *'Chakravarti'* ruler. Mutual religious tolerance, rather than inferiority of the Hindus was the basic reason of the stability of Muslim rule in a preponderantly non-Muslim milieu.

The economic life of the masses in medieval India was not much affected by the winds or storms of politics or the rise and fall of royal dynasties, Hindu or Muslim. The fortunes of only the warriors and their kin were affected by winning or losing in battle. The masses; the tillers of the soil, the workers and artisans, the money lenders, the scholars and priests, all continued doing their hereditary jobs, irrespective of who formed the links in the great chain of the power hierarchy. These links in the chain were not connected with religion. Thus, the ruler could be Muslim, his *'Dewan'*, Hindu, or vice versa, the military commander either a Hindu or Muslim, and so on, down the line. In general, however, central Asian Muslim nobility held the top civil and military positions, while the Hindu nobility dominated the revenue side. The sovereign allotted *'Jagirs'* for life to his trusted nobles, both Muslim and Hindu. These *jagirs* reverted to the crown at the death of the *'jagirdar'*, but the sovereign usually re-allotted them to the principal heir.

Trade and commerce were in Hindu hands, but the artisans and manufacturers were, generally speaking, converted Muslims. The moneylenders called the shots everywhere. But in point of prestige the trading community was far below the feudal class, both Hindu and Muslim. The converted Muslims were not accorded social equality with the upper class Hindus and Muslims. The Muslims of Rajput origin and the Muslims of central Asia extraction did not inter-marry though both enjoyed high status in society.

The Hindus always dominated trade, commerce and banking while Muslims dominated the military, police and the judiciary. The landed aristocracy was also, principally, Hindu in view of their far greater numbers. But the percentage of Muslim landed gentry and '*mansabdars*' was higher. To begin with, the artisans were mostly native Hindus. But a large number of artisans gradually and peacefully got converted to Islam, which must have definitely attracted them because of its worldly success as well as social egalitarianism. Forcible conversion was a rarity. The Muslim invaders were the pioneers in the manufacture and use of gunpowder and artillery that were the secret of their military prowess. Gradually the converted Indian Muslims came to dominate several sectors of industry, such as leather, textile, metal, wood, masonry and tailoring.

Social gradation cut across the distinction between Hindu and Muslim. Poor Muslims were in the employment of rich or affluent Hindus, and vice versa. Muslim rulers and feudal lords ruled over and commanded the genuine loyalty and admiration of Hindu subjects, no less than of Muslim, and vice versa. Friends and foes were not confined to any religion or caste, nor were creditors and debtors. There were business partnerships between Hindus and Muslims. The common man, both Hindu or Muslim, had the same experiences, pleasant or unpleasant, with the '*patwari*,' the '*kotwal*', the '*sahukar*', the '*qazi*', the aristocrat, the burglar, the artisan, and the dancing girl, mistress or prostitute who could be Muslim or Hindu. This state of affairs continued in the Lahore kingdom under Ranjit Singh, and the princely states of Hyderabad, Mysore, Baroda, Gwalior, Jaipur, and several others right up to the dawn of Indian independence.

Religious Interaction

The consolidation of Muslim political power in north India by the 13th century gradually created social psychological space in the sub-continent for the peaceful spread of the ideas and values of the new ruling class. Adversity induces the individual or a people to reflect on their situation. The military defeat of an old and well-established power by invaders, much smaller in numbers and far less intellectually cultivated could not but initiate a process of reflection and reformation of the native Indian mind. Sensitive and elevated souls pondered over the human situation: the destruction of life and property and the suffering caused by the perennial armed conflicts born out of the lust for power and wealth. Saints as well as common Hindus were also confronted with the claim that the repeated victories and success of Muslim invaders were a practical proof of Divine help to the victors. The *Bhakti* movement was the authentic Hindu response to the prevailing situation. The *Bhakti* saints, free from any bitterness, grudge or hostility against Muslims, realized that the failure of Hindu society was due to empty ritualism and the caste system. The saints candidly pointed out the contradiction between the theoretical professions of learned *Brahmans* that Reality was free from all duality, and at the same time defending the rigid and obnoxious caste system including untouchability itself.

The saints and poets of *Bhakti* distilled the ideas of Ethical Monotheism and humanistic love from the bewildering myths of folk religion, on one hand, and from abstruse *Brahmanical* Metaphysics, on the other. All sorts of ideas and cults had come to flourish in the garden of Hinduism and the *Bhakti* movement was a process of weeding out the useless accretions. Even the Upanishads, which reflect a high intellectual level, contained myths, occult beliefs and folklore. The Hindu elite made no attempt to educate the masses and raise their moral and intellectual level so long as the vital interests of the upper classes were not challenged. The caste system was a good protective institution, which preempted any possible 'revolt of the masses'. The *Brahmans* and the rest of the upper classes readily gave a supposedly rational justification of the caste system without having any qualms of conscience that the caste system violated human dignity and fraternity.

The impact of Islam on Hindu society initiated a new agenda and put a question mark before the, hitherto, unquestioned validity of the caste system. Likewise, the dialogue between Islam and Hinduism led the *Sufi* intellectuals and poets to a deeper probing into the *Brahmanical* idea of the Unity of Being and its relationship with the Islamic idea of a Creator God. This created the possibility of an organic fusion of the nuclear core of Islam (Unity of God and the oneness and equality of the human family) with the nuclear core of *Brahmanism* (Unity of Being and universal compassion for every form of life). This line of thought appealed to the philosophically oriented *Sufis*, but its general flowering did not take place in medieval times due to several political and historical reasons. However, a good beginning was definitely made.

Under the political and socio-economic conditions of medieval India it was very natural for the weaker sections of the land to gravitate either to the message of *Bhakti* or to *Sufi* Islam. The social function and practical thrust of both the movements were identical: the stress upon Ethical Monotheism, complete surrender to and trust in a personal God (by whatever name "He" may be called), inner purity, universal kindness and compassion, the universal brotherhood and equality of man, and lastly, seeking nearness to God, essentially, through spiritual meditation and discipline, and, optionally, through devotional music.

That some among the Indian masses gravitated towards Hindu *Bhakti*, while others got converted to *Sufi* Islam depended upon the religious identity of the spiritual mentor or mentors on the local scene. The degree of cultural resistance to new ideas and mundane considerations of material betterment also led to varying responses. In any case both *Sufism* and *Bhakti* spread in the entire land without any conflict or rivalry. Both Hindu and Muslim rulers welcomed these movements. But the orthodox among both *Brahmans* and Muslim *Ulema* resisted. This state of affairs prevailed right till the advent of British rule, indeed till very recent times.

The appeal of the *Sufi* and *Bhakti* saints cut across all religious communities. Common people, Hindu and Muslim alike, flocked to holy men or shrines, irrespective of their religious labels, to get solace and for spiritually resolving their mundane problems. This is, however, not to say that Hindus and Muslims had become fully emotionally integrated. Perhaps, the majority of conventional Muslims, under the influence of orthodox *Ulema* and jurists, continued honestly to believe in the exclusive salvation of Muslims, and that even the best non-Muslim remained inferior (spiritually) to the indifferent Muslim believer. This rather irrational and conceited approach must have diluted the healing potential of the balm of humanistic love and tolerance the *Sufis* and *Bhakatas* always extolled and applied to human relations.

The celebrated Muslim thinker, Al-Beruni (d. 1048) who was well versed in Sanskrit classics had fully understood the above point. He came to the conclusion, ten centuries ago, that idol worship was not tantamount to polytheism or atheism. This liberal and enlightened approach, however, was not intellectually appreciated by the orthodox Muslim *Ulema*, and therefore, did not percolate horizontally in urban Muslim society. In any case, the rural masses of India took the message to heart and lived accordingly.[5]

The great *Sufi* saints of medieval India, like Moinuddin Chishti of Ajmere, Qutub Sahab and Nizamuddin Auliya of Delhi, Baba Farid of Punjab, Mohibullah Shah of Allahabad and many others elsewhere functioned as spiritual magnets of Islam. However, their emphasis was always upon inner purification rather than conversion. The Muslim sovereigns too were not concerned with conversion. They wanted to exercise power, while the *Sufis* were quite content with educating the inner man and spreading the message of universal love.

LANGUAGE, LITERATURE AND ART

Every society has, in addition to its thought and value system, its distinctive artistic sensibility reflected in its literature, music and architecture. All these together constitute the inner spiritual world of the society. This inner world is reflected in the outer political, economic and legal structures of society, and these structures, in turn, also shape the inner world of the society. A continuing dialogue thus goes on between the inner and outer worlds of every society.

Like music, architecture also mirrors the soul of society. Architecture aims at both beauty of structure and functional excellence, and is correlated with the technology of the period concerned. Its changing styles also reflect shifts in political and economic power. Painting and sculpture also reflect the dominant concerns and interests of both the artist and his reference group. We find that the people of medieval India, irrespective of their religion, shared a common artistic sensibility, which varied according to region and class.

The Sultans and the nobility actively patronized music, the *Ulema* frowned upon this lapse, the urban middle class Muslims were divided on this issue, and the rural Muslim masses, along with their Hindu brethren, cultivated the folk music of their respective regions. Under *Sufi* influence '*qawali*' developed as a new art form on the pattern of '*kirtan*' and became immensely popular among both Muslims and Hindus. The Sultans and the Muslim nobility lavished favors on gifted artists without any distinction of religion or caste. The Hindu rulers and nobility did the same.

The Indian Muslim practitioners of music retained its original Indian complexion, but interaction with Persian and central Asian music led to the evolution of new melodies and airs. Muslim musicians freely accepted the stylistic conventions and even Hindu religious mythological themes. Schools of music (*gharanas*) arose and functioned like spiritual fraternities transcending religious and sectarian differences. The master or guru could be a Hindu, and his most talented pupil a Muslim, and vice versa.[6]

Great artists, just like the great saints, preached and practiced the brotherhood of man. Indian art and spirituality radiated the spirit of universal peace and emotional integration in the midst of all the strife and struggle, intrigue and rivalry, pomp and pelf as well as the poverty and suffering of Indian humanity.

The artists, craftsmen and artisans of ancient India were world famous for their skills. Muslim architects and builders fully utilized talented Hindus for building in the composite style of architecture that gradually evolved due to interaction between central Asian and Indian styles. The main features of Hindu architecture, on the structural side, were the heavy carved pillar or column, massive gateways and a high plinth. The main features of the central Asian style were sleek pillars, the arch and the dome. On the decorative side Hindu architecture relied mainly on icons, floral and animal motifs and also latticework. Muslim architects abjured all this with the exception of floral designs. Their favored forte was geometrical patterns and tile work. Interaction between the two styles led to the creation of the most exquisite architectural masterpieces such as the Taj, the Fathepur Sikri complex, the Rajput palaces, the Juma Masjid and Pearl mosque of Delhi, and so on. One has only to compare them with the great masterpieces of architecture in the rest of the Islamic world to realize the rich contribution from the Indian, rather the Hindu side. The artisans and craftsmen were all Hindus, to begin with, but gradually many of them got converted to Islam, while retaining many of their ethnic traits and social customs.

Since medieval Indian society had a monarchical and feudal character the great architects concentrated on palaces, castles, places of worship and mausoleums, all meant for the comfort and glorification of the mighty and the rich. The only item, which affected the common man, was the public ornamental garden. Building such gardens, in addition to hunting, were the royal and aristocratic hobbies. In fact, residential palaces themselves were a complex of pavilions, large and small, set in a vast garden having paved geometrical paths, fountains and flowing water. However, the monarchs liberally built utilitarian constructions for public benefit, such as, national highways, giant wells, tanks, rest houses for travelers etc. These constructions, no less than the palaces of royalty and mansions of the nobility reflect a common style and a common aesthetic sensibility. There is nothing Islamic or Hindu about Indian architecture of medieval India, apart, of course, from places of worship. The true artist was concerned with beauty, as he saw it, not with religion or caste. The rulers and the nobility, both Muslim and Hindu, patronized merit without any religious discrimination.

Concluding Reflections

Is the above interpretation of medieval Indian history a Muslim apologist's or Congress nationalist's defense against the charge emanating from *Hindutva* quarters that liberal, progressive, or leftist historians are given to concealing facts for the sake of vote bank politics? My honest reply is an emphatic - 'No'. The above interpretation (which I have come to accept after years of thought and reflection, in the light of the creative labors of internationally reputed and impartial scholars and savants) fully satisfies the most rigorous criteria of historical evidence, though, obviously, the evidence does not and cannot amount to proof in the logical or scientific sense. I have already said that historical interpretations are organically related to still more basic existential interpretations of the total human situation and such interpretations do not admit of proof in the conclusive scientific or logical sense.

It is incontrovertible that the Arab or Turkish tribes who invaded India were Muslim by religion. Therefore, if one insists upon emphasizing the religious identity of the invader, the invasion will always appear as an attack of Islam upon Hinduism. But if one surveys the human situation in general one will realize that dispersal of peoples and races on earth, and the struggle for power and wealth is universal and an integral part of the human story as such. Before Sultan Mahmud and Babar had turned their attention to India they had conquered or tried to conquer lands in central Asia that were inhabited by their own coreligionists. The Aryans and Hindus, in earlier times, had done the same in the vast stretches of the Indian sub-continent. So have all other races and peoples the world over, be they Egyptians, Greeks, Romans, Chinese or Europeans. Now this awareness can and usually does liberate the impartial and careful observer of the human situation from the habit of seeing every person or event under a religious label. The observer becomes open to the concrete quality of life as it flows in history and judges men and matters accordingly. This humanist interpretation of history not only has greater appeal for several well informed and noble souls but it is also more useful for promoting universal peace and harmony.

When one adopts the humanist approach to life the conflicts between different peoples, races, regions and religions in the past do not divide humans into permanently hostile in-groups and out-groups. One starts looking at the conflicts of the past as stages in the slow growth of the human family on a global scale. The victory of an Alexander and the defeat of a Porus, the devastation of a Halaku or a Nadir Shah, the compassion of an Asoka, the statesmanship of an Akbar, the aberrations of a Hitler all become achievements or failures of the human family. The true historian, from this angle, does not identify himself or herself with any particular group or adopt a partisan attitude. The rise and fall, achievements and failures, virtues and vices of all peoples and all times become his own. With charity for all and malice towards none he passes judgment on the deed, rather than the doer. His standard remains consistent, but takes into account that human ideas and ideals are subject to the law of evolutionary growth. In short, his range of sympathy gradually becomes universal instead of remaining congealed at a particular parochial level determined by his birth or early conditioning.

Notes: Chapter 9

India in Medieval Times

1. The well-established Hindu normative religious and social texts (*shastras*) including the *Manusmriti* contain the concept and ideal of a supreme overlord or sovereign emperor *(Chakravarti)* to whom all regional kings and rulers pay obeisance. Every Hindu king therefore aspired to this position and this naturally led to continual warfare in ancient India. Muslim rulers stepped into the same shoes and when successful in battle enjoyed the same legitimacy. Insurgencies and rebellions also continued as before.

Among other things, the *Manusmriti* also prescribes that girls should get married before the onset of puberty to enable them to become mothers at the earliest, that widows must not remarry, that women cannot inherit property etc. Laws or regulations governing marriage, prohibited degrees, succession and inheritance have always been an integral part of all religions. Muslim rulers and following them, the British also, on principle did not interfere with family laws of each religion. Both the Muslim and British rulers held that freedom of religious belief implied such non-interference, though this freedom could not be extended to other facets of civil and criminal law which, on principle, demanded uniformity of application. The British made a few exceptions in public interest, such as the abolition of sutee and child sacrifice. See Professor Devaraja's superb work, *The Mind and Spirit of India,* 1967.

2. The views of some people cannot be equated with the actual policy of the then government. Even today some Hindu fanatics or extremists do not mind spreading communal hatred and indulging in violence in the name of Hinduism. But this is not the message of Hinduism, nor the policy of the government of modern India.

3. The destruction of temples took place, primarily, during wars or armed hostilities, very seldom in times of peace. This happened when the monarch felt strongly challenged by rebellious forces and the government felt that strong punitive measures were called for to demoralize and crush insurgent quarters. In fact, genuine religious piety disfavored and opposed aggressive behavior both by Hindus and Muslims. Recent research by reputable Indian and Western historians employing the most rigorous methodology clearly shows that Aurangzeb had endowed many more temples (Hindu and Jain) in different parts of the empire than those he had ordered to be demolished for reasons, political or administrative, rather than religious bigotry. This applies to the Vishwanath temple at Varanasi and also the Keshadeva temple at Mathura. See, *Suba of Allahabad Under the Great Mughals*, by S.N.Sinha. See also, *New Cambridge History of India,* 1992. See also the remarkably rigorous and comprehensive research work done recently by Richard M.Eaton, *Essays on Islam and Indian History,* Delhi, 2000, and also his *Lives of Indian Images,* Delhi, 1999.

The Vision of an Unknown Indian Muslim: Part 2

4. Social Psychology shows that the typical character structure of an ethnic group is produced by generations of cultural conditioning of the child by the family and society at large. Religious conversion changes the previous Theology or some elements of the moral code, but the previous character structure and attitudes persist behind the new religious identity. The converted Muslims of Indian origin even after centuries retain their old marriage customs and patterns of family relationships. The Rajput and Bengali Muslims avoid marriage between first cousins on the father's side, though this was the favorite pattern in Arab society. Likewise, to date, the typical Indian Muslim attitude to divorce, widow remarriage, and other social relationships remains quite distinct from Arab attitudes. The Muslims of Malaysia and Indonesia have retained their own ethnic flavor even more strongly.

Comparative Studies in the Sociology of Knowledge also show there is a correspondence between an individual's ethnic traits of character and his religious approach. In other words, religious beliefs and values, formally the same, are understood and applied quite differently by different ethnic groups. Iranian Muslims, for instance, have always displayed a poetic and musical sensibility and have been inclined to the mystical speculative interpretation of Islam. The Arabs have been better known for their linguistic, mathematical skills, and capacity for accurate observation of the external world. Perhaps, this accounts for the fact that the overwhelming majority of the great *Sufis*, poets, artists and philosophers are of Iranian descent, while the majority of the great Muslim theologians, scientists, mathematicians, historians and geographers of Arab descent.

5. Al-Beruni was one of the geniuses of the human family. A native of Khwarizm in Central Asia, he spent several years in India mastering Sanskrit in order to study Hindu religious and philosophical classics in the original. His masterpiece, *Kitabul Hind* has been translated into several languages. It is a pioneering study in Comparative Religion just as Ibn Khaldun's classic, *Al-Muqadama*, is a pioneering work of genius in the field of Sociology.

Al-Beruni had observed that the Hindus who worshipped images nevertheless believed in one Supreme Being just as Muslims believe in one Supreme Creator. Again, he discovered that the practicing Hindu does not literally equate the material icon with his chosen deity (*Isht Devta*), but holds that the *Brahman* priest infuses the deity into the material icon consequent upon a special invocation. The priest could also de-infuse the deity from the physical icon, if necessary, through another prayer. From such studies and observations Al-Beruni concluded that idol worship does not, necessarily, clash with Monotheism. This was also the considered view of Gandhi. The abhorrence of religious pluralism came from the side of the *Ulema* and the jurists much before the rise of the *Sufi* movement. Even when *Sufi* thought and attitudes emerged and became a broad cultural stream in India and elsewhere it never could displace the hold and power of orthodox Islam in Muslim society.

6. Hindustani music of north India is, perhaps, the best illustration of the blending of the artistic sensibility of India and Iran. It is a flowering and creative growth of the original Indian musical culture. Both Hindu and Muslim lovers of music respected each other's religious beliefs. However, their hearts overflowed with spirituality. For them music was the prayer of the spirit and catharsis of the soul leading to communion with the Divine. Differences of creed dissolved in spiritual ecstasy associated with pure music. Muslims in

India in Medieval Times

India, *Sufis* and sultans, aristocrats and artisans, fell early and eager captives to the muse of Indian music, quite unheedful of the prohibition flowing continuously from Muslim orthodoxy. Sultan Zaynul Abidin (d. 1470) of Kashmir was a great patron of music. His court musician, Ludi Bhatt, was famous. Another *protégée*, Kali Nath wrote a commentary on the first authentic book on music, *Sangeet Tatnakar*, by the famous Saranga Deva of the Devagiri Kingdom in the 14th century.

The Sharqi king of Jaunpur, Sultan Husain (d. 1479) adopted the title '*Gandharva*'. The greatest Muslim musician and musicologist in pre-Mughal times was the famous poet and writer, Amir Khusro (d. 1325). In his famous work, *Ejaaze Khusrawi* he compared the technical aspects of the music of ancient India and Persia. He believed that Indian music was unbeatable for its spirituality.

The chief musician of the Gwalior kingdom under Raja Man Singh (d. 1516) was Naik Mahmud. He promoted the publication of the work, *Man Kauthal* that describes the melodies or airs first introduced by Muslim composers.

In south India Sultan Yusuf (d. 1510), Sultan Ismail (d. 1534) and Sultan Ibrahim II, all of the Bijapur kingdom, were dedicated to Indian music. Ibrahim even wrote songs dealing with Hindu mythology. Sultan Muzaffar Shah II (d. 1526) of the Gujrat kingdom was himself an accomplished musician.

In Mughal times Mian Tansen became a legend in his lifetime. The Awadh court at Lucknow produced several musicians and one of the most popular dance styles, Katthak. The modern era has produced several master musicians from among the Muslims. See, *Society and Culture in Early Medieval India* by Qamaruddin, 1985, and also *Society and Culture in Medieval India* by A.Rashid, 1969. See also *Musalman aur Sangeet* (in Hindi) by Acharya Brihaspati.

Chapter 10
British Rule in Modern India and The Transfer of Power in 1947

The Rise of British Power in India

By the end of the 17th century Western thought and technology had outstripped the Eastern. By the end of the 18th century no Eastern society could resist the military and industrial might of the developed Western nations. The British East India Company, which was merely a trading agency, to begin with, became the de facto ruler of the entire Eastern region of India just fifty years after the death of Aurangzeb. The independent regional states that had emerged following Aurangzeb's death in 1707 were always quarrelling among themselves and were no match to the superior organization, strategy and technical superiority of the rising British power in India. One after another they succumbed to a combination of British diplomacy and competence, and became client states or protectorates under British suzerainty.

The first Indian state to pass under British rule was the *Sultanate* of Bengal after the battle of Plassey in 1757. This was followed by the capitulation of Mysore in 1799, the defeat of Marathas in 1803, the annexation of Sind in 1843, of Punjab in 1846, of Avadh in 1856, and finally, the extinction of the titular Mughal monarchy in 1857.

Historical and sociological studies show that the passage of time transforms the ideas and values of a society, though the overt religious and cultural terms, symbols and rituals remain current as before. Thus while, under the impact of the industrial and scientific revolutions of the 18th century, the actual sensibilities or 'inner world' of the Christian ruling classes in Western Europe had greatly changed they, along with the populace, remained Christian in their own eyes no less than in the eyes of others. The 'style' of Christianity or the mindset of the British ruling class underwent a slow evolution or degeneration (according to the viewpoint of the observer) relative to that of Shakespeare's age three centuries back. Consequently, the policy makers of the East India Company, and later the British government, felt more interested in spreading the gospel of Westminster democracy in the Indian empire rather than propagating formal Christianity. Several British and other European intellectuals became deeply interested in the scientific or scholarly study of Oriental religions and cultures. William Jones, Elphinstone, Wilson, and, perhaps, the greatest of them all, Max Mueller, set this crucial trend of discovering the 'wisdom of the East'.

It was the missionaries, rather than the British rulers who plunged into the task of saving the souls of the teeming 'heathens' in India, be they Muslim, Hindu or tribals. The missionaries had followed the traders and had already built schools, dispensaries and churches in different parts of the country. The Company, as such, and subsequently the British Crown were least concerned to propagate formal Christianity that they themselves had gradually outgrown or which stood transformed under the impact of the scientific Humanism, and rationalism represented by Herbert Spencer, John Stuart Mill, Mathew Arnold, and Charles Darwin *et al.*

The British rulers honored and patronized Western educated Indian intellectuals or political leaders who were forward looking and in tune with modern liberal ideas that were being spearheaded on the world stage by eminent Victorians. The British rulers honestly tried to reform and develop the great cultural heritage of the Indian empire, apart from the introduction of modern transport and communications, public health schemes, and scientific agriculture. However, they were also determined (very understandably) to exercise sovereign authority. They were neither altruistic guardians of the Indian people, nor were they satanic imperialists out to suck the blood of the toiling masses to enrich 'home, sweet home'. At times they divided to rule, but these divisions were not produced like rabbits from the imperial hat of a magician. Indians themselves were a fractured people and diverse interests clamored for short-term gains without caring for the larger good. At times the rulers themselves were divided on what was right and just rather than merely expedient or useful for empire. And these were honest differences. Some of the ablest and noblest British minds squarely stood by the Indians when different perceptions prevailed in London and Calcutta, or when the provincial capitals or district headquarters were rather unwilling to fall in line with 'idealistic directives' from London or Calcutta.

Indian 'nationalist' historiography condemns Macaulay and British rulers for belittling and strangulating Oriental learning and taking calculated steps to destroy Indian self-respect, alienate Indian youth from their cultural roots and turn them into petty clerks and officers for helping the British masters to govern, without any tears, a vast empire with a minimum presence on Indian soil of the British rulers. Such historians always refer to and quote from the famous Minute on Education penned by Macaulay in 1832. This, however, is a highly distorted and selective interpretation of Macaulay's intentions and words. The great historian never belittled Oriental learning. In fact he greatly and sincerely praised Arabic and Sanskrit contribution to humanistic studies and favorably compared the great minds of the Orient with those of Greece and Rome. All that he had said was that in the sphere of experimental science a few modern textbooks on the shelf of a British schoolboy carried more accurate and useful knowledge than entire Oriental libraries. In other words, he strongly favored that Indian youth be given modern scientific education through the medium of English. He had also added that if and when the Indian educated youth, exposed to the new ideas taught by English masters also demanded the introduction in Indian society of liberal democratic institutions it would be a proud day for Britain.

The advent of British rule had naturally led to the emergence of a new class of Indians well versed in English, and also one or more of the modern Indian languages. The vastness of the empire and the ever expanding needs of efficient administration required the rapid growth of prose literature in the native languages. The Indian languages had a rich heritage of poetry, but not of prose. And the language of science, administration and politics is prose, not poetry. The Company founded the *Fort William College* at Calcutta to promote translations from English works into Urdu and Hindi and also the publication of original prose works on modern themes in the two Indian languages.

This was very useful and a wise move. But this could not but sharpen the hitherto slight differences of idiom and vocabulary between Urdu and Hindi into an ever widening or growing cleavage. The reason was that the quarry for coining new words was Arabic and Persian in the case of Urdu, and was Sanskrit in the case of Hindi. This was a more or less inevitable linguistic phenomenon, rather than a British imperial ploy to divide the nation. Perhaps, neither the rulers nor the Indians themselves fully understood the wide-ranging implications of the complex issues involved. In any case, the British rulers were not bothered by the social and political consequences of a growing cleavage between Urdu and Hindi. There was no Gandhi yet on the national scene. There was no agency or enlightened and aware leadership to steer the growth of a composite Indian language for the multi-lingual Indian family. By sheer default of situational compulsion, therefore, Hindustani was aborted and English proceeded, almost as a historic necessity, to become the all India link language of information, science, higher education, politics and commerce. By the time Gandhiji arrived it was late, if not impossible, to reverse the trend of history. Had partition not taken place Hindi-Urdu or Hindustani, in dual scripts, could have been saved. However, it is still open for us to create a consensus in favor of a naturally simple common language instead of stressing linguistic purism. This realism is, happily, gaining ground.

The British government's declaration of policy when Victoria was proclaimed Empress of India in 1858 said that the objective of British

British Rule in Modern India and the Transfer of Power in 1947

'Raj' was not the permanent subjugation of the Indian people but the granting to India of self-government within the British empire. The natural presumption was that democracy on the Westminster pattern would be introduced by stages, and that every Indian citizen would enjoy equal rights and responsibilities without any distinction of religion, caste or color. The Indian National Congress, founded in 1885, also had the same objective.

The idea greatly appealed to the Western educated persons (mostly progressive and liberal *Brahmans* who had already come to terms with elements of modernity the East India Company had already ushered in the three presidencies of India). Such English educated Hindus saw in the idea the promise of ready access to power by all citizens and the end of the multifarious evils of the feudal age. The small but dynamic Parsee community in the Bombay presidency was also thrilled. But the Muslim community as a whole was still living in the shadow of defeat and humiliation brought about by the failure of the great rebellion of 1857. They were apprehensive that the principle of one man, one vote could possibly, be misused by prejudiced or hostile sections within the majority community to harm the legitimate interests of the Indian Muslims. Sir Syed was the leader of this line of thinking. The Congress leadership, including prominent liberal and Western educated liberals like Badruddin Tyabji *et al* argued that parliamentary politics in self-governing India would be based on secular and commonly agreed upon social and economic policies, rather than upon religion based parties. They were quite logical and sincere. But they could not convince Sir Syed and his associates. There can be little doubt that Sir Syed was as patriotic as any other Congress liberal or Hindu patriot. It was a case of honest difference in perception and it would be most unfair to attribute motives to the great reformer and leader who was highly respected and admired by every section of the Indian people as well as by the British rulers.[1]

Sir Syed's perception was that the idea of secular parliamentary democracy was sound in theory but would not work properly in Indian conditions due to various reasons. He was apprehensive that Hindu-

Muslim harmony and unity that had long prevailed in a feudal society might not be able to survive the stresses and strains of competitive electoral politics in a purely republican system. He thought that the fraternal bond between Hindus and Muslims was to a large extent rooted in the traditional idea of the legitimate monarch as a father figure to all citizens, irrespective of race or religion. The subjects willingly obeyed the monarch and participated in his glory as the legitimate sovereign. The position in a democratic society on Western lines would become entirely different, said Sir Syed. Every citizen, irrespective of social rank, education, religion or caste would be a decision maker and be pitted against everybody else in the race for power. Thus a sphere hitherto reserved for a tiny elite would become free for all and every candidate for election will be tempted to mobilize one's own community or caste to support him in the name of caste or community. In this exercise the Muslim minority would be at a permanent disadvantage in relation to the much larger and educationally more advanced Hindu community. Sir Syed, therefore, opted to work for the educational and cultural uplift of the Muslim community rather than plunge into political activity or agitation for ending the colonial status of India. He stood in the company of several liberal reformers and patriots, including eminent Hindus. Their view was that the national agenda should give priority to education over agitation.[2]

It seems Sir Syed's thinking was considerably influenced by the actual working of modern secular democracy at the municipal level in the presidency cities. There was no reservation of seats and no separate electorates for Muslims and other minorities. Very few Muslims got elected. Perhaps, this fact prompted Sir Syed to conclude that the same would happen at state and central levels in the years to come. Sir Syed was certainly sincere, but there can be little doubt that this was a rather hasty and over simplified inference.

The principal reason for the poor showing of Muslim candidates was that they were not sufficiently equipped in terms of Western education and political skills required of a modern corporator. Even the upper caste Hindus were backward in comparison with the Parsees, who were returned in high numbers in Bombay. It is a matter of history that as the upper caste Hindus caught up with the Parsees in education and political consciousness the high percentage of Parsee representation started declining. It seems Sir Syed responded with the caution of a practical politician rather than the insight of a political sociologist. His fears and apprehensions were not without foundation in view of the plural character and composition of Indian society and the unequal levels of modern education among the different segments of the people. But, perhaps, he despaired too soon of the chances of success of secular liberal democracy rooted in the essential unity of the human family and the essential unity of all religions. However, it would be unfair to dismiss Sir Syed as a communalist or as the father of the two-nation theory, later on propagated (most unfortunately) by the ideologues of the Pakistan demand.

After Sir Syed's death in 1898 his cautionary stance gradually developed, among his close followers, into a radical opposition to the Congress movement for home rule. The British rulers were quick to exploit this situation. They partitioned Bengal in 1905. They definitely encouraged and blessed the founding of the All India Muslim League in 1906 and gave a sympathetic hearing to the demand for separate electorates. The concept of separate electorates destroyed the sap of the tender plant of secular humanist approach to democratic politics. Whether the idea was a sinister imperial technique to divide and rule or a British error of judgment in trying to be fair to a Muslim David pitted against the Hindu Goliath need not be debated here. The plain fact is that the concept of separate electorates is the axe, which destroyed the tree or rather plant of national emotional integration of the Indian family.[3]

The constraints of the First World War in the early years of the 20th century impelled both the British rulers of India and the Indian National Congress, the main agency for promoting Indian self-governance, to go slow on the issues concerned. British gradualism was matched by Indian patience and the basic trust of Indian liberals in the sweet reasonableness of the British rulers and the immense prestige of the British Parliament. Almost all sections of the people of India contributed to the imperial war effort. Attacks by German submarines on British shipping had greatly affected trade and commerce and sea transport. This naturally set in motion the process of Indian industrialization and greatly boosted Indian economy. It also raised Indian aspirations and expectations from the British government, officially committed to granting self-governance to the Indian people. The question of the future of the *Turkish Caliphate* after the German and Turkish defeat in the war also became a crucial issue for the Indian Muslims who had always cherished sentimental concern for the welfare of the widely scattered Islamic community.

Gandhiji sincerely and enthusiastically supported the movement launched by the Ali Brothers, and Abul Kalam Azad *et al* for giving moral and material support to Turkey. After the notorious *Jallianwala Bagh* massacre at Amritsar Gandhi created a joint front of the *Khilafat* and Congress organizations and launched a common struggle for achieving both the objectives through direct action. Indian liberals (including Jinnah himself, then a Congress stalwart) dissented from Gandhi. Gandhiji stood for peaceful '*satyagraha*', but it, inevitably, took a violent turn, and the British establishment, naturally, treated the agitation as a law and order problem.

The twenties and thirties were spent by different Indian political parties and factions, in haggling over their share of power in free India; rather than in joint efforts for securing freedom as such. 'All Parties Conferences', peace talks, official 'Round Table' meets were held from time to time and every group participated in the discussions. But every group was adamant on getting its own pound of flesh and adopted an all or none approach. The British rulers, justifiably, found a valid excuse for maintaining the status quo.

THE PARTITION OF INDIA:

The Muslim League at its annual session held at Lahore in March 1940 passed a resolution that the only satisfactory formula for the equitable sharing of power by the Hindu and Muslim communities in independent India was the establishing of an independent sovereign state or states where the Muslims constituted the majority. From 1940 onwards India divided or India united became the one point debate for the Indian Muslims and the country as a whole.

The demand for the partition of India was consistently opposed by the Congress and also by a large section of the *Ulema*, who from the very inception of the freedom struggle, had sided with the secular freedom fighters. British liberal opinion also did not favor partition. Lord Wavel till the very end of his term as Viceroy tried, in his straight-forward way, to preserve Indian unity. The British Cabinet Mission sent by the Atlee government to negotiate with Indian parties did its best to allay the Muslim fear of Hindu domination in a united India.

The Cabinet Mission plan had envisaged a loose federal structure based on the principle of 'grouping' of contiguous states. Each group was to constitute a sub-federation of the existing Indian provinces. The basic idea of the plan was to decentralize power in order to allay the fears of hegemony by one group or the other, and simultaneously preserve the unity of India.

The Muslim League's initial acceptance of the plan was a constructive compromise in a spirit of give and take. The Congress also accepted the plan to begin with. This must have been the happiest moment in the life of Maulana Azad, the Congress President, who had labored hard and long, more than anybody else, in the entire country, to hammer out a solution acceptable to both the Congress and the League. But alas his joy was short lived. The new Congress President, Jawaharlal Nehru, soon after taking over from the Maulana at a very crucial moment declared at a press conference at Bombay that the proposed Indian Constituent Assembly will function as a sovereign body without being bound in any way whatsoever.

This statement brought the wheels of constitutional progress to a sudden grinding halt. Jinnah instantly denounced the evil intentions of the Congress and the total unreliability and hypocrisy of Hindu leaders, with whom, he alleged, it was impossible to deal with in a straightforward manner. A fresh impasse was created and the dark clouds of mutual bitterness and distrust started hovering all over again on the all too brief reconciliation between the Congress and the League.

The British government, initially, chose the policy of wait and see and allowed matters to drift rather than take a clear-cut stand on the correct interpretation of the relevant clause on grouping. Eventually, it upheld Jinnah's interpretation as correct. But before the Congress leadership could make a definite response in the light of the British declaration the League annulled its previous acceptance of the Cabinet Mission plan, and went back to the original demand for Pakistan, as a sovereign state. Thereupon the Congress, at the instance of Nehru, and to the profound sorrow of Azad, also rejected the Cabinet Mission plan. This unfortunate development brought back negotiations for an agreed constitutional and political settlement to square one again. Soon thereafter the Viceroy, Lord Wavell was replaced by Lord Mountbatten.

The deadlock could be broken only when Jinnah was forced to agree to the bifurcation of Punjab and Bengal as a pre-condition to the partition of India as a whole. The Congress held that it stood for a united secular federal India with adequate safeguards for all minorities and provinces. If, however, partition had to come, the Congress held that the logic of partition would have to be applied to Punjab and Bengal, since contiguous areas of both these provinces had a predominantly non-Muslim population. This meant that the eastern region of Punjab and the western region of Bengal would have to be excluded from the proposed Pakistan. Jinnah was extremely reluctant to accept this pre-condition as it amounted to a substantial reduction in the size and resources of the proposed Pakistan. He, however, preferred this 'truncated' Pakistan as a lesser evil to a united India, where, according to Jinnah, the Muslims would be condemned to live at the mercy of the majority community. This is the zigzag path, which eventually led to the partition of the Indian family.

Some quarters hold Jinnah's intransigence primarily responsible for partition. Some hold the British policy of divide and rule to be the crucial factor. Some squarely blame the Congress policy of appeasing Muslims as the main factor, which paved the way to partition. Others add the role of the economic crisis of post-war Britain and the unholy haste of Lord Mountbatten, Nehru and Patel for the transfer of power. Azad points out that Nehru's pronouncement at the Bombay press conference in regard to 'grouping' was an unfortunate blunder that led to Jinnah's *volte face* on his earlier acceptance of the Cabinet Mission plan and the renewal of the demand for Pakistan. In what follows I shall endeavor, as best as I can, to make a balanced appraisal of the responsibility, rather the degrees of responsibility, of the main actors concerned.

The demand for partition, obviously, came from the Muslim side and was consistently and powerfully opposed by the Congress. But it is equally true that at a particular stage the League did give up the demand in favor of a united India. Admittedly, this was on a trial basis and it did not amount to an absolute and unconditional waiver of the idea of Pakistan. Jinnah had made this quite plain.

Though Jinnah did not have any spiritual pretensions and could never appreciate Gandhi's spiritual halo and political style, all impartial observers, Indian and foreign, agree that Jinnah was a forthright person of great integrity and force of conviction. Though arrogant and hungry for power he was not given to deceit or intrigue. I, therefore, submit he should be given due credit for showing genuine flexibility in his approach towards the Cabinet Mission plan. Nor is it insignificant that the British government concurred with Jinnah's interpretation of the Cabinet plan on the issue of 'grouping'.

It is, therefore, quite fair to hold that if Nehru had not reacted the way he did in regard to the issue of 'grouping', the Cabinet Mission plan would have been put into practice, at least on a trial basis. The experiment might have failed and partition may eventually have followed. But, at least, it would have been delayed. And in the interim trial period some understanding, conceivably, might have evolved in favor of a united India. But the, then, rather brusque posture of the Congress, under the stewardship of Nehru, changed the entire political climate and scenario at a most critical moment.

To say so, however, does not mean that it is Nehru rather than Jinnah, who is responsible for partition. Just as Jinnah thought that a truncated Pakistan was a lesser evil than no Pakistan at all, Nehru thought that conceding a truncated Pakistan was a lesser evil than accepting a virtual 'caricature' of a united India fractured into three compulsory groupings. In other words, Sardar Patel and Nehru honestly thought that a united but weak federal India, divided into three sub-units would become a bigger evil than partitioning India subject to the bifurcation of Punjab and Bengal.

Whether the above judgment or assessment was right or wrong is another matter. It is arguable that this judgment was mistaken. Left to themselves, neither Gandhiji, nor Maulana Azad would have accepted the above reasoning. It is also arguable that the sub-continent would have fared much better if Nehru and Patel could have yielded to the wisdom of the Mahatma and the Maulana, rather than what actually did happen. What is beyond dispute is merely this: Precisely, when the League reluctantly agreed to the unity formula of the Cabinet Mission, soon, all too soon, the Congress went back upon the formula, because (rightly or wrongly) it honestly preferred the evil of partition to the evil of an illusory unity. In other words, therefore, the full responsibility for partition cannot be placed, exclusively, on any one individual, party or community. Indeed, historical causation is always too complex for any impartial observer to apportion blame or responsibility without making numerous qualifications. What any person or group chooses is never a free first choice, but a more or less constrained 'package' choice in a crisis situation.

BRITAIN'S ROLE IN PARTITION

A factor, which played a crucial role in the unfolding of the partition drama, was the extreme British impatience to get rid of the imperial burden of governing post-war India. The 'brightest jewel of the British Crown' had, indeed, become a festering sore on the British body politic. The once strong imperial hand was impatient to transfer its burden of power and governance to Indian hands, even if this spelt chaos due to Indian in-fighting. The British 'fear of responsibility' and the virtual abdication of the sense of 'imperial duty' was the consequence of the world war Britain had won, at the military and political level, but lost at the economic.

The paramount consideration for the wounded British lion was quickly to regain its own economic strength and vitality after the travails of war rather than go on indefinitely carrying 'the white man's burden, and adjudicating impartially on the claims and counter-claims of the warring communities and interests in the Indian empire. In short, British national interest prevailed over the real good of the dying empire. Peaceful as was the transfer of power from Britain to India and a unique event in the history of Imperialism, as such, this signal achievement has not been sufficiently appreciated by the world at large. It is, however, tragic that Indians had to go through a blood bath in spite of the peaceful intentions of the players concerned.[4]

It is now generally accepted that the Mountbatten's played a crucial role in bringing round Sardar Patel and Nehru to reconciling themselves to the idea of partition with a view to ending the agonizing suspense of the unending negotiations and averting the escalation of violence should the uncertainty continue longer. The plain fact of the matter was that both Nehru and Patel had lost their political will to resist partition on the assumption that partition was a lesser evil than the compulsory 'grouping' of the provinces under the scheme. The husband-wife team of the Viceregal magicians had persuaded (in a very subtle manner) the team of the 'gentle colossus' and the 'iron man' to let political realism prevail over sentimental idealism over the issue of Indian unity. The Mahatma, however, was beyond the magnetic pull of the Viceregal magicians and plenipotentiaries of the British government, impatient to cast away its Indian burden from weary shoulders, come what may.

THE TRAGEDY OF GANDHI AND NATIONALIST MUSLIMS

The Mahatma continued to walk alone after having declared that partition could only be brought about on his dead body. But he had been sidelined within the Congress itself by his own *protégées* and pupils, barring the Muslim members. They still looked up to the deserted Mahatma rather than to the Nehru-Patel team running the government in the last days of the Raj. Perhaps, the most agonizing decision the Mahatma ever made in his life was made, when in the throes of a tortured conscience, he finally decided to side with Nehru and Patel, rather than to continue the struggle for Indian unity with the help of Azad, Ghaffar Khan, and Purshotum Das Tandon *et al*. Gandhiji's close associate and biographer of his last years, Peareylal, has faithfully revealed the tortures the Mahatma went through during this crisis.[5]

Once Gandhiji decided, most reluctantly, to support Nehru and Patel who already had (reluctantly) swallowed the bitter pill of partition, therapeutically recommended by the Mountbatten's, consequent upon Jinnah's reluctant acceptance (in sheer desperation) of bifurcating Punjab and Bengal as a precondition of partition, Azad had no spirit or motivation left in him to challenge Gandhi himself in order to protect an ideal already sacrificed by the high priests themselves. This was the tragic denouement of the long drama of partition.

Denounced as a traitor by a large section of his own community, ridiculed as a show boy by the *Quaide Azam*, not much appreciated by some influential elements within the Congress, it was most likely that Azad's efforts to resist the joint decision of the Congress Supreme Command would have evoked more amusement than admiration or acceptance. There are some who hold that had the Mahatma and the Maulana been truly as great souls, as their ardent followers claim them to be, the two of them should have carried on a rightful struggle for Indian unity, irrespective of the dilemma in which they found themselves due to the joint stand of Patel and Nehru, acting over the head of their common mentor. But this is hardly a balanced view.

What is not generally known or fully appreciated today is the heroic resistance of some Congressmen (specially Muslim Congressmen) to avert partition. When the All India Congress Committee met to ratify the earlier decision of the Working Committee, jointly taken by the Sardar, Nehru, and others who had consented to partition, Maulana Hifzur Rahman, one of the most clear headed intellectuals among the *Ulema*, voted against the resolution. The case of the Frontier Gandhi, Khan Abdul Ghaffar Khan, is the most tragic of all those who strongly and honestly resisted the idea of partition, but failed to avert the day when there was '*darkness at noon*' on August fifteenth.

The division of the Indian family must have been an inner torture for all Indian nationalists, but there were some silver linings of subjective satisfaction that their long struggle, appreciated by their own people, had borne some fruit. Gandhi became (very rightly) the father of independent India, Nehru its Prime Minister, Sardar the architect of its consolidation, Rajendra Babu the President of the Union, Azad the conscience keeper of the Party, Rajagopalachari, the wise old pilot of the '*Rath*' of modern India, and so on. But Badshah Khan, the brave tragic hero, became a villain and traitor to his own countrymen and was put into prison in his own land by those he had liberated from foreign yoke. A tragedy of this sheer poignant intensity is, perhaps, without parallel in world history.

Little did the architects of a sovereign homeland for Indian Muslims realize that slightly less than half of the total Muslim population of India would be excluded from the proposed 'homeland'. In other words, that almost half the Indian Muslims, even after the creation of the homeland, would still remain at 'the mercy of the Hindus' in independent India. Little did the ardent champions of Pakistan in Uttar Pradesh, Bihar and other areas of Hindu dominance realize that the logic of Pakistan, as a Muslim homeland, would precipitate the parallel idea that India was or ought to be a Hindu homeland. Little did the ardent dreamers of Pakistan belonging to and living in India realize that those who did not go or could not go would have to live under the shadow of a continuing suspicion of divided loyalties.

Little did the young hearts and minds of the dreamers understand the logic of politics and of human passions. The argument they gave was twofold. One, that saving one half of the population was better than the destruction of all; second, that the presence of minorities on both sides would act as a check upon the tyranny of the majority. I recall my revered father's observation that this argument was absurd and that the Muslims in India would have to pay a heavy price, in installments, for their folly. He just could not digest the irony of the fact that Muslims living in Uttar Pradesh, Bihar etc. were clamoring for a Muslim homeland (which, by definition, would not include their actual homeland), while the Muslims living in the actually Muslim majority areas of Punjab, Bengal, and Sind etc. (that were going to comprise Pakistan) were not at all enamored of the idea. The Muslims of the Muslim majority provinces joined Jinnah's bandwagon rather late, only when they realized that partition was just round the corner.[6]

It was as if the Muslims of Uttar Pradesh, Bihar and other Muslim minority provinces in India behaved as a suicide squad paving the way for a sovereign state, which, by definition, would not include their own hearths and homes. A tiny fraction of such Muslims might well have played with the idea of immigrating to the 'golden land' after its birth. But the vast majority of the Indian Muslims had never given any thought to the political and sociological ramifications of their irrational and confused dreams that they quite innocently equated with being good Muslims or with fidelity to Islam.

That they had lived in their Indian homeland for centuries in amity with their Hindu brethren and had evolved on this very soil a common language, art, music and culture and even a common spirituality did not seem to be of much moment. Such was the hypnotic effect of the personality of one man and the power of religious appeals and sentiments on the Muslim psyche. A crucial factor was fear of competition in politics and business with the relatively more educated and better-placed majority community. A combination of the above factors produced the mirage of a Muslim homeland for even those young and innocent Muslims of urban India for whom the idea of leaving their hearths and homes in India had, perhaps, never entered their wildest dreams. The immortal speech delivered by Maulana Azad in the precincts of the *Juma Masjid* at Delhi soon after bloody riots had broken out in Delhi and elsewhere in the wake of partition captures the tragedy of their situation.[7]

The longed for birth of Pakistan was a pyrrhic victory for the Muslim League, because it soon became a traumatic disenchantment for Muslims in India, condemned to live 'at the mercy of the Hindu majority'. These elements were thrown into utter confusion and insecurity in their own land of birth. They found themselves in a predicament for very obvious reasons.

Several proactive protagonists of Pakistan promptly migrated to the country they had helped to create, some had to do so by force of circumstances in the way of communal riots resulting in serious loss of life and property of Muslim citizens. Many Muslims migrated because Pakistan held brighter prospects of business or service rather than any love for Pakistan. Many thought it prudent to join the Congress bandwagon under the changed circumstances. This political realignment suited both the ruling Congress and the erstwhile supporters of the League. The Congress umbrella gave protection to the erstwhile Muslim Leaguers, while the Congress rulers, presumably, expected that the neo-Congressmen would make more pliable colleagues than nationalist Muslims who had lost the battle for a united India but not their fighting spirit. This political cynicism led to undesirable results in the long run.

The nationalist Muslims, deep down in their hearts, had apprehensions about the natural psychological reaction among the Hindus to the fact that the so-called nationalist Muslims had stood repudiated by their own folk. Broken and crushed, they bent all their efforts and energy to do relief and rehabilitation work in the riot hit areas. This was their finest hour in the prevailing darkness and tragedy. Their record of secular nationalism and their old associations with Congress and other freedom fighters gave them proper credentials for successfully redressing the just grievances of the citizens, specially of the Muslims, who were feeling rather orphaned under the changed conditions.

The transfer of power into Indian hands, however, diluted the traditional moral idealism of the Congress party members. Competition among Congressmen (mostly Hindus) for loaves and fishes at different levels gradually marginalized Muslims and pushed them into the backwaters of mainstream politics. Muslim politicians, including Congress activists, tended to retreat into areas of exclusive Muslim concerns such as the affairs of the Aligarh Muslim University, the status of Urdu, control of communal riots, Muslim personal law, *Waqf* and *Hajj* arrangements etc. Muslim politicians were fairly effective in these limited spheres. But with the exception of the Communist Party Muslim politicians in India found their role reduced to being 'political extras' in the game of power.

Skeletal as it is, the above account is accurate and impartial. It would be simplistic and misleading to pin the responsibility for partition on any single individual, political party, community, or the British policy of divide and rule. Different factors and different persons at different times contributed to the complex causal matrix that led to partition. However, in my honest and non-partisan view the largest share of responsibility will have to be placed on the Quaid-e-Azam. Liberal humanist and secular to the core as he was in his early and middle years, Jinnah had developed, in his later period, a total and inflexible distrust of the Hindu character in politics. Honest, straightforward and a person of unimpeachable integrity and character, he developed a passion for absolute authority without any challenge from any quarter, be it religious or secular. Yet, I submit, the honest observer must combat the growing tendency in India to simplify matters and regard the Muslim community of India as the villain of the piece in the complex and tragic drama of the partition of India.[8]

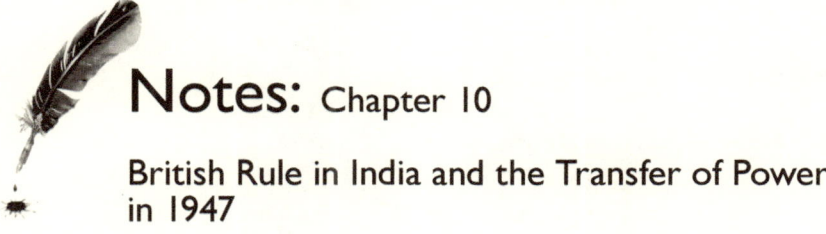

Notes: Chapter 10

British Rule in India and the Transfer of Power in 1947

1. See A.G.Noorani's well-researched biography of Badruddin Tyabji in the *Builders of Modern India* series. The book gives the letters exchanged between the two great leaders on the subject concerned.

2. Eminent Indian leaders who gave top priority to education and social reform without bothering to speed up political advance in the absence of an adequate social base include liberals such as Surendranath Banerjee, and, to, some extent, the great Gokhle himself. See Nehru's balanced assessment in his *Autobiography and Discovery of India*.

3. There is no contradiction in holding that his motive was both administrative efficiency and political containment of the Congress clamouring for instant freedom under the impatient B.G.Tilak. Our purpose here does not require a definite verdict. Beck, the dynamic Principal of the MAO College, Aligarh, was indeed close to the ruling British circles. As an Englishman wedded to the principle of 'gradualism' in politics and society he could not appreciate the impatience of Tilak, in view of the internal complexities of the Indian situation and the unequal progress the two principal communities had made in the field of Western education and democratic politics. It is, therefore, quite understandable that the perceived self-interest of the Muslim community coincided with the British perception of both imperial interests as well as imperial responsibility to a relative minority group (the Muslims) despite its vast numbers and cultural dominance in the past. Under these circumstances Beck may have drafted (in all good faith) the memorandum of the Muslim League submitted to the Viceroy, Lord Minto, at Shimla in 1906.

4. The British imperial record in India is a unique phenomenon of world history. A critical balanced appraisal from the Indian side has yet to come. It is significant that many top Indian freedom fighters, despite years of imprisonment in British jails, retained genuine admiration for the British character and achievements in India. However, the middle and lower ranks of freedom fighters hardly suspected this ambivalent attitude in the top leaders like Gokhle, Gandhi, Nehru, and Jinnah *et al*. The American philosopher journalist, Walter Lippman, praised in glowing terms Britain's statesmanship and balanced wisdom in the planned transfer of power to India and Pakistan in 1947. To view the known British stand on preserving the unity of India as window dressing is rather unfair to the British, though it is true that a section of British opinion was not averse to thinking that partition might benefit British interests. Abundant literature, secret official correspondence, memoirs, responsible journalistic accounts, and well-documented books on the course of events resulting in partition are now available, and the honest and impartial reader can draw his own conclusions. The 12 volume official British publication, *The Transfer of Power* is a masterpiece of documentation. Also noteworthy are the *The*

The Vision of an Unknown Indian Muslim: Part 2

Transfer of Power by V.P. Menon, and *A Viceroy's Journal*, edited by Sir Penderel Moon, and Moon's own very valuable writings.

5. See, *Mahatma Gandhi: The Last Phase*, by Peareylal.

6. Far from spearheading the demand for partition the Muslims of Punjab, Sind, NWFP (North West Frontier Province) and Bengal joined Jinnah's bandwagon rather late in the day on realizing that partition was coming after all. Sir Sikandar Hyat dominated Muslim politics in Punjab until his death in 1942. He and Sir Chotu Ram were the stewards of the secular Unionist Party. Sir Sikandar's speech in the undivided Punjab Assembly on March 11, 1941, is a powerful critique of the two-nation theory. This remarkable speech is quoted in full in V.P Menon's, *Transfer of Power*.

After Sikandar Hyat, Khizr Hyat became Premier and remained so right till March 1947, until a few months before partition. He too resisted partition. However, after Lord Wavell ceased to be Viceroy the 'Jinnah wave' engulfed all concerned. In Bengal, Fazlul Haq and in Sind, Allah Bux opposed partition almost till the end. The Frontier province was a stronghold of the Frontier Gandhi, as is well known. But the Pakistan wave, helped by a strange concatenation of factors, ranging from internal Indian short sightedness to British economic collapse, swept aside all opposition. Paradoxically, the most vociferous support for partition came from areas like Uttar Pradesh, and Bihar etc., which by definition, stood outside the promised 'land of deliverance for Muslims'.

The Muslim League did win a literally overwhelming victory in terms of the number of seats in the Central and state legislatures. But this high number did not reflect the considerable percentage of votes cast against the Muslim League's demand for Pakistan. Moreover, the franchise was very limited. It is highly plausible that under universal adult franchise the majority of Muslim voters in the country, as a whole, would have opted for a united federal India with suitable constitutional safeguards for the minorities.

7. The speech is given in the original in the multi-volume *Collection of Maulana Azad's Speeches*, edited by Malik Ram.

8. There is yet another harmful tendency to project the ideas, ideals and attitudes of one's own age on those of earlier times. Thus, both some critics and admirers of Sir Syed dub him as the spiritual father of Pakistan, though the fact is that he had never even dreamed of Pakistan. Likewise, the great philosopher poet, Iqbal, had never advocated a sovereign Islamic state separate from India, but only the consolidating of a Muslim majority state or province inside India. This is quite clear from the poet's correspondence with his friend, Professor Thompson, of Oxford University. The original letters were with his son who donated photostat copies to Professor Irfan Habib of the Aligarh Muslim University. These copies are preserved in the archives of the Aligarh University. (Late) Professor Hasan Ahmad, who taught Political Science at the AMU, published facsimiles of Iqbal's hand written and signed letters in his book, *Iqbal: His Political Ideas at Crossroads*, Aligarh, 1979. It is unfortunate, that many in Pakistan think it fit to dub the original letters and their photostat copies as forged.

Chapter 11
Candid Reflections on the Indian Political Scene, 1947-1992

The Gandhi-Nehru Vision

The Gandhi-Nehru vision is the invaluable heritage of modern India. Nehru was outstanding among the great architects of modern India. Remarkable integrity of character, the balanced sensitivity of a keen intellect, intellectual honesty, capacity for appreciating different points of view, a deep and wide grasp of history and appreciation of diverse cultures and civilizations, a scientific temper, a capacity for warm human relationships and respect for human ability, irrespective of caste, color or creed, his team spirit and tolerance of the failings of comrades, accessibility to the common man, a capacity for hard labor, and, last but not least, his charismatic charm: all this made Nehru the phenomenon Jawaharlal was.

Nehru's ethical approach to politics (inspired by the spiritual genius of Gandhi), his commitment to world peace and the peaceful resolution of all international disputes, his Humanism, his solicitude for the have-nots and the oppressed, were the product of his creative application of the Gandhian vision without caring to remain a carbon copy of his mentor. He attempted to blend the Western liberal humanist tradition with the quintessence of Gandhian spirituality. Genuinely admiring British political culture he leaned towards Westminster democracy but he was no imitator. He also admired Marx and Lenin, but he was not willing to dilute democracy and the stress on right means, despite pressure from textbook socialists and communists to compromise on democracy for the sake of rapid economic development or the speedy removal of social evils.

The integration of over five hundred princely states, the rehabilitation of refuges from Pakistan, the introduction of universal adult franchise, the principled adherence to secularism and a composite Indian culture, despite reluctantly agreeing, on freedom's eve, to divide the Indian family, the concern for the weaker sections, the attempted synthesis of democracy and socialism, the stress on economic self-sufficiency, the rapid development of different infra-structures throughout the country, the promotion of scientific Humanism and scientific research are the seminal features of the Nehruvian era. However, all the above initiatives and achievements have failed to yield optimum results. This is not merely because the real always falls short of the ideal, but also because the 'gentle colossus' could not cut deep into the unhealthy flesh of poor implementation of plans and policies. The capacity and will to monitor and regulate the administrative machinery had eluded the overflowing treasury of Nehru's natural gifts. His mentor had combined the solicitude and tenderness of a mother with the severity and tenacity of a slave driver, but Nehru could not reach that rare condition. Perhaps, without Sardar Patel the integration of princely states might also have been impeded.

The honest observer will have to a concede that during Nehru's regime as also to date the common man is fleeced by the police, the small farmer is exploited by various state agencies, Harijan women are raped by the higher castes, the litigant is forced to pay under the table for every little movement of files and papers, and has to suffer from the manipulations of unscrupulous lawyers, patients in state hospitals live in filth, no contactor can survive without illegal gratification at various levels, no fully sanctioned loan or pension (even to a widow in distress) can be disbursed without palm greasing, no house plan can be approved without unaccounted payments, examination centers flourish where mass copying is the rule, schools exist without black boards or chalk, power brokers arrange appointments, postings and promotions, octroi posts and police stations are auctioned to the highest bidder, commercial trucks are not allowed to pass check points without their driver entertaining the local staff to 'tea and snacks'. Much more could be added in this list, but it is already sufficient for my purpose.

Thanks to the genius of India's functioning anarchy industry developed, commerce thrived, education expanded, consumerism spread, democracy thrived, the concern for social justice and women's rights grew, and expectations soared. So did petty corruption and a general decline in the quality of life as a whole.

The most perceptible decline occurred in the spheres of education and politics. The process of decline gathered momentum in the late sixties and early seventies. Till then politicians used criminals or shady characters for their own nefarious purposes, and suitably rewarded them for services rendered. But criminals themselves did not aspire to political positions. Gradually the commanders of muscle power turned into politicians instead of being content with mere pull or influence in the corridors of power. The universities that had once been seats of learning and centers of enlightenment turned into shops and factories that mass produced graduates and whose administrators ever tried to please power hungry politicians and ministers.

The Congress party is not the first or the only offender. However, as the premier party from the dawn of independence, one should have thought that it would abide by higher standards of political conduct befitting the tradition of Gandhi and Nehru. Soon everybody started doing what the other did, and all became naked in the bath, as it were.

This was tragic for the country. There is no doubt that Indira Gandhi's vision was as broad and her mind as sensitive as her father's. But while the father, despite the vicissitudes and temptations of politics, managed to preserve the Mahatma's ethical approach to politics till the very end, the daughter, after a few rebuffs and disillusionments from political opponents, took to the devious shortcuts of power politics. I would still call it tragic even if it be conceded that she did so in national interest, as she saw it. The real danger of this approach is that it tends to blur the distinction between national interest and self-interest.

Rajiv Gandhi tried to arrest the moral decline in public life. But it was too late to stop the rot. However, he realized very early that social justice was empty and sterile without high productivity. Nehru and Indiraji were also well aware of this truism. But both were rather too close to the era of high expectations from the panacea of socialism. By the time of Rajiv several developing countries following the model of market economy had left socialist counties far behind in the race of rapid all round development.

The tragedy of Rajiv was that he succumbed to the charge that while he was soft to Muslim sentiments on the issue of Muslim personal laws, he was indifferent to Hindu sentiments on the *Ram Janmbhumi* issue. Rajiv was, thus, lured into a destructive exercise in appeasement on the *Ayodhya* issue. Principled firmness, without fear or favor, would, perhaps, have won the day for him, even if all the voices of discontent could not have been silenced. When he himself came to this view it was too late.

The position to date is that all the organs of state and infrastructures, with the exception of the apex judiciary, stand as before, but their inner life has been blown out. The candle is still there and it also burns but there is little light. The darkest hour was, not when the *Babri Masjid* fell to the last mighty push of some misguided fanatics, but when the Prime Minister of India did not care to offer his resignation when the repeated assurances of its protection had been flagrantly violated before a dazed India and the world. The British Parliamentary convention of constructive responsibility was thrown to the winds. No matter, how the event happened, it was beyond dispute that the Prime Minister's trust was misplaced and his judgment wrong. Had the then Prime Minister, Narasinha Rao, offered his resignation from his high office, in pursuance of the notion of constructive responsibility to Parliament, I dare say the ethical quality of Indian democracy in the following decades would have risen to tremendous heights instead of taking a sharp plunge, as it did, after the willful demolition of the mosque. In the final analysis, honest and effective government in a democracy flows from the possession of genuine moral authority.[1]

In short, independent India has achieved many remarkable results in the past fifty years. Several general elections have been held and peaceful transfers of power have taken place. The Indian family has, broadly speaking, assimilated the idea of a secular state, democracy, social justice and human rights, though, obviously, there are discordant notes in several quarters, and also lapses in implementation of principle and policy. Agriculture and industry have prospered. The technical manpower of India is among the top countries of the globe. India is a member of the nuclear, space and Antarctica clubs. The fighting forces of India are second to none. Despite all this and more the quality of life in India is far below what should and could have been the case, had our politicians and leaders built upon the Gandhi-Nehru heritage, in reality rather than in appearance.

Any honest and dispassionate observer will have to concede that expediency and short-term goals have triumphed over basic values. Norms and codes of conduct have evaporated in the heat and dust of the struggle for power for its own sake. The unscrupulous use of caste, money, and muscle power has become part of our political culture irrespective of political parties. The flag of every party bears the cynical confession that politicians will be politicians; say what you may.

All political parties, without exception, organize mass rallies that indulge in looting food shops, vandalism, ticket less travel, and gross misuse of state transport and immense dislocation of normal civic life. No party takes effective steps to check these grave social evils and such flagrant prostitution of the freedom of association and of organized expression.

Parliamentary opposition has degenerated into parliamentary obstruction. This malpractice amounts to keeping the outer shell of democracy: periodic elections, majority party rule, debates and voting, but throwing away the kernel of the democratic spirit, namely, the moral and legal right of the government to function without intimidation or obstruction. All political parties stand equally guilty in this regard. The presiding officers in Parliament and the state Assemblies, indeed, deserve protection against cruelty of this sort. This amounts to playing a game without any rules. The party in power accuses the opposition. But when the opposition of today becomes the ruling party tomorrow both change their roles almost as naturally and mechanically as a car does when its gears are changed.

Educational standards, specially, in the sphere of humanities and liberal arts have declined even as there has been an enormous growth in numbers of degree holders. Codes of conduct have become ancient myths. Palm greasing has become the accepted mechanism of making the wheels of the system move smoothly. It has become the lubricant for success in almost every sphere of life, including success in matrimonial alliances of daughters with suitable boys.

The above state of affairs pains many a patriotic soul. At times they feel tempted to enter into politics out of a sense of civic duty. But intuitively sensing that the rule of the jungle prevails under a democratic disguise they restrict themselves to 'social work'. The plain fact is that in the game of politics, where guts count for more than conscience, tough-minded persons push out the 'tender hearted' persons. What is, therefore, needed in public interest is social work that goes beyond curing or reducing social evils to social and political restructuring without however involving the social worker in political activism as such. This type of social work may be termed 'metapolitics' which, I submit, is as important for democracy as an independent judiciary and a free press.

Democratic politics, at its best, implies a proper concern with 'metapolitics' in the above sense. However, very few politicians can rise to this high and exalted level of statesmanship. The vast majority have neither inclination, nor ability for this type of work. Some of the pressing 'metapolitical' challenges in India today are the prevention of adulteration in food and drugs, non-interference by politicians in educational institutions, the promotion of communal harmony, reduction in election expenditure, reduction in judicial delays etc.

Gandhi was the greatest 'metapolitician' of modern times quite apart from his role as fighter for India's freedom. Gandhiji was a moral genius who forged his own techniques of 'moral pressure' for winning freedom from foreign rule. But blindly following those techniques in a free democratic India is hardly feasible. We need new tools in a new situation. We are called upon to break the resistance of vested interests to a continuing process of social, political and cultural reformation without destroying or weakening the moral fabric of our society. It is most unfortunate that many well-intentioned reformers and patriots after Gandhiji have misused his idealistic concept of *'satyagraha'* for achieving political power or various objectives quite unrelated to wider moral or humanitarian issues.

The Gandhian concept of *'satyagraha'* (holding firm to truth) implied that that truth was God and that man was, basically good, despite being swayed, at times, by evil forces. Religion, at its best, purified the human soul and thus brought about a just society based on truth and non-violence. The Mahatma was, however, quite clear that various social evils would not end without some form of struggle between the forces of good and of evil. But he insisted that this struggle should be against evil, rather than the evildoer. *'Hate the sin but not the sinner'* was his motto. The applying of 'moral pressure' through self-suffering and altruistic dedication to moral principles was the essence of the Gandhian technique. But modern day socialist and communist direct action and agitation resorts to plain and simple psychological and physical coercion, blackmail for imposing one's own *'diktat'* upon others, including elected representatives of the public.

Political parties have failed to take a detached and objective view of the requirements of Indian democracy. They have hankered after the fruits of power and ignored the ethics of seeking power. When the central government, under Indira Gandhi, did partly address itself to the problem of election costs, the government committed the grave blunder of banning political donations by the public sector. The evil went underground and the remedy proved worse than the disease. Rajiv Gandhi rightly removed the ban and tried other remedies. In fact, he was wiser than his mother in this regard. Political sociologists have shown how in the early twenties the votaries of prohibition in the USA had ruined the moral fiber of the American society in their blind passion to eliminate totally the evil of alcohol from American society.[2]

The present system of one man, one vote, has led to strange anomalies in the distribution of political power. Parties have won parliamentary majorities without winning the majority of all votes polled. Likewise it is in theory possible for a party to win the maximum number of votes in the country as a whole, but fail to win the largest number of seats in Parliament. The matter at issue is of enormous complexity. However, the solution that promises to be the least harmful should be adopted.

SOCIALISM AND SOCIAL JUSTICE

Enlightened thinkers both in India and the West, until recently, had come to accept socialism as the panacea for all human ills. The victories of Communism in Eastern Europe and China and the decline of the once mighty British empire after the second world war led many to believe that Karl Marx was right after all, and that Socialism and Communism were the inevitable destination of the grand world historical process. This dream, whether we like it or not, stands shattered by recent events in several parts of the globe.

The high productivity, horizontal prosperity and social egalitarianism that has come into being in several democratic societies that opted for some form or other of the model of free market economy in preference to the Russian or neo-Russian socialist model have forced numerous informed and dispassionate observers and social thinkers to revise their economic theories in the light of actual evidence. This has happened not only in the Western world but also in the Mecca of Communism itself. Today the clay feet of the once powerful and dominating ideologues and lawgivers of the Communist world stand plainly visible to all. Perhaps, the clay feet had been dangling all the while, but the audience stood hypnotized, if not blindfolded. Some of the best Communist minds have, at last, awakened from their 'dogmatic slumbers', which have caused no less harm than the slumbers of those addicted to the 'opium of the masses'. The shattering of the great expectations from textbook Socialism shows the futility and danger of abstract or 'ideological' reasoning instead of free empirical enquiry in the sphere of economic theory. Marx had himself insisted upon the unity of theory and practice and honestly declared that he was not a Marxist. Unfortunately, his policy formulations came to be turned into axioms no good Communist was supposed to question.

The perils of 'ideological economics' (no matter what the ideology may be) have become clear just like the perils of the 'dictatorship of the proletariat/party'. No rigid system of politics and society derived from any closed source (sacred or secular) can properly claim validity or infallibility without passing the test of actual experience. The Communists did not heed this basic truth and suffered. The advocates of 'Islamic Knowledge' or the Islamization of society on an a priori basis commit the same type of fallacy without being fully aware of the logic of their stand.

Nehru's concept of a mixed economy was also a textbook idea rather than a model that had been tried and tested in the crucible of experience. It appeared to combine the advantages of both Capitalism and Socialism and some of the best informed, enlightened and humanitarian thinkers had come under the spell of this idea. Nehru was, indeed, in excellent company. It is true that some very able minds remained skeptical of the assumed advantages of the middle path of Capitalism and Socialism and experience has confirmed this insight, rather than the theoretical projections of Nehru. However, Nehru cannot be blamed for his advocacy of the Socialist dream that had captivated the imagination of an entire age or era. After all, the idea of Socialism, both in its early British humanist version and the later Russian Communist version did put the full focus of attention and concern on the open and hidden evils of the early Capitalist phase of Western society. The tenacious fighters for a worker's state and labour power did release mighty energies for conquering the said evils. The Communist Manifesto certainly did play a substantial role as a midwife to the birth of the idea of a welfare state and welfare economics. Several social ills, both open and hidden, were removed or reduced under the impact of the socialist critique of Capitalism. And this is not a negligible contribution. Some ills are still there, but there seems to be no way of achieving a perfect or ideal society. In the final analysis, human welfare will best come about, not through ideological based economics (be it Socialist, Capitalist or Islamic or Vedic), but through empirically testable analytical economics. Utopian conditions should never be expected to obtain. One problem solved will beget another, and so on and so on.[3]

Nehru's approach to the issue of population control also got blurred due to his being unduly influenced by the Russian apathy and ideological indifference to the strategic control of population as a necessary condition for sustainable development. Until the late fifties the Communist perception was that the slogan of control of population was a 'bourgeois' strategy for diverting the attention of the oppressed workers from the real causes of their poverty and suffering. Perhaps, the great leader was swayed by this particular Communist perception, though he stood as a rock against the Communist theory of the dictatorship of the proletariat. As is well known the Nehru government never gave high priority to population control, despite strong advice from the highest advisory quarters that this was essential. Population control became a top priority for the Government only during the emergency period. Unfortunately it was translated into practice in a deplorable manner that proved disastrous in its consequences. Even the present strategy needs a more effective combination of incentives and disincentives for making amends for past failures. Many enlightened quarters hold that stressing family planning in the present state of educational backwardness would be putting the cart before the horse, and that families will automatically become smaller as education expands. This debate is sterile, since both requirements are crucial and will have to be attended to with equal urgency. Education required for smaller and happier families will never catch up with the natural increase of numbers unless top priority is given to reducing the natural growth rate.[4]

THE SHADOW OF THE CASTE SYSTEM

It is a platitude to say that the great Hindu community, constituting over eighty percent of the total population, has always been a fractured society based on hereditary caste gradations. Each caste had its own distinctive duties and rights (*swadharma*). Even if it be accepted for argument's sake that early Aryan society was not rigid and permitted movement from one caste to the other, the plain fact remains that the entire historical period of Indian society was marked by a rigid and shockingly unjust vertical stratification, despite a remarkably high degree of doctrinal tolerance.

The uninterrupted political and cultural presence of Islam in medieval India greatly influenced Hindu sensibility and also triggered various reform movements among the Hindus. But none could suffice to remove the ugly thorn of caste from the fair rose of Hindu society. The Muslims themselves adopted a caste-based perspective, even though they never went to the full length of the Hindu caste system. No significant improvement took place in the economic and social status of the lower Hindu castes until the advent of British power in India.

The constitution of free India dethroned the demon of caste, but the introduction, at one stroke, of universal adult franchise has empowered a very vicious false god—an insatiable mass clamor for instant material gain. This state of affairs is the result of two main factors; the unfortunate decline in the quality of top leadership, after the Nehru years, and the sudden revolution of expectations of the terribly long suppressed weaker sections of Indian society. They now demand concessions and special treatment to compensate for their misery and suffering in the centuries past. This naturally reduces the share of the upper castes in the national cake. The end result is not only mutual recriminations, but also conflicting notions of the actual content or meaning of social and distributive justice. The needs and interests of each group unconsciously shape this notion. The conflict of interests leads to differing perceptions and theories honestly and passionately held. But this inevitably intensifies and acerbates caste consciousness and conflict.

Caste based reservation and quotas in state services and the legislature do violate the abstract principle of equal opportunity. However, the quota system is an instrumental necessity for speeding up the transition of the submerged and stagnant weaker sections to a level field from where they could, later on, take off on the path of equal opportunity. In other words, the classical notion of social justice as equal opportunity must be qualified by equity or compassion for the weak. Otherwise, the fruits of planned development will reach them at too slow a pace to be called fair or just to the weaker sections. The quantum and modalities of reservation is, however, a different matter that should be fixed after the most careful deliberation on the totality of social consequences of the adopted policy. The choice of the quantum and modality of reservations should be guided by the principle of maximum utility for the beneficiaries of reservation compatible with the minimum social costs (a decrease in productivity and excellence) to the nation at large. The Supreme Court has already spelled out this abstract principle but the Supreme Executive follows its own logic.

Reservation, as an instrumental measure or tool of social justice, should not be equated with the timeless ideal of equality of opportunity. Other related and ancillary schemes (such as special employment centers, coaching institutes, credit and grants in aid facilities etc.) for the exclusive welfare of the weaker or backward segments of the nation should also be treated as social medicine, not as a staple diet for Indian society. Reservation is a pill rather than a cereal. How long the pill will be required by Indian society, as a patient, is too difficult to indicate.

The entire nation should rejoice at the newly acquired vertical mobility of the long suppressed *Dalits*, though negative depth attitudes linger on in the psyche of the higher castes. Suppressed hostility spills over in the rather frequent carnages and atrocities against *Dalits* and other weaker sections in Bihar, Assam and elsewhere. However, what the *Dalits* have gained after a dark night lasting thousands of years is the firm promise of a new dawn.

Regional and Communal Tensions

Indian states or provincial regions are as large or even larger in area than several sovereign European states like France and Germany. Under these conditions exclusive regional concerns can easily acquire the mass appeal and respectability, which the modern mind attaches to nationalism as such. Indeed, the dividing line between nationalism and sub-nationalism is somewhat thin. At times even populism puts on the garb of social justice. Great and responsible leaders or statesmen however often succeed in reconciling national and regional interests and loyalties. Some quarters hold that the creation of linguistic states after independence has destroyed the possibility of inter-regional emotional integration. The continuing inability of some states to settle disputes over water utilization, allocation of new industries etc. is cited as proof. However, the various states are inter-dependent in regard to agriculture, industries and scientific or technological education. The essential unity of Indian culture and religion is also a mighty bond. The Hindi speaking areas will have to convince other regions, by deed and not word alone, of their respect for the plural languages and sub-cultures of the land.[5]

Regional parties reflect the ethnic, linguistic and cultural diversity of India and also great disparities in their economic, industrial and educational development. The different states of the eastern region, Punjab, Kashmir and Tamil Nadu (for a very brief period) in the southern region were misled into the politics of secession from the Indian union. This was, obviously, a political issue and it was accepted as such. However, the issues of Punjab and Kashmir acquired religious overtones.

The Central Government's policy in the post-Nehru era has led to the continual erosion of the constitutional authority and dignity of state Governors, and several state governments' non-cooperative and evasive dealings with the Centre have, severally and jointly, greatly harmed national interest. How to orchestrate the perceptions and priorities of the vast and fragmented Indian society has become today a baffling challenge before all political parties due to past blunders or wrong priorities in the past.

Emotional integration of the vast regions of the land requires that leaders identify themselves with every region and segment of the Indian family. Nehru and his great colleagues had this capacity and vision. This era has slipped past, it seems. The complexity of the issues precludes a definite judgment. But, perhaps, the present model of Indian federalism will have to yield in favour of decentralization and devolution of power to the states or regions. It is not paradoxical to say, in the same breath, that the Centre is too strong and too weak at present.[6]

A constitutional reduction in the powers of the central government would definitely hamper and even prevent India from emerging as a military superpower in the comity of nations. But is not the quality of life of a nation more important and more worth pursuing than it's being or becoming a superpower? Superpowers cannot survive without super leaders and the latter emerge rather infrequently on the human scene. I, as an Indian, long for the day when outstanding men of vision and integrity emerge in India in the days ahead as had happened in the past days of the modern Indian Renaissance. Should this not happen I, for one, will prefer a confederation of small but beautiful and truly creative sovereign or semi sovereign states to an amoral regional or super Power. The momentous structural changes in the Soviet Union, Eastern and Western Europe have an enduring message for the perceptive observer of the human scene.[7]

THE KASHMIR ISSUE

The issue of Jammu and Kashmir brims with contradictory interests and clashing ideals. There is no doubt, whatsoever, that terrorism is an insufferable and monstrous evil that has to be eliminated from India as well as the world at large. But it is equally essential to understand the 'roots of terrorism' wherever it has spread. Terrorism is playing havoc at all levels in Jammu and Kashmir. A vicious circle of 'political terrorism' and 'state terrorism' has been activated in that part of the world. Life for literally every individual and group inside Jammu and Kashmir has become a curse in some sense or other. Elections have been rigged, innocent people have lost their lives, the security apparatus has been brutalized, civil liberties have been strangulated, innocent Kashmiri Pundits have been rendered homeless in their own homes, corrupt practices have peaked to an extent unparalleled in the rest of the country, security and defense requirements have enormously eaten into the extremely over-stretched resources of the land. This has been going on and on as an endless vicious circle. Both India and Pakistan blame each other for the deadlock. There are internal differences of approach also in both the countries as well as in Jammu and Kashmir itself. Some militant Hindu voices decry Indian restraint and patience as docility against Pakistan and want India to make a pre-emptive strike against terrorist bases located inside Pakistan.

I do believe that when Nehru took the stand he did at the time of the provisional accession of Kashmir to India and also subsequently, his authentic concern was not for a bigger India but a better India. Sentimental reasons apart, he believed that the inclusion of a state having a predominantly Muslim majority in the great Indian family would give strength to the forces of liberal secular Humanism in the plural Indian society, in addition to benefiting the Kashmiri people as a whole. And Shaikh Abdullah too thought on the same lines. However, as we all know, dreams often get shattered and broken. Even when they bear fruit the reality does not turn out to be exactly the same as the dream.

I hold that India and Pakistan simply must give up the approach of imposing one's own will upon the other or upon the people of Jammu and Kashmir. The challenge today is to convince rather than to bulldoze the other. All Indian citizens, irrespective of religion and politics, are called upon to contribute to this task. Indian Muslims cannot be singled out for this purpose, since they are equal citizens, not hostages in their own country.

Prime Minister Atal Bihari Vajpayee was earnestly concerned to break the vicious deadlock and open a new chapter in international cooperation and peace. It would be rather presumptuous on my part to suggest any guidelines to the parties concerned. All that is axiomatically clear to me is that a military solution is an exercise in total futility, and an irreversible slide into mutual destruction. Secondly, the turmoil in Kashmir is also not reducible to a mere law and order problem to be solved by police action by India. It is a highly complex political challenge to the parties involved. Thirdly, the genuine representatives of the people of the state, in every ethnic region, must participate in the peace process and in determining their future. The elections that have been periodically held to the legislature of Jammu & Kashmir, most unfortunately, were vitiated by *realpolitik* and violated democratic norms. It is, precisely, this more or less internationally accepted conviction that has cost India dear in the eyes of world opinion, including several genuine friends and admirers of India.

I would like to close this section with recalling the stand taken by Nehru just before he passed away. It is not generally known what exactly had transpired between him and Shaikh Abdullah when the latter, shortly before Nehru's death, proceeded to Pakistan to explore the ground for a stable reconciliation between all the parties concerned. True, much water has flown down the Ganga since then. But I dare say the Gandhi-Nehru vision remains as fresh, vital and relevant today as it ever was.[8]

THE HINDU-MUSLIM QUESTION IN INDIA

Right till the partition in 1947 the Muslims, though numerically considerably less than their Hindu brothers, were very well entrenched in the administration, army, police and also, politically, in five or six Indian provinces. All this dramatically changed for Indian Muslims after partition. Whatever partition might have done for Muslims of western Punjab and Sind or those Indian Muslims who migrated there, the Muslims in India suffered an enormous loss of power, influence and opportunity in every sphere of life. Every religious or caste group in India has some problem or grudge, but nobody questions their loyalty to the nation at large. But ever since they fell into the trap of the perverse two–nation theory all Muslims in India now have to answer the awkward question why should they not migrate to their separate and sovereign homeland whose creation cost tremendous pain and suffering to millions of innocent Indians. Militant Hindu quarters now charge them with the crime of desecrating 'Mother India' and making them scapegoats for all ills of the country. The more fanatical and militant elements go to the extent of daring the embarrassed Muslim to migrate to the 'holy' land of their dreams and of their own making.

Equality of political and economic opportunity is guaranteed to all Indian citizens by the constitution, but is not available to Muslims in actual practice due to the psychological fallout of their foolish advocacy of the two-nation theory. The post-independence abolition of reservation for Muslims in the services and the legislature greatly reduced their entry into them due to much stiffer competition from better qualified and also better politically placed Hindu brethren. Muslims had always excelled in the police and military services. And it was here that they suffered the most at the higher levels of service.

Muslims also found it hard to compete with their Hindu counterparts in big business or industry under the 'permit-license raj' (that prevailed till the late eighties of the last century) since obtaining a government license was unthinkable without political patronage or clout. The private sector was unable to do much for Muslims, not because of any discrimination or hostility but because of sheer apathy for an out-group. After all, their own kith and kin were better qualified, and they had a prior claim for help. Only those Muslim youth got encouragement and help in their careers as were close to powerful or influential Hindu patrons. Numerous ambitious Muslim young people migrated to Pakistan not because of any love for the Muslim country but purely in search of greener pastures in a land where competition was less and they could expect better patronage.

Endemic communal riots and violence in towns and cities in the northern regions of the country have posed a major problem. High powered commissions of enquiry recommended short and long term corrective measures, but they were hardly implemented. In general, administrative drift, downright failure of nerves, pious platitudes without follow-up action, appeasement now of one and then of the other went on doing tremendous harm to the nation at large. However, the Communist governments in Kerala and Bengal, the Telugu Desam government in Andhra and the Janata government in Bihar have the best record in this regard. Now at long last the lesson seems to have sunk in all political parties that communal violence harms the entire nation, not merely the immediate victims. Now the Christian minority has to face the ire of Hindu fanatical elements.[9]

Despite the virus of episodic communal violence in north Indian cities Indian Muslims have succeeded in making their voice heard and heeded in the corridors of power. All secular political parties and now even the *Hindutva* family has awakened to the importance of paying due heed to Muslim perceptions. Indeed, democratic leadership in a plural society is a very challenging and difficult job. It requires the ability to see things from several viewpoints and different perspectives in order to reconcile them constructively without appeasing any one particular group or different groups at different times. This task requires insight into the human situation and a sincere concern for the principled accommodation of different interests without falling into the trap of ad hoc appeasement or populism.

The educationally and socially backward classes, the artisans and self-employed small manufacturers among Muslims, however, have fared very differently from the upper class Muslims in the newly emerged setup in independent democratic India. The abolition of feudalism, the introduction of adult franchise, and the state encouragement of small and middle scale industries, facilities for loans and export promotion drives etc. have all contributed to their rapid and sustained economic improvement and rise in their status and level of expectations. Indeed, even political leadership has passed on to this section of Muslims from elitist Muslim quarters. From olden days Muslim artisans and small entrepreneurs had been well entrenched in industries and trade related to leather, handloom, brass and steal wares, carpentry, motor repairs and transport, carpets and shawls, tailoring etc. Muslims continue to prosper in all the above spheres of industry and trade.

The Muslim peasantry has also done well along with their Hindu counter-parts due to the general betterment in rural conditions and the benefits of adult franchise. However the semi literate urban Muslims whose main source of income and sustenance was domestic service or class four jobs have been or are being pushed out by others enjoying the protection of reservation or general political patronage.

To sum up, the sudden abolition of reservation for Muslims in the legislatures and services, the greatly reduced recruitment to the army and police, the abolition of the *Zamindari* system, the drying up of political patronage, the exclusion from previous concessions now passed on to non-Muslim weaker sections of society, stiffer competition for admission into professional courses, all these and some other factors combined to produce an undercurrent of discontent and despair in the upper class Muslims, though not in the artisan and rural segments of Indian Muslims.

Upper class Muslim discontent would have become greater still were it not for the developmental revolution in West Asian and Gulf countries. The Indian Muslims got a very good chance of highly remunerative professional employment in a far less competitive atmosphere. Timely and welcome as was this unexpected economic boon to Indian Muslims they still feel confused and perplexed on returning home when they face various social evils: poverty, casteism, Hindu chauvinism, money power, corruption etc.

Continuance of such ills and evils even fifty years after independence makes Indian Muslims despair of the capacity of democratic institutions to reform society. Indian Muslims have traditionally looked up to a strong and good Muslim leader or charismatic figure for delivering society from evil forces. The foreign Muslim states that provide them with economic salvation are not democratic societies and, therefore, unable to provide any political education to the Muslim expatriates.

This state of affairs pushes these rather disillusioned Muslims into a protective Islamic shell in their own country. They long for a great Muslim leader or, failing that, even some non-Muslim charismatic figure, but they find none equal to the task. They want quick results, but they hardly have a clear and consistent secular vision requisite for solving social problems in the long run rather than in the short term only. As a result they fall easily into the laps of pedagogues hailing from various quarters, Muslim as well as others.

STRATEGY FOR MINORITY GROUPS

The right political strategy for minority groups is to realize that different religious/caste groups are not monolithic entities, each pitted against the other without any common needs or interests. In reality, each group is internally differentiated into sub-groups having different perceptions and interests. A wide spectrum of attitudes is present in every group. Thus, while committed Humanists among the Hindus actually fight for the legitimate interests of the oppressed, regardless of the caste or creed of the oppressor and the oppressed, others stoke communal passions for political gains. In general, liberal Hindu intellectuals and the entire Left mean well for the minorities.

The Hindus, as a group are quite friendly to the minorities; the Muslims or Christians, as a group, are certainly loyal to the country. In fact, the silent majority in all communities seeks mutual harmony. They face common problems. Poverty, disease, unemployment, corruption, judicial or administrative delays, pollution etc. make life miserable for all, not for this or that group alone. The struggle to overcome these problems brings different groups together on a functional basis. Diverse 'functional identities' do not weaken genuine religious faith but merely remove the intrusive presence of religious, caste or regional labels from our secular concerns and problems. No single identity (religious or functional) should displace other identities that jointly constitute the complex fabric of human relationships. This would be like reducing a rose to one of its petals, as it were. How irrational it sounds if, say, a victimized worker, clerk, nurse or teacher always kept in mind the religious or caste or regional identity of the wrong-doer and ever indulged in puerile generalizations about this or that group. This approach would harm, not help redress of the wrong.

The normal growth of society makes it increasingly complex both in terms of structure and function and dilutes the exclusive power of the traditionally dominant group that becomes apprehensive that other growing interests and ties might dent its present status. But, sociologically speaking, it is impossible to check the growth of multiple functional identities in modern society.

That Hindus constitute more than eighty percent of the Indian nation is, obviously, true. It, would, however, be preposterous to suppose that democratic theory justifies brushing aside the concern for the remaining 20% of the population. A political majority that violates the principle of equity and natural justice in dealing with concerns or interests of the minority or minorities becomes guilty of the charge of 'the tyranny of the majority'. In other words, the argument of some Hindu quarters that to serve and promote Hindu interests exclusively is the demand of democracy will not hold water. Any concept of Hindu solidarity that tends to weaken Indian solidarity, in the broad sense, and leads to inter-religious confrontation in Indian society is not patriotism but the 'communalism of the majority religious group'. Eminent thinkers and statesmen, both Western and Eastern, speak of the 'tyranny of the majority' when it attempts to ignore and trample upon the sentiments or interests of any minority. Proponents of *Hindutva* who equate national interest and Hindu dominance and decry 'minorityism' should realize that Hindu 'majoritarianism' could become even more perverse and vicious. Wisdom lies in following a proper sense of proportion.

The Muslims may be a minority group in India, but so large are they in absolute numbers that their Hindu brothers tend to become apprehensive of Muslim power, especially because of the rather growing threat of religious fundamentalism in neighbouring Muslim countries. The fact of the matter is rather different. The classical Hindu ethos (though always plagued by the caste system) has been tolerant of religious plurality; the secular political parties are well entrenched in the public life of the country; political democracy (though not free from traces of the ancient caste system) has become an integral part of the Indian psyche; the vast majority of the leading Hindu intellectuals and professional groups stand for communal harmony and social justice, inclusive of 'affirmative action' for creating a level field of equal opportunity for the weaker sections. All this augurs well, indeed, for the eventual success of the ideal of liberal Humanism and the strategy of secular or functional unity. The slogan of 'Hinduism in danger' is, thus, a perverse or, possibly, even a 'pathological' fear in some extreme cases.

There never has been and there is no conflict in Indian history between Hinduism and Islam, or any other religion for that matter. All religions have functioned and flourished on Indian soil. The real quarrel is over the issue of political power that gives control over the means of production and distribution of wealth. The various religious groups or communities failed in the past to reach an agreement on the terms of sharing of power. The partition of the land just on the eve of independence was a tremendous blow to the process of emotional integration of the Indian people and the ideal of humanistic democracy. But the genius of India survived this tragedy. More than eighty percent of the Indian people were Hindus, yet India opted for a secular state. The vast majority of the Indian people continued, as ever, to live in peace and amity on the time hallowed principle of live and let live. Communal violence and riots occurred mainly in areas where refugees from either dominion had been forced to flee due to insecure conditions. The Indian nation, as a whole, retained its sanity and religious tolerance.

As things stand in India today a large section of backward Hindu classes and backward Muslim groups have become natural allies in their struggle for vertical mobility in an intensely competitive society where the upper caste educated Hindus are much better positioned. The 'forwards' and the 'backwards' look from different perspectives in the continuing debate on the meaning or definition of social or distributive justice. The 'forwards' lay stress on merit: the 'backwards' on reservation. If the backward classes from all communities combine politically they outnumber the forward and the elitist combination. This is the predicament of contemporary Indian politics.

The politics of *Hindu Rashtra* is, in the final analysis, a desperate ideological attack upon all those who are perceived as being oversupportive to the weaker sections, be they Hindu, Muslim or Christian. This approach leads not merely to historical distortions but even to the irrational fear that the present Hindu majority will turn into a minority due to Muslim opposition to family planning and the practice of polygamy. The *Sangh Pariwar* apprehends that power-hungry de-Hinduized politicians may combine with foreign assisted Muslims and Christians to sideline the true Hindus who alone are the devoted sons of Mother India. This mindset is absolutely misconceived and sterile in the modern age.

The Muslim segment of the Indian family cannot be suppressed by force. Nor is it in national interest to keep them down economically. Such policies only push the Muslims or other disliked groups into the arms of religious fundamentalism and the promise of dubious redemption through militancy. Likewise, Muslim militancy and fundamentalism polarize politics to the general detriment of the Muslims themselves. It is absolutely immaterial whether *Hindutva* politics is the reaction to Islamic fundamentalism, or the other way round. The crux of the issue is that both feed upon each other. The rejection of the mix of religion and politics does not amount to rejecting religion or spirituality as such. All that is needed is to outgrow those versions of historical religions that produce or stand for communal polarization and emotional distance between their respective adherents.

Unity cannot be produced by legislation or force. Unity is bred in the minds of men who jointly share, through the passage of time, the joys and sorrows, victories and defeats in collective life. This had happened in medieval India, despite the religious divide. The Hindu concept of '*Isht Devata*' and loyalty to the monarch had produced the ethos of live and let live. The legitimacy of the ruler was independent of his religion. Different religious groups remained loyal to a common king. Legitimacy was decided in the field of battle, not the legislature that just did not exist. Occasional revolts and rebellions did take place but they were overcome by military force. Alternatively, a new king emerged and a new dynasty came to be established. There is no reason why the same pattern and rhythm of power and governance should not continue in the plural Indian society under secular democratic conditions in place of the ancient and medieval monarchy.

What is required for the above goal is to give priority number one to removing the sense of insecurity among the different minority groups and providing them with facilities for overcoming their backwardness. The framing and application of a common civil code is certainly not a priority matter, on a balanced sociological perspective. The real damage to emotional integration and the solidarity of the Indian family occurs, not when a Muslim woman suffers due to Muslim personal laws, but when she is widowed or orphaned due to communal violence anywhere in the country. Every time this happens the poison of criminality enters the arteries of the entire nation and its moral fibre is torn asunder. This destroys the roots of national solidarity as also of economic health.

The Politics of 'Hindutva'

Hindutva politics is, in part, a reaction against the powerful currents of Islamic fundamentalism in different Muslim countries, and, in part, due to more or less conscious memories of Muslim domination in medieval times. Some well meaning Hindus might honestly hold that *Hindutva* is not anti-Muslim or anti-Christian. But this could hardly apply to the several newly born militant Hindu organizations as ancillaries to the old RSS (Rashtriya Swayamsevak Sangh). In the final analysis, *Hindutva* politics obstructs the flowering of the scientific outlook, the humanistic interpretation of history and of internationalism. It condones some Hindu values without the willingness to revise and redefine them in an ever-changing world.

The founder of the RSS, Dr. Hedgewar (d. 1940) was sincerely dedicated to the welfare of the great Hindu community in India, but his historical vision and general outlook on life was greatly deficient in the universality and humanist appeal that characterized a Ram Mohan Roy, a Tagore, a Gandhi or even a Vivekananda. All the above giants were great Hindus, without being parochial or narrow-minded. Thus, despite his undoubted sincerity and goodness Hedgewar's approach could not flower into universal concern and humanist empathy radiated by the great spiritual humanists of the Indian family.

The simple unsophisticated heart of Hedgewar overflowed with tender concern for the gentle cow and the poor but intellectually gifted Brahmin in a merciless competitive colonial setup. He also had a measure of concern and sympathy for other weaker sections. But the burden of his passionate lament was the moral and spiritual decline of the once powerful and prosperous Hindu society. Had Hedgewar given attention to the human situation, as such, rather than only to its Hindu wing, he would have clearly seen that rise and decline, glory and defeat have been the common lot of all races and nations. When one looks at history from this humanist perspective one develops a concern for the welfare and resurgence of the entire human family, rather than for any particular section. This was Gandhi's vision and the secret of his universal appeal.

The vision of Hedgewar's successor, Guru Golwalkar (d. 1973) gradually became even more exclusivist and blurred due to his misreading of Indian history and his greater involvement with political activism as compared with the relatively more pietist Hedgewar. Golwalkar's work, *A Bunch of Thoughts*, is an essay on Hindu resurgence addressed to a pure Hindu reference group, which he equates with the Indian nation. It is not an essay on Indian Renaissance addressed to a multi-religious nation in the making. Several well-informed and enlightened observers, both Indian and foreign, have pointed out the serious errors and limitations of the above work.

The embryonic political activism of the early years of the RSS has now developed into a much broader and rather turbulent political stream in a cross section of modern Indian society. The present constituency ranges from sober intellectual and professional groups to petty shopkeepers. Its youth wing (*Bajrang Dal*), are muscle men who prefer their own brawn to the *Brahman* brain to promote the politics of *Hindutva*. Indeed, the older generation of the RSS at times feels uncomfortable and restricted while operating at the control panel of the sprawling family.

On the theoretical side the political pundits of the RSS family desire to change the concept of secular nationalism (as enshrined in the Indian constitution) to 'cultural nationalism'. But they barely suspect that 'cultural nationalism' tends to turn into the monster of 'cultural imperialism'. They decry the rising tide of religious fundamentalism but forget that 'cultural nationalism' could easily degenerate into 'cultural fundamentalism' opposed to humanist democracy. What happened on December 6, 1991 might have saddened some highly sensitive souls in the RSS or its political wing the BJP which claims that it stands for truly secular politics and berates the pseudo-secularism of the Congress. But the brutality and violence involved in the episode resulted in a shocking mutation of 'cultural nationalism' into the worst form of 'cultural fundamentalism' and collective hysteria.

The root limitation of the RSS philosophical vision and interpretation of Indian history is its 'a historical' and totally abstract notion of the '*Rashtra*'. From the RSS (Rashtriya Swayamsevak Sangh) angle of vision the '*Rashtra*' is some eternal and pure Aryan collective entity that is the special creation or manifestation of the *Absolute Brahman*, and is, thus, something apart from the common rung of humanity. The RSS intellectuals and ideologues hold that the *'Rashtra'* is the pure historical microcosm of the *Brahmanical* macrocosm and *Bharat* is the territorial locus of this historical process. This stand implies that the language, thought, culture, customs, institutions of the Aryans of *Bharat* during the golden period of its sacred history (before the scourge of foreign invasions and conquests) were all perfect. Muslims and Christians corrupted them and attempted to destroy the soul of *Bharat*. The Muslims and the British eventually conspired to vivisect the body of 'Mother India' before being compelled to vacate the unholy aggression against India down the centuries.

The RSS vision goes on to claim that the soul of India is immortal and destined to conquer all opposition. It is for *Bharat* to teach and for all others to learn the infallible wisdom and truth eternally enshrined in the Vedas. The wisdom of the Vedas is complete and needs no further growth through exposure to and dialogue with other thought systems, cultures and religions. In fact, all these are cultural or conceptual aberrations to be swept aside by Vedic wisdom of a resurrected *Bharat*, freshly emancipated from centuries of accursed foreign rule.

The above philosophical and historical vision and interpretation of Indian history is a species of a closed 'ahistorical' pattern of understanding the concrete growth of the Indian people in history. This type of conceptualization of history completely ignores the concrete processes of the growth of nations and the evolution of human ideas and ideals through continual interaction and dialogue. This approach totally brushes aside the mutual give and take between different wings of the human family in both peace and war. It also ignores the fact that the invader or foreigner of yesterday becomes the son of the soil tomorrow, provided he settles down, works, dies and mingles with the air and dust of his chosen land, just like those who may have arrived earlier on the common soil.

Unfortunately, some RSS (Rashtriya Swayamsevak Sangh) ideologues have gone to the extent of flatly denying some of the hitherto established basics of pre-history concerning the place of origin and subsequent migration of the earliest Aryans from Afro-Asia to Europe in the West and India in the East. Such intellectuals or ideologues question hitherto accepted basics or assumptions of Anthropology, Ethnology, Archeology and the evidence of empirical studies in history. Free enquiry is, indeed, a precondition of advance on the endless human quest for truth. But the motive of such questioning should be pure search for truth rather than defensive rationalization of unexamined traditional beliefs. Moreover, there should be coercive or crucial evidence in favor of a new theory. In view of the above considerations, wherever highly technical issues and procedures of verification are involved, the honest seeker of truth must give far more weight to the consensus of detached experts than to political or religious spokesmen. Finally, one should always keep an open mind. It is significant that Western pre-historians and ethnologists who had until recently held the central Asian region to be the cradle of the earliest homo sapiens have now veered to the view (in the light of new and strong empirical evidence) that Africa, not Asia, was the earliest cradle of the human species.

Last, but not least, official RSS thinking ignores the plain historical fact that Aryan India, specially the once creative *Brahmans*, had entered upon the state of declining vigor and creativity much before the advent of Muslims on the Indian stage. Indeed, Jainism and Buddhism themselves had arisen in ancient India as powerful and authentic protests against the moral laxity and empty conventionalism that had come to encrust the once bright flame of *Brahmanical* spiritual and intellectual creativity. Several centuries elapsed before the *Brahmanical* corpus regained this creativity in south India through the inspiring life and creative labors of the Adi Shankaracharya.

Different races or nations reach peak levels of energy and creativity at different stages in the forward movement of humanity as a whole. Human culture is a team achievement, grand relay race of torchbearers of ideas and ideals that grow and mature over centuries in the womb of the human quest for values ever more. And every nation, religion and culture is called upon to contribute to this never-ending quest. No nation, culture, language, scripture, or era, therefore, may lay claim to perfection or hold that no further growth of ideas and ideals is needed or even possible. This truth applies to all religions and thought and value systems, including my own cherished religion of Islam. This was also the Gandhian approach to Hinduism.

I submit that Hindu resurgence in India is natural and inevitable in a democratic state having a preponderant Hindu majority. There is no question of Hinduism being in danger or Hindus being reduced to a minority due to the machinations of hostile Muslims. Such fears are grounded in irrational fear and an irrational interpretation of history or the rejection of sociology. Every sane Indian, irrespective of religion or region, welcomes Hindu resurgence on rational and liberal lines. But Indian resurgence is more than the resurgence of any of its component parts. The circle is greater than any arc, no matter how large the arc might be. Muslims, Christians, Sikhs, Buddhists and Jains, Parsees and Jews are all sons of the soil with equal rights and duties and equal dignity. No distinction may be made between religions that originated in India and those, which originated elsewhere. The ancient Aryan, Iranian, Turkish, Arabic and European cultural streams, call them by whatever name, Brahmanical, Islamic, Christian or modern, are all constituent elements and ingredients of an ever-evolving Indian society and culture. The exclusive devotion to the Aryan content will diminish the wonder and the sweetness and light (drawn from many sources) that India was and should remain in the ceaseless pursuit of universal values. The Indian genius for diversity in unity and unity in diversity must remain the chosen destination of the Indian family.

Despite the colossal tragedy and brutalization in Gujrat in 2002 it is my honest and firm belief that the Gujrat will again bounce back to the ethos of liberal democracy. The common Indian, no matter what his or her religion or politics, instinctively realizes that the fire of hatred, if it is allowed to spread, will engulf and destroy the entire nation. The Hindu majority has always been tolerant of religious plurality, though, unfortunately, they have remained trapped in the bog of caste.

As is well known, the political architect and founder of Pakistan, Jinnah, was himself a very modern and Westernized Muslim and he had no sympathy whatsoever with what is termed 'Islamic fundamentalism', in modern parlance. The other Muslim League leaders at the top, and the professional classes, in general, also had a liberal Islamic outlook in varying degrees, though they were highly confused on some basic religious and political concepts of modernity. This conceptual confusion prevails in Pakistan to date. One thing is, however, clear. While religious fundamentalism is an active and highly organized movement possessing considerable money power in Pakistan, the vast majority of the Pakistani Muslims do not care to join or even to follow 'Islamic fundamentalism', in Mawdudi's sense. The Indian Muslims are even less bothered to listen to the talk of Islamic fundamentalism. Their political commonsense has already convinced them that the mixed society of India in which their Hindu brothers form 85% of the population is ill suited for the politics of religious fundamentalism. The vast majority of Indian Muslims have cast their lot with the direction set by Gandhi, Nehru and Azad.

Many Indian Muslims do feel inwardly uneasy with the modern idea of de-linking politics with religion because they have been used to the idea that *Shariah* covers every aspect of life. But they have reconciled themselves, in all good faith and sincerity, to make adjustments in the traditional or classical idea of Islam in view of the realities of the Indian situation. I submit that this approach is a half way house rather than a full or unqualified commitment to spiritual Humanism and secularism. But, then, inner attitudes require centuries to grow and evolve in the minds and hearts of men enjoying security and freedom. Gandhi and Nehru understood the human condition and showed patience and generosity to all. Perhaps, the votaries of *Hindutva* politics today are impatient and their insight into the human condition is blurred, and this makes it hard for them to arrive at a proper and balanced evaluation of the genuine Muslim response to the Indian situation.

The doubts and fears in *Hindutva* quarters arise, more because of Islamic terrorism outside India than because of the religious fundamentalism among Indian Muslims. Since Muslim terrorists in Pakistan, and elsewhere carry on the heinous crime of killing innocents in the name of Islam, non-Muslims are led to accept this claim at its face value. But the truth is entirely different. Religious fundamentalism, as such, springs from cultural isolation and a closed society that hampers free enquiry. Political terrorism, on the other hand, springs from existential anxiety and despair in the face of perceived injustice and the tyranny of the strong over the weak. Moreover, political terrorism cuts across different religions. Here an unexpected parallel exists between Hindu and Muslim perceptions.

A considerable section of urban Muslims in united India had been swayed (under the influence of the absurd two-nation theory) to demand Pakistan, but they were traumatized and suddenly left in the lurch by its creation. They are becoming increasingly insecure in India due to the rising Hindu fascist trends in Indian politics. The Hindus more or less totally dominate the politics and economics of the land. Yet, they do not feel inwardly secure and in full control of the situation in India. They are scared of the dangers latent in Islamic fundamentalism and terrorism.

The Muslim logic is that Hindus do not behave like a 'big brother', as they should. The Hindu logic is that, far from being a younger brother, the Indian Muslims are members of a mighty Islamic power bloc stretching from North Africa to South East Asia located right on top of the Indian land mass. In other words, the Hindus do not perceive the Muslims as a weak younger brother but as a potentially powerful world community. A fear seems to lurk in the depths of the Hindu psyche that neither the Western world, nor the Islamic world wants the clever but mild Hindus to live in peace under their own sky from the Himalayas to the Indian Ocean. And fear is the mother of hate and aggression. This is the root cause of the rising incidents, in recent years, of physical violence against Indian Christians in several parts of the land.

Whatever Christian missionaries may or may not have done in the past to 'save' lost souls in India, the Christian church today has nothing to do with the theory or practice of forcing Christianity on the throats of infidels or of bribing them to join the flock of Christ. The plain truth is that the vast majority of Christian missionaries in India today are models of selfless service, piety and religious scholarship. Even the Pope has accepted plural paths to salvation. The adversarial approach to other religions has undergone an internal revolution in the contemporary Christian value system. On this point all the major religions of the world are fast converging. It is a pity that some *Hindutva* quarters still nurse or air old grievances against Muslims or Christians.

There is no dearth of compassionate and fair-minded Hindus or Muslims in India and Pakistan. They are, in fact, the silent majority. A vocal minority may be said to have hijacked the role of spokesman for Hinduism or Islam, as the case may be. However, in the long run the relative dominance of good over evil in the human heart will make the fair-minded liberal vanguard in each community, score over the forces of negativity and stagnation. This will pave the way for removing ignorance and prejudice. This has happened several times in history though new tensions and conflicts arise with the passage of time. But this is the limitation of humankind. The human pursuit of truth, goodness and beauty knows no boundaries of religion or race. I have no doubts that an inclusive approach to religious and cultural diversity will gradually score over an exclusive approach, be it Hindu, Muslim or Christian. This is the destination of man in the modern age. However, temporary ups and downs, setbacks and spurts in the movement of history can never be ruled out.

To close this chapter, let me state what may be called the 'paradox of growth'. In the process of growth or development success in solving some problem or challenge breeds some other problem or challenge. This cycle is inbuilt and is repeated indefinitely. The phenomenon may be called 'the partial resolution-involution cycle in human life'. Let me give a few random illustrations.

Planned small families solve the economic problem at the micro level. However, one child or childless families lead to a drought of fraternal affections and virtues. Consumerist societies make the home comfortable and the work environment productive. However, beyond the optimum level, people become addictive or compulsory hedonists and tend to lose their creativity and drive. Gender equality removes social evils and gives women an equal chance of creative self-realization. However, a strictly tit for tat relationship between the sexes destabilizes the family. Democratic governance respects and promotes the development of autonomy and authenticity in the individual. However, excessive individualism weakens social cohesion and solidarity. A caring state fosters citizens from the cradle to the grave and is the peak of social justice. However, beyond a certain point, state intervention or control tends to result in the devaluation of personal initiative and merit-based reward. Technology gives man mastery over nature. However, subjugated nature turns toxic and disturbs the inner peace and emotional balance of its arrogant conqueror. Developing societies are compelled to spend huge sums on several fronts at the same time, such as public health, education, housing, administrative infra-structures etc. However, every sector appears as priority 'Number One' on the wish list of some person or other. And to satisfy everyone on every score is just not possible in reality. And so on and so forth. This is the paradox of growth. In other words, all plans are vitiated by the inherent cycle of resolution and involution. Eternal vigilance is the price of virtue. And the essence of virtue or justice (in its widest sense) is a 'proper sense of proportion'.

Notes: Chapter II
Candid Reflections on the Indian Political Scene, 1947-1992

1. Much water has flown into the Ganga and oceans of ink have gone into the attack and defence of partisan positions on the Ayodhya issue. A person who has no axe to grind, however, can safely affirm only three things. First, there is no uniform belief as part of the Hindu faith that Rama was born at the exact spot where the Babari Masjid was raised five hundred years ago. Second, the reopening of the issue was an exercise in political strategy, rather than religious piety. Such exercises at all times gravely harm the nation, rather than boost national pride or glory. See the well-researched and perceptive work, *The Anatomy of A Confrontation*, edited by Sarvapalli Gopal, Delhi.

2. Prohibition was introduced in USA a few years after World War I ended, and was withdrawn a few years afterwards. The law had been passed in the teeth of opposition from quarters that had predicted the extremely harmful consequences of the measure. No single legislation has ever done greater harm to public morality in the USA than this ill-considered exercise in ethical idealism without taking into account grass root realities.

3. The Communist experiment broke down, principally, because of the inevitable long term consequences of controlled ideological reasoning in place of free empirical enquiry and cross checks by ndependent observers. The genuine Marxist approach was based on free enquiry, but Stalin had begun to impose his own *diktats* on the Party and society at large. He abjured all opportunities of a free dialogue with the outside world that was painted as a capitalist devil bent upon destroying Russia. Reality was, thus, shut out or concealed under the cloak of an infallible ideology. Unfortunately, the same type of dangerous game is being played out (unconsciously, of course and with all good intentions) by fundamentalist Muslims preaching and practising the gospel of hate and violence against the Satanic non-Muslims dubbed as the 'enemies of God'.

The sociological approach to politics means that policy decisions are made in the light of objective data, supplied by social sciences pursued in the spirit of free and independent enquiry. The pure ideological approach (whether religious or secular) on the other hand, resorts to 'closed' reasoning. This type of reasoning is a species of rationalization. Sociology respects accurate data, even if it be unpalatable or unacceptable. Ethics and philosophy start where Sociology ends. But there is no confusion of roles or functions. Those who follow the ideological approach, whether religious or secular, mix up facts and values and (with the best of ntentions) cause great harm to society. The sociological approach is quite compatible with religion and spirituality. But it does demarcate the proper jurisdiction of religion. See the insightful work, *The End of Ideology*, by Daniel Bell, 1988.

Candid Reflections on the Indian Political Scene, 1947-1992

4. The countries of the third world have yet 'to awake from their dogmatic slumber' on the crucial need of population control as the foundation for building a planned welfare society. Only when Communist China abandoned its old line on population control and resorted to the one child family norm did the country take a new turn for the better. It is doubtful if China could have achieved this breakthrough without a drastic reduction in the birth rate.

5. Muslims are the largest, while Parsees the smallest religious minority group in India (apart from a handful of elderly Jewish families left behind in Kerala or Mumbai after Jewish emigration to Israel). The Parsees are not permitted to marry outside and are struggling to survive in the Indian family. Insignificant in numbers (less than hundred thousand) the Parsees have produced a galaxy of eminent leaders, industrialists, scientists and lawyers. They are a creative minority facing extinction. However, no external agency can help them resolve their demographic crisis. They have to hit upon a solution on their own.

The Christian wing of the Indian family is the second largest minority after the Muslims. In terms of education, economic prosperity and modernization they are far ahead of the Muslims. The rich network of educational institutions, hospitals, voluntary organizations, foundations and trusts created by Christian missionaries are a contribution to the welfare of the Indian nation as a whole.

Until very recently the Christian community felt quite secure and comfortable in secular India. The politics of *Hindutva* has created tensions and fears. The crimes against nuns and other Christians, the charges against missionaries of forcibly converting or giving the lure of material gains, the attribution of extra-territorial loyalties, the proclaimed apprehensions of collusion between Western powers and Indian missionaries for harming Indian national interests have all befouled the hitherto peaceful atmosphere. Some quarters have also expressed concern that mass conversion of Adivasis to Christianity might lead to a political alliance of Christians, Muslims, *Dalits* and other backwards to oust the upper caste Hindus altogether from the corridors of power. In addition to the above depth fears or apprehensions the prosperous condition of Christian institutions and those running them stand in sharp contrast with the poverty and backwardness of the weaker Hindu sections of the Indian family. Calm and critical reflection on these fears would readily expose their essential hollowness. But the heat and dust of politics hardly allows dispassionate analysis in *Hindutva* quarters.

The Adivasis constitute a substantial proportion of the Indian family. Because of their long isolation from mainstream culture and politics Western anthropologists better know their condition than most Indians themselves. The eventual destination of Adivasis is full emotional integration with mainstream India. This, however, does not mean absorption or assimilation at the cost of their distinctive local culture, which must be respected. Emotional integration or healthy nationalism does not demand uniformity and the obliteration of variety, but only genuine respect for each other. The idea that 'seamless uniformity' is essential for or integral to nationalism and patriotism is both erroneous and dangerous. Given the historical conditions in India it is very natural for the Adivasis in several regions to gravitate to Christianity in the course of their modernization. Equally natural it is that Hindu resurgence should aim to spread a modernized enlightened version of

The Vision of an Unknown Indian Muslim: Part 2

Hinduism in the cultural space of Adivasis. Muslim missionaries too are justified in the task of 'saving souls' from their own point of view. What is crucial that the modernization process is carried on peacefully.

6. One should not rule out the desirability of a further reorganization of the states of the Indian Union, or the desirability of formally instituting 'sub-regions' within a state as such. What is crucially important is that all change be brought about peacefully in the ambience of a liberal humanist system, rather than of caste or communal considerations. The idea is very clear though its implementation is, certainly, a difficult and delicate task. At present no act passed by the state legislature becomes operative without Presidential consent. States are greatly dependent financially upon the Centre. On the other hand, states can directly or indirectly obstruct Central laws and directives, not to their liking. The power and accountability structure in India is, thus, highly ambivalent.

7. The political unity and integrity of the Indian union will survive only if the country throws up leaders of vision and stature who could reconcile conflicting perceptions and interests of the diverse regional, religious, caste groups constituting the sea of Indian humanity. This will have to be done with supreme artistry and genuine empathy for all rather than skill in playing one group against the other. I honestly think that if this crucial condition is not operative the Union could well break into smaller regional Unions. If this happens the cultural and economic unity may still survive but the political clout of India in the comity of nations will be adversely affected.

8. The Kashmir imbroglio has placed the Indian Muslims in a political predicament. They desire and long that Kashmir, 'the paradise on earth', should remain a part of India, both in their own as well as national interest. But they feel utterly helpless in the matter of shaping the course of events inside Kashmir due to the rise of strong regional aspirations and international developments following Pakistani aggression. Indian Muslims feel doubly inhibited lest their honest response as Indian patriots be misconstrued as partiality for Kashmiri Muslims or for Pakistan. Some intellectuals and journalists on both sides of the border, however, have made a promising beginning. No matter what the short term results, the effort to resolve the issue peacefully with the consent of all concerned, including the people of the region and also Pakistan, must go on. The lesson of history is that worthwhile goals take their own time for realization.

9. The government, from time to time, appointed several high powered commissions of enquiry that have produced excellent reports. Perhaps, the most monumental of all is the multi-volume Madon Report which is breath taking in its scope, accuracy and objectivity without fear or favour. All reports carried considered recommendations for preventing the evil of communal violence, but the governments concerned had their own priorities and concerns.

CHAPTER 12

THE DREAM OF AN INDIAN MUSLIM

BACKGROUND OF MY DREAM: THE LEGACY OF THE BENGAL AND MODERN INDIAN RENAISSANCE

A great and promising cultural inter-action between Islam and Hinduism at the folk level had already started in medieval India under the auspices of the wide spread *Sufi* and *Bhakti* movements in the 13th and 14th century. Given more time they might well have flowered into an intellectual enlightenment that occurred in Western Europe in the 18th century. But the sudden decline of the central Mughal authority shortly after Aurangzeb's death in 1707 led to chaos and anomie in the entire country. This invited the infamous incursions and invasions of Nadir Shah and Ahmad Shah of Central Asia and also numerous internal adventurers and thugs of different hues. By this time the British lion had started to roar and it did not take Great Britain very long to fill in the power vacuum in India.

To my mind, the British rulers did a magnificent job of uniting the vast and diverse Indian family and placing it on the path of modernization and progress. I say so in all humility and with full intellectual honesty. However, the modernization of Indian society under British rule proved to be a mixed blessing. The introduction of modern democratic institutions at the local level and the emergence of new power structures from among the English educated classes made Indian

Muslims deeply apprehensive of their future prospects in a setup very different from the old feudal establishment. Muslims had belonged to the ruling class before the British took over, but the situation became very different after the advent of British rule. The communal problem in colonial India was, at bottom, a product of harsh competition for jobs in a plural society in which the upper caste Western educated Hindus had stolen a march over the educationally backward but culturally dominant Muslim segments from pre-British times.

The partition of the country in 1947 on religious lines was the end result of the failure of Indian Muslims to keep pace with their Hindu brothers in the ongoing transition from a medieval outlook to the modern. Later on they could not achieve mutual agreement on the sharing of power in a modern secular democratic state and society. It is now futile for Hindus, Muslims or the British to play the blame game. It was no mean achievement that the galaxy of Indian leaders who steered India into freedom and later drafted the constitution of India saved her from sliding into authoritarian rule or anarchy that befell her neighbors who had won freedom from colonial rule along with India.

While nationalism is a considerable and necessary advance from regionalism or populism it is itself incomplete and unfulfilled unless territorial nationalism flowers into humanistic inter-nationalism. The Western type of nationalism which sidelined Christianity in 19th century Europe amounted to treating a segment or arc of humanity as the unconditional focus of devotion without reference to the full circle of humanity or to the Creator. Several bloody wars between regional or great powers and two world wars and the experience of a nuclear holocaust, however, led the ablest and noblest minds of the human race to see through the limitations of territorial nationalism. Thinkers like Bertrand Russell, Freud and Einstein have even defined territorial nationalism as a species of tribalism. Marx and many religious fundamentalists of different religions also decry nationalism as a divisive principle. However, the organized religions have little justification to criticize a territorial nationalism as divisive since they themselves divide the human family into believers and non-believers. Only full democratic humanists do justice to the ideal of the oneness of the human family.

Nationalism in the territorial sense is only a transitory stage in the consolidation of Humanism. Technological and economic factors are slowly but steadily changing adversarial nationalism into internationalism and the idea of sovereign independence into cooperative inter-dependence. The human family will take considerable time and will have to pass through great turmoil to reach this goal. But the direction of the long journey is in little doubt.

Muslims in India (with notable exceptions, of course) have failed to understand the sociology of politics and religion. Unexposed to the concepts and values of modernity and the changed concept and function of religion in the scientific era, allergic to Godless Communism, disillusioned with the Congress government's failure to protect and implement the rule of law on numerous occasions in independent India (especially the Babari mosque issue), apprehensive of the long term consequences of aggressive *Hindutva*, plagued by fears of progressive political marginalization on the national scene, large sections of the Muslims, began to suspect that the Congress party had started to take Indian Muslim support for granted. This disillusionment led to their drifting into the camp of the *Other Backward Classes* (OBCs) who had just been galvanized into a new life under Yadava leadership soon after the implementation of the *Mandal Report*.

Exuberant at their spectacular success in humiliating the Muslims as well as their Congress patrons the BJP felt emboldened to forge a united front with the *Dalits* against the hitherto ruling Congress, now in disarray. However, the coalition failed because the motive of the *Hindutva* camp was political expediency and opportunism rather than genuine humanistic care and concern for the *Dalits*. And political instinct made the *Dalits* and OBCs rather ambivalent and skeptical of the overtures and allurements from the Hindu side. It was not easy for the *Dalits* and other backward classes to forget that

Hindutva, historically speaking, has always been weighted in favour of the upper castes. The *Dalits* have now tasted real power on their own in Uttar Pradesh after centuries of exploitation and deprivation. But is the present Dalit leadership really inspired by genuine humanistic ideals and values of modernity? Or is it merely moved by deep-rooted and festering resentments against the upper caste Hindus? The rather unbridled aggression and ambition of a Mayawati seems to flow more from negative feelings and hurt pride than from a mature and selfless commitment to humanistic values. She allowed a much larger than life personality cult to grow in her circle. In all humility, I submit that this is not the way to realize the genuine dreams of Dr. Ambedkar who was a genuine reformer and visionary, even if he could not see eye to eye with the great inclusive vision of the Congress.

More or less the same remarks apply to the political successors of Charan Singh, who, unfortunately, have totally failed to imbibe his genuine concern for the Jat community and the farmers, in general, under the inspiring leadership of Gandhiji. Instead of furthering the cause of social justice and the uplift of the weaker sections the Jat, Yadav and *Dalit* leaders have been forging and breaking opportunistic alliances and coalition governments for the sake of sheer power. As a consequence, though the nation has steadily developed in terms of industrial production and infra-structure as a modern welfare state, India stands rather low on the scale of the Human Development Index (HDI), as we all know.

The country is condemned to go through the tortuous and thorny path of short-lived coalitions, midterm polls, constitutional breakdowns, ineffective and corrupt governance, crises of economy and of law and order. However, the ancient land which in the past produced a long line of saints, sages, philosophers and other intellectuals, and, not less importantly, the sublime and spiritual music and dance of India, has arrived at a turning point of history. Sheer disgust with the system of democracy, as it has come to be practised in recent years, the common man, irrespective of religion or caste, seems to have learnt, at last, to wake up to his right and duty to monitor his rulers rather than merely vote.

Hindutva quarters will soon begin to realize that it is self-defeating to try to check Islamic fundamentalism/terrorism by raising slogans of Hinduism in danger, just as Islamic quarters will realize the futility of working for Islamic hegemony in the modern age of science and humanistic democracy. The common man can be fooled for some time, but not forever. Voters, irrespective of religion, caste or region, will gradually realize the wisdom of electing only those who genuinely respect the common man, and who work for the welfare of all segments of the population. If a widow has to give a monthly cut to some fixer for getting her mandatory pension, the religious or caste identity of the fixer or the ideology of the ruling party is immaterial to her. If medicines allocated to state hospitals find their way into the open market, if fake drugs are sold in abundance, if electricity is stolen with impunity, it is immaterial who robs the sate or society.

The birth of the Indian National Congress in 1885 was a turning point in our history. But due to various reasons this insight reached the Muslim mind very late and even then in a diluted form. They still have to catch up with their Hindu brothers in a secular India. And they are gradually advancing on the road to the modern idea of religion as a personal matter that should not be mixed with politics. The traditional conception that Islam is a complete code of life that should govern every aspect of life is still strongly entrenched in Muslim thinking. Intellectually honest Muslims must now show the moral courage to question this long held approach. The Hindus did so long ago when modern Hindu intellectuals and reformers questioned the deeply entrenched Hindu caste system and some other traditional values.

Political agendas that flow from fear of or hostility to 'the other', (which are negative human emotions) will never remove the evils and sufferings of humanity. Only the positive force of all inclusive love, compassion and human brotherhood, transcending all negativities, achieves permanent solutions. This was the basic message of Gandhiji to the modern world.

Broadly speaking, the Western educated Hindu urban elite, under the impact of the Bengal and Indian Renaissance (much before Gandhi's time) had already accepted a spiritually based humanism that included the modern idea of the separation of politics and religion. The Indian Muslims, on the other hand, remained tied down to the classical Islamic view that the *Shariah* was supreme in every sphere of the Muslim's life, Even during the early twenties of the 20th century when Gandhiji's twin agenda of winning political freedom and defending the *Caliphate* of Islam had captured the imagination of India the inner motivation and the life vision of the top leadership among the two great communities was very different. They were, indeed, united in their common aim to be free of foreign rule, but there was little understanding or vision of what was to be done after winning freedom.

We all know what happened in the thirties and forties of the 20th century. Due to the great disparities in the educational and economic development in different regions and segments of the great Indian family and the relative backwardness of Muslims on the scale of modernization the dream of Gandhi ended in the nightmare of partition and colossal hatred and suffering on both sides of the border. Partition (and I say this with all respect to all concerned and in all humility) was a quack's remedy, not a farsighted and holistic prescription. However, there is no point now in crying over spilt milk. Yet, we can and simply must learn from it.

The national interests of both India and Pakistan now demand that citizens of both the countries become fully aware of the folly and the danger of doing politics in the name of religion. To my mind, while the free mixing of the sexes may or may not be harmful to social health, free mixing of politics and religion is, certainly, suicidal, no matter what the religion may be.

Confining myself to India, I am absolutely clear that the Congress concern for the welfare of minorities through some form or other of 'affirmative action' is perfectly compatible with the concept of secularism. The habitual rather compulsive tendency of *Hindutva* quarters to mis-interpret this genuine concern as vote-bank politics and to dub it as pseudo-secularism is a matter of regret. The *Sachhar Report* is a notable step in the right direction and it should be promptly and meaningfully implemented. The state must help all under-developed sections to learn how to help themselves in a truly welfare state. The government must further ensure that full benefits of affirmative action actually reach the intended beneficiaries. Rajiv Gandhi's honest and perceptive observation at what actually happens at the grass roots should have shocked and shamed the nation into immediate action. Unfortunately, we lost him. We should heed him now. Irreversible history has made the welfare of all minorities an integral part of the welfare of modern India, and this welfare is indivisible. The promoters of exclusive interests, whether Muslim or Hindu, are living in a fool's paradise, completely oblivious to the facts of life.

The modern humanistic approach to religion and the idea of secular democracy hang together. Both the American constitution and the constitution of India are informed by this basic approach. This approach, which I call 'religious liberalism', will gradually become the standard Indian approach in all religious communities in India and elsewhere. To point out the limitations or faults of 'others' and glorify one's own virtues helps no one. Inter-religious cooperation between different historical faiths must replace adversarial relations between them. Though extremely slow and tortuous and, seemingly, irrational the march of history is in the broad direction of spiritual pluralism and representative democracy. This expectation gets enough support from a balanced and impartial study of history.

In an essay, *The Dream that Failed*, I have described some of the well known facts of modern history that justify this optimism. Another supporting argument is the irrepressible existential conviction of humankind all over the world that human nature is a mixture of good and evil, but good preponderates. This belief is not an axiom nor is it deducible from any self-evident truth. Yet, this faith is an undying inner voice and a light that shows the way to humanity in the darkest nights of the soul.

After ten to fifteen years from the date of writing the multi-religious people of India, the vast majority of whom are, obviously, Hindus are likely to get totally disgusted with the present religion/caste based pattern of voting at elections. The politics of integrity and functional ability will, then, replace the politics of religious or caste identity at every level. Millions of our long suffering and patient weaker sections who throng the voting booths with a smiling face are steadily learning this truth at every general election in our country. Every general election in India is silently working as a spiral staircase to bring the long suffering and deprived sections of our people to higher levels of humanistic democracy. However, there is a great need for creative thinking by competent sociologists and political scientists to ensure that the political party or coalition that becomes the legitimate ruling power actually gets the majority of the total national vote, not merely the majority of seats in the legislature. Introducing this concept in the body of our constitution should greatly improve the quality of Indian democracy.

THE EMERGING DREAM OF AN INDIAN MUSLIM

I foresee that the leaderless Indian Muslims (presently confused, demoralized, in the grip of a besieged mentality) after two or three general elections will join the mainstream of secular Indian politics instead of functioning as vote banks for political managers, be they secular or religious. The bewildered Indian Muslims (including the erstwhile champions of a separate homeland for Muslims) are now realizing the tremendous folly they committed in 1947. They are fast coming round to the view that they should vote for the man who is honest and has the right agenda in view (irrespective of his religion or caste). I am pretty confident that well educated Muslims having a broad humanist outlook and vision will soon emerge on the Indian scene. The same applies to *Dalits* and OBC's (Other Backward Classes). Nitish Kumar of Bihar has already captured the imagination of the people of India, while Narendra Modi of Gujrat is more likely to take on the image of a boss who gets things done rather than of a statesman and democratic leader. And it is my faith in the genius of India that the common man is soon going to see through the dirty tricks as well as honest deceptions of our establishment. Young India is developing the clarity, courage and conviction to embrace the politics of integrity without importing religion, region or caste into the game of power.

The persons who win the free and fair vote of the people must honestly view themselves as servant leaders of the great Indian family, rather than the leader of any particular group. The servant leader will be fully alive to the fact that the Indian family, in its own turn, is an arc (a very large one indeed) of the still larger circle of humanity. Accordingly, he will fully understand the limitations of the dictum, 'my country, right or wrong' and will take the lead in applying the Gandhian-Nehruvian ethical approach to national and international politics. Today several Christians, upper caste Hindus and Muslims who are compassionate humanists stand rather marginalized in the corridors of caste-centred Indian politics. This must go and the 'Obama Moment' should arrive. Reinhold Niebuhr and Gandhi inspired Martin Luther King. Likewise, Gandhi inspired Nelson Mandela. When will Gandhi inspire another Indian after Jawaharlal? When will it be? Who will it be? Where in India will it be? All I know is that it will be.

Much earlier, Rabindra Nath Tagore had described the land of his dreams in his prayer in the *Gitanjali* in the immortal lines:

Where the mind is without fear and the head is held high;
Where knowledge is free;
Where the world is not broken up into fragments by narrow domestic walls;
Where words come out from the depth of truth;
Where tireless living stretches its arms towards perfection;
Where the clear stream of reason has not lost its way into the dreary desert sand of dead habit;
Where the mind is led forward by thee into ever widening thought and action:
Into that heaven of freedom, let my country awake.

And I, as an Indian Muslim, dream of the day when every Indian Muslim heart will resonate with Tagore's prayer and will cease to bother whether the poet was a Muslim or a Hindu.

APPENDIX 1

Fascmiles of three Letters Addressed To The Author

1. Letter from Jawaharlal Nehru

2. Letter from Indira Gandhi

3. Letter from Rajiv Gandhi

Appendix 1: Fascmiles of three Letters Addressed To The Author

No. 2313-PMH/61

PRIME MINISTER'S HOUSE
NEW DELHI
November 29, 1961

My dear Jamal,

I got your letter of the 28th November this morning. I appreciate what you have written to me. It is difficult for me to advise you as this is a matter which much depends upon the judgment of the individual concerned and his urges. I was looking forward to your continuing in Parliament. If, however, you feel that you would be more usefully employed in carrying on productive work in the University, then I would not like to come in your way. Work in the University is certainly of importance. As to which type of work one chooses, University or the Legislature, must necessarily depend upon the inner urges of the individual concerned.

I agree with you that humanism, which is so important, is neglected in India at present. It might be said that it is largely neglected in other countries too, except for pockets in the Universities or elsewhere. It is not clear to me, however, how the building up of an organisation would help in this matter. It might a little, but I doubt if it will have any powerful effect. Probably a first-class Weekly or Monthly dealing with this aspect would be more helpful. Anyhow, there can be no objection to an organisation devoted to humanism.

Socialism, as I understand it, must include the humanist approach, but I realise that it seldom is so now-a-days. It is really the Universities that should nurture the humanistic spirit as they should encourage the scientific spirit. Indeed the Universities are supposed to deal specially with the humanities. You have, of course, my love and good wishes.

Yours affectionately,

Jawaharlal Nehru

Shri Jamal Khwaja, MP,
77, South Avenue,
New Delhi.

Appendix 1: Fascmiles of three Letters Addressed To The Author

PRIME MINISTER

New Delhi
November 25, 1981

Dear Jamal,

    I have your letter of 16th November, 1981. I am so sorry to hear of your mother's passing away. She lived a full life and was a devoted partner and helpmate to your father. May her soul rest in peace.

    The erosion of the values of Gandhi and Nehru is of considerable concern to me. Every endeavour to preserve and protect those values, indeed to restore them, is obstructed or thwarted on political considerations. At the same time we must not forget that a nation, like a human being, has to go through certain stages of development. Some are pleasant, others unpleasant.

    Your suggestions regarding electoral reform are useful. There is deep thinking these days on this topic. I hope we can have some definite changes in the future.

                                 Yours sincerely,

                                 (Indira Gandhi)

Shri Jamal Khwaja
Sami Manzil
Aligarh

Appendix 1: Fascmiles of three Letters Addressed To The Author

RAJIV GANDHI
10 Janpath, New Delhi-110011

April 04, 1991

Dear Prof Khwaja

You have in the past few months shared your views and suggestions with me and your letter has given me some thought provoking ideas.

In the past fifteen months of 'political experiment' we have all undergone 'political turmoil' and our country has been left directionless. Our problems have increased greatly with the uncertainty which has vexed everyone. Non-Congress Governments have failed and they have brought the country to the brink of disaster. Internationally too, we have lost our standing and the credibility which had been consolidated by Panditji and Indiraji has been eroded.

We took the decision to support the Janata Dal (S) last year because the atmosphere was charged with communal tension and our country could ill afford elections. We trusted the Janata Dal (S) despite certain policy decisions taken by that Government which were against the basic tenets of the Congress.

Unfortunately, there was a total breach of trust when we found that surveillance was being carried out at my home. Our request for action against the persons involved was not acceded to by the very Government we supported.

Total trust and faith is very important for effective functioning in Government and when such a breach takes place it is extremely difficult to restore any such relationship. And yet, we reiterate that we did not withdraw support and exercised great restraint. It was the Prime Minister's unilateral decision to resign.

For any country to progress there has to be a stable Government with clear cut policies. We, the Congress have in the past displayed such stability whereas other Governments have failed to do so.

I am confident that with your support and the support of your friends and colleagues we can form a stable Government at the Centre and can work hard together to build a strong and progressive India - the India of our dreams.

With best wishes.

Yours sincerely,

APPENDIX 2

Some Random Personal Memories of Abdul Majeed Khwaja

Part A:
A Personal Statement:

My father, Abdul Majeed Khwaja (1885-1962) was born at Aligarh, Uttar Pradesh, educated at Cambridge University, and called to the Bar in 1910. Under Ghandhiji's inspiration he gave up his flourishing legal practice at Patna in 1919, joined the struggle for Indian freedom and suffered imprisonment for his role in the Civil Disobedience and *Khilafat* movements. He actively opposed the partition of the country in 1947 and dedicated his entire life to the promotion of Hindu-Muslim harmony and the attainment of a united free India.

He was one of the founders of the *Jamia Millia Islamia* that was established at Aligarh in 1920, under Gandhiji's and Maulana Muhammad Ali's inspiration, to provide higher Western education on nationalist lines as an alternative to the British system of college education that prevailed in colonial times. He permanently shifted from Patna to Aligarh to give full time attention to the infant institution. This meant immense financial sacrifice on his part, but he undertook the task as a labor of love and as a part of his patriotic and Islamic duty. He incurred huge financial debts during the period 1920-25.

Appendix 2: Some Random Personal Memories of Abdul Majeed Khwaja

In 1925, with Ghandhiji's and Hakim Ajmal Khan's concurrence and blessings, Khwaja Sahab shifted the institution to Karol Bagh, Delhi and handed over charge to Dr. Zakir Husain, who had just returned from Germany after completing his higher studies in Economics. I was born in 1928 and father, after a long gap of six years, resumed legal practice at the High Court at Allahabad. Domestic and health reasons kept him out of active politics until the end of 1943, though he continued liberally supporting the *Jamia* and the Congress party. The raising of the demand for Pakistan stirred him into actively opposing the partition of the motherland on religious lines. He and some close associates founded the umbrella *All India Muslim Majlis* to co-ordinate the activities of all Muslims opposed to partition on the basis of the 'two-nation' theory and Khwaja was unanimously elected as its President. In this capacity he met the British Cabinet Mission at Delhi and also extensively toured the country to influence Muslim public opinion in favor of preserving the unity of India. He and others like him patiently bore the ire of the separatist forces without losing faith in their mission, which, however, failed to materialize. But for him *Bapu's* assassination was a shock he could never overcome and thereafter Khwaja almost faded out of active election politics in independent India.

In 1949 he somehow managed, at great personal sacrifice, to send me up to his old *alma mater*, Christ's College at Cambridge University, for my Moral Sciences Tripos. In 1953 I was appointed lecturer in Philosophy at my *alma mater*, Aligarh Muslim University (AMU). Father was not very happy at my choice of the teaching profession, but he had to accept the facts of life. I worked as a teacher for four years and was tinkering with the idea of getting a doctorate in philosophy from Germany or some other foreign university. Meanwhile I was almost picked up, as it were, by Jawaharlal Nehru, to contest for a seat in the Second Lok Sabha (1957-62) as a part of his declared desire to induct fresh blood in the Congress party. I was one of the four or five young or youngish persons so selected. Once again father was not enthused by the idea because of financial and other reasons, but after some initial reluctance he accepted the sudden change in my life situation.

Appendix 2: Some Random Personal Memories of Abdul Majeed Khwaja

There is no doubt that Jawaharlal's choice fell on me because of his love and regard for my father; his old comrade from Cambridge days and also deeply committed to Gandhiji's ethical approach to politics. There is also no doubt that it was the power of the Congress ticket in those early days that ensured my success at the polls.

I was, obviously, a political moron though I certainly cherished high ideals and also entertained some illusions about myself. I completed my full five year term in Parliament, but I realized that I was not gifted enough to combine the pursuit of knowledge or wisdom with the pursuit of power. With a heavy heart I had to disappoint my mentor and beloved leader who wanted me to continue in politics. I returned to my old teaching job in March 1962. Shortly afterwards father passed away in December of the same year.

All the family members deeply mourned father's passing away and numerous friends and members of the public and prominent leaders and public figures sent messages of condolence to us. It was quite natural for a large number of father's old associates and friends to suggest that some suitable person or persons should be asked to compose a biography of Khwaja Sahab to provide for posterity a written record of the life and achievements of an eminent person. Being the eldest son of my parents and also in view of my academic background I should have embarked upon this work as a labor of love. But I must confess that I felt myself to be unqualified to undertake this task since I had no personal knowledge of the major achievements and contributions of my father that had taken place much before my birth in 1926. I was also aware that father had been very careless and unconcerned to keep proper records. I did seek the consent of some old colleagues and friends of father to contribute to a proposed collection of essays on my father but they also needed records and references that I could hardly manage.

My younger brother, Raveend, had much greater personal knowledge of some events and incidents connected with father's political activities in the period 1944-48. He had also played a very active role

Appendix 2: Some Random Personal Memories of Abdul Majeed Khwaja

as a student leader in the Aligarh Muslim University (AMU) in the middle forties of the last century trying to combat the politics of separatism and partition. He accompanied father on an extensive tour of the country to oppose the idea of partition. But he was in the same boat as myself in regard to the much earlier golden period of our father's rich contributions to the Indian freedom and *Khilafat* movements, his constructive work under the auspices of the *Hindustani Culture Society*, Allahabad, and his efforts to reform the Muslim law of divorce. The youngest among us brothers and sisters, Ajmal, knew the least in the matters concerned. My sisters, all considerably older than the brothers had seen father function together with such stalwarts and luminaries, as Gandhiji, the Nehrus, Ali Brothers, Sarojini Naidu, Hakim Ajmal Khan, Dr. Ansari and many others, but they too did not have any records to rely upon.

As time passed by and no work was done on the project (for which I felt personally responsible) father's close friends and associates who had consented to contribute to the memorial project started to pass away, one by one. As of today there is only one person alive who had promised to write a chapter for the proposed book and actually handed over the Urdu composition to me. Meanwhile the Aligarh University launched an Urdu project, *Eminent Aligarians*, in several volumes, and included father's name in the said project. A high level editorial committee selected competent writers to write on the life and achievements of different personalities. It is most unfortunate that the person who had been commissioned to write on Khwaja Sahab failed to complete the job not once but thrice. Later on he assured me that he would compensate for this lapse by writing a full length well researched work on the subject. However, even after the lapse of some ten years or more he has failed to deliver.

Under the above circumstances I have been compelled to abort the project as it had been conceived several years ago. However, since I have already crossed eighty and can exit into the other world any moment without any notice I have solemnly ventured to pen an essay on my father, under the title, *The Islamic Vision of Abdul Majeed*

Appendix 2: Some Random Personal Memories of Abdul Majeed Khwaja

Khwaja. This would have been my own contribution to the proposed volume had the project materialized. This essay would also serve to supplement an earlier long essay of mine: *The Islamic Vision of Sir Syed.* This piece forms a critical introduction to an Urdu anthology of the writings of the Father of the Aligarh Movement. The book was published by the *New Aligarh Movement*, in 1988.

This essay on Khwaja Sahab is an attempt to bring alive the living thoughts and attitudes of Khwaja Sahab to religion and politics. I have written from intimate and inside knowledge of father's life and character. I have not consulted any book, nor given any references, as this was quite unnecessary for my purpose. In any case, no references on this subject exist, apart from Khwaja Sahab's foreword to the printed Convocation Address Sir P.C.Ray delivered in 1923 at the *Jamia Millia Islamia*, Aligarh when Khwaja was its Vice-Chancellor.

My father was a man of great integrity, moral courage and intellectual clarity, though he had no pretensions to scholarship and was definitely averse to sitting down and undertaking the pains of putting his thoughts on paper. In all humility, sincere admiration and gratitude to my father I would like to say that my book, *Living the Quran in Our Times*, is at bottom, a systematic and philosophical elaboration of the essence of Islam as Khwaja Sahab used to express his ideas and thoughts in the natural course of time in personal conversations with family members, personal talks or discussions with friends or associates and also at public gatherings. However, I must add that my presentation of the ideas and views of our father is my 'take' of what I heard him say in personal conversations or public talks. Others including our own family might not have exactly the same 'take' as mine. In any case I have aimed to be a faithful reporter.

Furthermore, I hold that Khwaja's vision of Islam has a permanent value for all Muslims and others in the task of the proper and balanced understanding of the function of religion, as such, in the modem age. I should like to say the same about the already well acclaimed contributions of Abul Kalam Azad, Iqbal, Muhammad Abduh, Shibli, and

Appendix 2: Some Random Personal Memories of Abdul Majeed Khwaja

Aslam Jairajpuri *et al* and of course, to the father of modern Islam in the Indian subcontinent, Sir Syed. I would like to pay a special tribute to the unwritten but subtle and very positive contribution, Zakir Sahab, the first Muslim President of the Republic of India, and his brilliant team comprising Abid Husain, Muhammad Mujeeb, K.A.Hamied, made in this regard. Here I must also express my admiration for the solid intellectual contribution made by Ghulamus Sayidain and Rafiq Zakaria, and the unwritten contribution of Bashir Husain Zaidi, as Zakir Sahab's immediate successor at the helm of the Aligarh Muslim University (AMU). I honestly maintain that he sincerely tried to steer the boat of the AMU in the direction solemnly set by his predecessor. Zaidi Sahab achieved a lot despite the strong winds of opposition due to cultural lag of the Aligarh community in general: a quite natural and innocent sociological phenomenon in all developing societies.

Unfortunately, Muslims from the very beginning have practiced the 'monolithic' approach to Monotheism and the revealed Scripture instead of the 'pluralistic' or 'conceptually permissive' approach to the human spiritual quest. The resultant 'fear of persecution or heresy' has ever hovered over the Muslim believer's quest for authenticity and conceptual clarity. The fear of persecution simply must go if we want Muslim believers to be authentically committed to Islam. The core of the Islamic faith, to my mind, is the belief in Monotheism and a genuine commitment to the mystery of Quranic revelation plus the total sincerity and integrity of Prophet Muhammad.

The illustrious personalities I have mentioned above, each in one's own way, had integrated this core faith with basic modern concepts and values that include secular democracy, polymorphous human rights and complete tolerance. They were all authentic persons, who had genuine religious faith (the core of the Islamic faith) and they were also committed to the core values of modern democracy. However, every individual Muslim will have to discover the paradigm that best suits him or her as a unique individual. The patient search for the 'personalized paradigm' of religious faith without fear or favor and the atmosphere of abundant loving tolerance, are the basic needs of

Appendix 2: Some Random Personal Memories of Abdul Majeed Khwaja

all humanity (including Muslim believers, be they citizens of secular societies or Islamic states) in the modern age of science and technology. These two, as such, are neutral to religious faith provided the believer chooses such a paradigm of the concerned faith as does not clash with the 'methodologically legitimate' jurisdiction of science. This insight is the indispensable foundational truth on which humanity has to build its future and the direction in which we must move, failing which we are likely to perish.

In view of the above considerations I do hope and trust that the Vice-Chancellor of *Jamia Millia Islamia* would kindly consider devising ways and means, as he thinks best, for the preparation and publication of a suitable full length memorial volume on the life and contributions of a person who was an authentic Muslim, an equally authentic secular patriot, a major benefactor of the Jamia from its birth, and had the unique honor of being Chancellor of the Jamia for a quarter of a century.

PART B:
SOME RANDOM OBSERVATIONS AND PERSONAL MEMORIES OF ABDUL MAJEED KHWAJA:

1. About 5' 8" in height, Khwaja had broad shoulders, a radiantly fair and smooth complexion (right till old age), medium sized dark brown eyes, a well proportioned straight nose, an elongated cast of face with well filled cheeks, a finely chiseled mouth and a shapely chin bearing a French-cut beard, the only minor flaw in his almost perfect body was, a, relatively, short neck. His striking personality made many say that he was even more handsome and physically magnetic than his friend and comrade Jawaharlal.

2. As a youth I once referred to 'Nehruji' in the hearing of my father. This was at Allahabad. Father immediately chided me for not saying 'Jawahar *Chacha*', and proceeded to relate his own childhood experience long back in Aligarh. In the nineties of the 19th century

Appendix 2: Some Random Personal Memories of Abdul Majeed Khwaja

he was playing near the main entrance of his father's house when a spacious horse carriage arrived and some distinguished looking visitor alighted and enquired if Molvi Sahab (my grandfather) was at home. The young child (my father) did not know the visitor's name, so he first quietly asked a servant who the visitor was and then rushed to inform his father that *Raja Sahab*, Mursan had come. Immediately he received a slap from his father for not calling *Raja Sahab* as Uncle from Mursan.

3. Our first-born child (a boy) was born in 1950. According to tradition the grandfather selected the name, and father chose 'Jawahar Kabir'. He left the choice of name to me when our second son was born. We named him 'Sundar Habib'. Our third child was a daughter. Again, father selected the name 'Geeta Anjum'. For our youngest child (a boy) born two years before Khwaja Sahab passed away we selected the name, 'Nasser Navin'. Father put into practice his long held view that throughout social space and time personal names had come from the language of the tribe or clan belonging to a region rather than from any religion. He always reminded his fellow Muslims in private as well as in public that when the earliest Arabs of Mecca first accepted Islam they did not change their pre-Islamic names to some supposedly Islamic name. Among his children my younger brother, Rasheed, and I had inwardly accepted father's approach early in our youth. My spouse and I, therefore, welcomed and rejoiced at father's choice of Indian or Hindi names for his grandchildren, first for our son, and then for our daughter. When several persons in our circle of friends and the family mildly objected to a Muslim child being given a 'Hindu' name father pointed out that Jawahar was actually an Arabic word, and not Hindu or Muslim. He also added that he stood for adopting Hindi names that were sweet and short, not Hindu names having a religious significance

4. Father loved to invite his dear friend, Pandit Sundarlal, the famous disciple of Gandhi, to address Muslim gatherings for commemorating the birth and character of Prophet Muhammad. The Pandit's transparently sincere and soul stirring speeches and the tears

Appendix 2: Some Random Personal Memories of Abdul Majeed Khwaja

he shed kept large audiences captive for hours at a stretch. I have heard and experienced his magical sermons several times. Sundarlalji's younger friend and disciple, Bishambar Nath Pandey, who edited the presentation volumes, *The Spirit of India*, in honor of Indira Gandhi, and also served as Governor of Orissa, had learnt his speaking skills from Sundarlal himself.

5. Gandhiji's elder son, Harilal, converted to Islam in the mid thirties of the last century. This event caused a sensation and much controversy in the entire country as was to be expected. Some Muslim quarters celebrated this event by lionizing the young heroic son of the Mahatma, and showered gifts of money and invitations to speak at public functions, while others, presumably, felt embarrassed that the Mahatma's own son had repudiated the great leader. In the midst of the crisis Gandhiji wrote a four/six page letter in his own handwriting to his dear friend and admirer, Khwaja. I found the letter in father's papers in the late sixties and read it, fascinated by every word Bapu had written.

Most unfortunately I handed over the said letter, along with some other letters of Gandhiji to my brother, Raveend, who is unable to trace them now. I am told that the letter must have been copied and preserved by Gandhiji's personal staff before being posted to the addressee. Nothing will give me greater joy if the copy in fact survives; I am going to make farther enquiries at the earliest.

It is well known that Harilal was a profoundly disturbed and unhappy soul who hankered after peace of mind but could never win it. He took to blaming his father for his own limitations and failures in life. His conversion to Islam was far from being a genuine spiritual experience. It was a mere pathological reaction to his inner frustrations and after a few months or weeks of basking in the dubious adulation from some short sighted Muslim quarters; Harilal reverted to his earlier depressed state of mind. Gandhiji had foreseen the result and had merely taken his true friend and follower into confidence. The letter was a moving and transparent document written by an authentic and committed soul, firmly rooted in his own faith, but full of loving tolerance for the genuine faith of all others.

6. Khwaja was a man of high integrity and extra-ordinary moral courage and unswerving determination. He stood by the truth, as he saw it, without fear or favor. He never hankered after any position though he did seek constructive power as a man of action rather than merely of words and dreams. When political power eluded him after independence due to the passing away of his mentor Gandhi and his own reluctance to play second fiddle to those in power at the national level, he confined himself to exercising power in the affairs of the Aligarh Muslim University as a member of the Executive Council and as Honorary Manager of the *Islamia College*, Etawah. He also did not interfere with the affairs of the *Jamia* at Delhi although he remained Chancellor until his death in 1962 due to the insistence of old comrades.

Khwaja was extremely liberal in helping friends and even his critics when they sought his help in some just cause. His donations to Congress party funds, educational, cultural and other public institutions were very generous in relation to his actual assets. He donated his inherited family house in Aligarh to a local school, his rich personal library to *Jamia Millia Islamia*, in addition to spending continually huge sums on its maintenance from 1920 to 1926, his huge Law Library to the AMU, considerable land to the Barasehni Degree College, Aligarh, and a huge chunk of land for constructing the proposed Medical College of the AMU. He also gave several scholarships and stipends to deserving students for studying in India and abroad or for establishing small-scale business or production units. He also gave grants and loans to those who approached him for help, but never talked about such matters. A lot of his time was taken up in such works instead of pursuing his own serious work of writing his memoirs and editing his scattered Urdu poems and verses of no ordinary quality. It is, indeed, a pity that a person of his intellectual brilliance, integrity and varied contacts and experiences could not put his thoughts on paper.

7. Father often expressed his strong disapproval of the well-known grudge of the *Shia* Muslims against the first three *Caliphs* who suc-

Appendix 2: Some Random Personal Memories of Abdul Majeed Khwaja

ceeded as the heads of the Islamic state after the death of the Prophet. Khwaja could never digest the open and public abuse of the first three *Caliphs* or the doctrine of habitually concealing one's inner convictions. However, he ardently admired the moral courage and principled stand of the Prophet's younger grandson, Husain, against the establishment. I had often heard father expressing this sentiment. But the intensity of the sentiment came to my knowledge only when I heard father address a *Majlis* function at the residence of my sister's father-in-law, Ali Hasan Khan at Gadhi Samdabad, District Pratapgarh. This was in the late thirties or early forties of the last century. The other speaker was the renowned orator, Syed Kalbe Abbas of Allahabad, who was known to cast a spell on his hearers. In any case, Khwaja never allowed polemics to stand in the way of his warm relationships with several *Shia* friends. I cannot help thinking that his self-proclaimed distrust of *Shias*, in general, was more an exercise of his irrepressible wit and a pose that he enjoyed enacting before Sunni fanatics rather than serious prejudice as such.

8. Khwaja Sahab loved to hear Urdu and Persian ghazals, *bhajans* and *sitar* recitals. However, to the best of my memory, I never heard him praise or admire Western music. He firmly rejected the orthodox Muslim view that music was the gateway to moral corruption. On the other hand, he regarded music as the gateway to spiritual catharsis. In view of his greatly developed musical and poetic sensibilities his spiritual mentor, Mir Qurban Ali of Jaipur of the *Naqshbandiya* order, had exempted him from the traditional orthodox restriction on listening to music. Khwaja was drawn to *Sufi* thought and poetry, but he disliked credulity and the uncritical acceptance of miracles and the granting of boons by saints and holy men. He believed in seeking help directly from God and exhorted Muslims to combine piety and prayer with rational action.

9. My father's parenting style was marked by the traditional oriental aloofness of the father from his children, specially the sons. He expected them to obey their father in all matters, though he never reprimanded them if and when his children failed to do so. He, how-

Appendix 2: Some Random Personal Memories of Abdul Majeed Khwaja

ever, felt a silent hurt when his wishes or expectations were not met with. I vividly recollect how unhappy I made him when I offered him a gift from out of the first salary I received as lecturer in philosophy at the AMU. I knew well his fondness for Turkish cigarettes that he used to purchase from the famous Macropolo firm of Delhi. I, therefore, asked the firm to make a gift packing of an assorted carton of the finest brands they sold. I placed the impressive packet with an attached loving note in his bedroom and thought what a good deed I had done. But it turned out that father thought that I had blundered into wasting my money on expensive cigarettes. He refused to accept the gift and I had to request a local dealer at Aligarh to buy them back. Likewise, he insisted that I should keep my wife and children at the family house at Aligarh instead of moving them to Delhi after my election to Parliament. However, at my insistence he reluctantly allowed my request. His parenting style was the same with his other children. At the same time he was full of concern and solicitude for his family and friends and was ready for liberal financial help at the cost of his own comforts.

10. Among his fads was his habit of ad hoc constructing buildings without previous planning or consultation from architects. This led to the need of frequent alterations or demolitions and waste of money. He was extremely fond of throwing grand parties to friends and public figures. He loved sweet dishes and insisted on at least one sweet dish being on the table at both lunch and dinner. However, he ate very little of the sweet dish. He loved mangoes, but his main criterion of their good quality was their sweetness rather than flavor. He was not fond of hills and hill stations, but he enjoyed the sea beach.

11. Among his habitual weaknesses was his last minute packing before travel, poor time management and also poor filing of papers. He never resorted to weeding of papers with the result that important and useless papers got badly mixed up as a matter of routine. All the family members and his old and faithful valet, Chotey, who was completely illiterate, then embarked upon a search campaign to retrieve the needed paper. The weakness that I, as a son, wish he had overcome, was his

Appendix 2: Some Random Personal Memories of Abdul Majeed Khwaja

utter disregard for preserving his poetic compositions in Urdu. There can be little doubt that his poetic gift was considerable. He used to scribble verses, or complete *ghazals* on any piece of paper he could lay his hands on and then not bother to preserve them. At times he noted them down in mini pocket diaries but the contents were almost illegible due to incredibly small handwriting. Likewise, he never properly filed his correspondence papers though I managed to salvage what I could and passed them on to the Nehru Museum, Delhi.

12. Here are some examples of Khwaja's wit and his gift of quick repartee:

Father once invited an English couple (an old Cambridge friend and Judge of the High Court and his wife) to dinner at his residence at Allahabad and served a very sumptuous meal. The desert was delicious mangoes. Father himself sliced the mangoes before offering them to the guests, but he did not help himself to the desert. The lady guest noticed this and asked her host why was this. Father answered that he was too fond of mangoes to eat them in the company of European guests. The answer made the guests all the more curious to know the full reason. Father hinted that mangoes are a special fruit and they taste best when eaten in a special way. The lady guest became curious to know the proper way. Father than ordered a servant to bring a large bowl filled with water. He then removed his Indian jacket and rolled up his shirtsleeves, peeled a mango to the full and started biting into the fruit, to the merriment of all.

Father was once a guest at a dinner party hosted by Mr. and Mrs. Jinnah at Bombay and was seated next to a Muslim public figure who held rather orthodox views about the proper dress code for Muslim women. Father and he were on friendly terms. In the course of polite dinner conversation father heard him quietly curse the devil in the traditional Islamic manner. When father asked him why he was doing so he slyly answered that the low-neck design of the dinner gown the hostess was wearing was prompting him to do so. Father kept quiet for the moment, but soon after he quietly started praising Allah in the traditional Islamic manner. Now it was the turn of his conservative friend to know the reason. Father mischievously answered back that he was admiring the elegance of the dress of the hostess.

Father smoked cigarettes having Turkish tobacco instead of the usual Virginian brands. Some of his friends specially asked for his brand just for the sake of change and he readily offered his German Silver case to them. One day his friend, Sir Wazir Hasan, who after retiring as Chief Justice of the Avadh High Court had joined the Allahabad High Court Bar, asked him for his special brand of Turkish cigarettes. Father took out one from his case and handed it over to Sir Wazir, who demanded an explanation for this rather odd behavior. Father replied he was afraid of the *Shia* touch.

13. Muhammad Hadi, a very close associate of father in Aligarh and a fellow Gandhian worker during the heady *Khilafat* days related to me on May 18, 1963 the following two incidents. He told me that these were in his personal knowledge:

(a) In 1921 Mr. Liddard, then Collector of Aligarh, accompanied by a few constables, came in person to Khwaja's house, Habib Bagh, to confiscate the arms license of Khwaja. Motilal Nehru was at the time staying with Khwaja as his guest. When the Collector asked Khwaja Sahab to surrender the arms and the license Khwaja replied as follows:

"Mr. Liddard, In so far as I am non-violent I don't need my fire arms. When I choose to become violent, I shall not need your license. So, both your license and my fire arms are useless for me".

The Collector had no answer, but he collected the license and the arms and left.

(b) Khwaja Sahab had made a general appeal to the Muslims of Aligarh not to sacrifice any cow on the *Eid uz zuha* (in the period, 1921-22) as a mark of respect and solidarity with the religious sentiments of their Hindu brothers. The appeal had worked. But one gentleman (probably named Sheikh Abdur Raheem) from the city announced

Appendix 2: Some Random Personal Memories of Abdul Majeed Khwaja

before a large gathering at which Khwaja was also present, that he had sacrificed a cow to irritate the leader concerned. Khwaja quietly took out a five-rupee note from his pocket and offered it to the gentleman with the following remark: "You did so not to please God, but to displease me. Please, now sacrifice a goat for the pleasure of God".

PART C:
THE ISLAMIC VISION OF ABDUL MAJEED KHWAJA: INTRODUCTION

Abdul Majeed Khwaja (1885-1962,) was one of the galaxy of selfless freedom fighters, public figures and patriots inspired by Gandhiji in the first quarter of the 20th century. His father, Khwaja Muhammad Yusuf, (d. 1902) was a close associate of Sir Syed Ahmad Khan, the principal architect of the Aligarh movement for the social and cultural regeneration and modernization of the Indian Muslims after 1857. Khwaja's early education and upbringing took place under his father under the influence of Sir Syed and Sami Ullah Khan. He studied Arabic and Persian with competent private tutors at Aligarh but he did not pass any formal examination until he left for *Christ's College, Cambridge* in 1906. This was the College where Sir Syed had sent his son, Syed Mahmud, some thirty years earlier. Young Khwaja's considerable grounding in Arabic and Persian and his subsequent studies in modern history and comparative religions under world renowned intellectuals and scholars at Cambridge gave him an authentic insight into the modern scientific outlook. Khwaja returned home in 1910 after graduating in History and having been called to the Bar. He was two years senior to Jawaharlal Nehru in Cambridge.

In Cambridge he associated with the famous Islamists, E.G.Browne, Nicholson, and the romantic anti-imperialist Arabist and liberal author, Wilfred Scawen Blunt. He also came in close contact with Muhammad Iqbal, Jawaharlal Nehru, Muhammad Wasim, and Haroon Khan Sherwani at Cambridge and with T.A.K.Sherwani, and Syed Mahmud, among others, at London. It was also in Cambridge that he first saw

Appendix 2: Some Random Personal Memories of Abdul Majeed Khwaja

and almost immediately came under the spell of one, M.K.Gandhi, who happened to be there to address a student gathering. Gandhi was then a famous Barrister and champion of human rights in South Africa. Gandhi returned to his chosen place of humanitarian work in South Africa and Khwaja returned home to practice law, first at his native Aligarh and later at the Patna High Court. His practice flourished and he had bright prospects of being raised to the Bench. But then, all of a sudden, his life took a u-turn at the magic touch, as it were, of Barrister Gandhi now turned into Mahatma Gandhi. He was then staying (to the best of my knowledge) with Barrister Mazharul Haque, and after finishing his day's work at the High Court Khwaja often dropped in at Haque's place to call on Gandhiji.

One evening *Bapu* jokingly pulled at Khwaja's lawyer's collar bands and asked when were they going to disappear from his neck? And lo! Khwaja, the ardent admirer who until a few minutes earlier, was hopeful of shortly being elevated to the Bench at the Patna High Court, decided to give up his legal practice then and there. This is what transpired in those fateful moments. Khwaja told Gandhiji that he would resign soon after he was actually elevated to the Bench, since this would make a much greater impact upon public opinion and promote the national cause. His mentor gently reminded him that this was his ego whispering in his soul, not the way of *'Nabiji'* (Prophet Muhammad). And Khwaja's mind was made up in this split second. The *Khilafat* movement was already on and the Ali Brothers, along with Maulana Abul Kalam Azad and others were in detention.

More and more Indian Muslims began coming under the magnetic spell of the Mahatma. The rising new leader of the august Indian National Congress was eager to make the Muslim cause of *'khilafat'* an integral plank of the National Congress, in addition to the government rectifying the 'Punjab atrocities' at the Jallianwala Bagh and the demand for the speedy transition to self-rule under Dominion status. After the annual session of the Congress at Nagpur and later at a special session at Ahmedabad the hitherto Indian National Congress was transmuted, as it were, into Mahatma Gandhi Congress. From

Appendix 2: Some Random Personal Memories of Abdul Majeed Khwaja

then onwards Khwaja became one of the most prominent among the younger lieutenants of the Mahatma, next only to the Ali Brothers, Hakim Ajmal Khan, Dr. M.A.Ansari, and Maulana Azad. On the other hand, the liberal and more or less modernized wing of the Congress, including the hitherto 'ambassador of Hindu-Muslim unity', Muhammad Ali Jinnah, parted company from the great organization. Thus began the 'Gandhian era' of the Congress that was, in origin, the product of British liberalism, at its best, symbolized by A.O.Hume, and the Indian Renaissance symbolized by Ram Mohan Roy of Bengal and Dadabhai Nawroji of Bombay and the great Tagore's.

The induction of Muhammad Ali, an Oxford educated, scintillating Muslim into the 'Gandhianized' Congress led to the blowing of a new wind in the MAO College of Aligarh, the great legacy of Sir Syed, whose Aligarh Movement performed the same function for north Indian Muslims as the Bengal Renaissance, about a century earlier, had done for the country as a whole. Genuinely captivated by the moral genius and the spiritualized politics of the Mahatma, Muhammad Ali accepted *'ahimsa'* as a strategy though perhaps not as a principle. He stood disappointed with the political and cultural stagnation of the Muslims the world over and the slow pace of India's advance from colonial rule to full independence. Under Gandhiji's inspiration and the blessings of the old Deoband patriotic old guard, symbolized by the highly venerated Mahmudul Hasan; Muhammad Ali established the *Jamia Millia Islamia* at Aligarh in 1920. His active role in the growth and survival of his own baby, however, was short lived, thanks to his over active public engagements and activities at the national level.

In 1921 Muhammad Ali handed over temporary charge for a few months to Muhammad Alam Sahab and then finally to Khwaja. It was Khwaja Sahab who steadily nursed the infant with his lifeblood and tremendous financial sacrifices till 1925, before himself shifting the *Jamia* to Karol Bagh at Delhi. With Gandhiji's concurrence and blessings Khwaja then handed over charge to Dr. Zakir Husain. Zakir Sahab was a student leader of the Aligarh Muslim University who

Appendix 2: Some Random Personal Memories of Abdul Majeed Khwaja

had joined the *Jamia* at its very inception as a graduate instructor and then left for Germany to pursue higher studies in Economics. It was Zakir Sahab who from 1925 onwards piloted the boat of the *Jamia* in the stormy seas for the next two decades and more until he was asked by the Muslim Doyen of the Congress organization, and Education Minister at the Centre, Abul Kalam Azad, to head the Aligarh Muslim University shortly after independence.

The period, 1925-30, saw mutual disillusionment settle between Muhammad Ali and his supporters on the one side and the top Congress leadership, including Gandhiji and Motilal Nehru, on the other. The fateful '*Nehru Report*' is the landmark document of this crucial period. However, Khwaja, along with Ajmal Khan, Dr. Ansari, T.A.K. Sherwani, Abul Kalam Azad, Dr. Syed Mahmud, Rafi Ahmad Kidwai and some other stalwarts firmly remained in the Gandhian camp, though domestic reasons induced Khwaja to withdraw himself from active polities for a pretty long period. However, he was back at centre stage once again from 1944 to 1947 in his vain bid to prevent the partition of the country on religious lines.

This period was very trying and painful for all Indians, specially, Indian Muslims who were opposed to mixing religion with politics. When the Congress High Command made a compromise with the Muslim League these honest and brave souls felt tragically deserted by all sides. Few among the Hindu public have ever understood the pathos and tragedy of those Indian Muslims who were ridiculed as 'traitors to Islam', 'Hindu lackeys', 'Congress show-boys', and 'political orphans' in this period, while, on the other hand, their loyalty to their cherished motherland was soon to become questionable the moment Pakistan was born. The simple truth of the matter is that the Indian Muslims are the greatest losers, emotionally, politically and economically by the partition of the country. They were not less eager; their sacrifices were not less than others for the cause of national freedom of the motherland. But when freedom came they were condemned to drink the cup of political marginalization on the logic of the two-nation theory. However, I submit, in all humility, that the most poignant suffering fell to the lot of the 'Frontier Gandhi', Khan Abdul Ghaffar Khan. 'Darkness at noon' was his lot. A tragic finale, indeed, to the symphony of the freedom struggle: the strangulation of personal liberty in the very first embrace of national freedom!

KHWAJA'S APPROACH TO ISLAM:

Khwaja's views on religion and politics were not a patchwork response but an organic synthesis of religious liberalism and secular politics. I do believe that his blending of the two is of permanent relevance to all Muslims in the modern age. He was a product of the Aligarh Movement in the second half of the 19th century, but he also enjoyed the advantages of a Cambridge education. In retrospect it is pretty evident that the Aligarh Movement had a two-fold agenda, the spreading of modern education among Muslims, and also the inner growth of their idea of Islam. Sir Syed achieved considerable success in the first objective and this greatly enabled Muslims to gain materially and professionally under the British rule. But his success in the second objective was just marginal, The English educated Muslims certainly became 'Westernized' in their dress, style of living and eating and entertainments, etc. but this was not the same as accepting the rational or scientific outlook on life (in the higher sense) that had 'modernized' Sir Syed and the most enlightened of his close associates. Many Aligarians, 'suited-booted', as they were, did not, or could not change orthodox social attitudes and mind-sets. Consciously or unconsciously, they had learnt to live in two split compartments, by turns. Their 'religious compartment' was presided over by the 'ulema' while their 'worldly compartment' by modem thinkers and writers (Western or Indian). This was very different from Sir Syed's own vision of Islamic liberalism that involved a radical 'demythologization' of Islam. His objective was to distil the nuclear core of the Islamic faith out of the social and cultural gloss that, in the natural course of time, had accumulated around the Islamic faith. This happens in the case of all religions, and, therefore, creative followers of all religious traditions try to discover and rediscover the core of their own religious faith.

Appendix 2: Some Random Personal Memories of Abdul Majeed Khwaja

Sir Syed believed that being a good Muslim meant nothing more and nothing less than pure Monotheism and faith that the Quran was, in some sense or other, the revealed 'Word of God' rather than the product of human reflection and linguistic formulation. Belief in myths and miracles and various social, cultural, political and economic institutions and practices in different Muslim societies were not integral parts of the nuclear core of the Islamic faith, as such. Even the putative sayings of the Prophet, though worthy of veneration and authoritative (up to a point) could not claim the same binding power and authority of the revealed scripture. Khwaja had fully and honestly absorbed this liberating insight of Sir Syed as had Amir Ali, Iqbal, Azad, Shibli and many other enlightened and liberal Muslims from Aligarh and other centers of modern education.

Khwaja Sahab's thinking was rooted in the Quran over which he had a good grasp due to his familiarity with Arabic. He remembered by heart numerous Quranic texts, which he readily quoted in his conversations and discussions with friends and in public speeches. However, he was ever careful to distinguish between Divine revelations and their human interpretations. For instance, he held that the Quranic prohibition on eating pork did not necessarily rule out using lard as a cooking medium or using bristles in toothbrushes. One may or may not agree with this line of thinking. But what is significant is Khwaja Sahab's rational approach to Quran and Islam and his awareness that the revealed text was amenable to plural interpretations. And this is the starting point of tolerance and of a rational approach to the human situation.

Khwaja was, thus, opposed to the idea that to be a good Muslim the believer must follow a closed and rigid interpretation of the Quran and the *Sunnah*. He held that one could be a true Muslim without losing one's freedom of choice in an ever changing society, provided one adhered to the spirit of the revealed text and the basic values reflected in the character and conduct of the Prophet. This, I submit, was a very different proposition from the traditional Islamic piety into which he, his parents or Sir Syed had been born and brought

Appendix 2: Some Random Personal Memories of Abdul Majeed Khwaja

up. The reason was his father's very close association with the Islamic reformation initiated by Sir Syed at Aligarh. Khwaja's later exposure to modernity during his stay in Cambridge led the young Khwaja to the enlightened and liberal approach to all religions, including Islam as such. His historical approach to different human civilizations and cultures, belief and value systems had deeply convinced him of the presence of one cultural constant underlying plural forms of worship and different patterns of social behavior.

Khwaja's style of Islamic piety centered on being truthful, honest and adhering to the spirit of the Quran and the character of the Prophet rather than on lengthy liturgies, prayers at shrines and tombs, seeking boons from holy men and saints. He said the Quran was a Divine medical prescription that ought to be used rather than reverently kissed. He was strongly drawn to Sufi thought and poetry but rejected popular Sufi lore and belief in miracles. He appreciated music, painting and dance as art forms. He was the first Muslim in the Aligarh region to bring out his wife and daughters in mixed gatherings without the traditional veil, though he shunned ballroom dancing and free mixing of men and women.

Khwaja held that to be a good Muslim did not entail that Muslims should think in terms of being superior to the rest of their fellow countrymen whose souls had to be saved from eternal damnation. He honestly held that that Quranic injunctions dealt, primarily, with spiritual and transcendental beliefs and articles of faith together with basic moral values, and only, marginally, with political, economic, social and cultural matters that belonged to the secular sphere of human life. In other words, he was totally and firmly opposed to the 'totalist' function of religion as a complete code of conduct in every walk of life. This liberal approach to Islam was the legacy of the great Syed himself after he had outgrown the earlier impact of his former mentor, Shah Waliullah of Delhi.

Khwaja repeatedly mentioned before family, friends and in public that different religions were different paths to a common goal, or

Appendix 2: Some Random Personal Memories of Abdul Majeed Khwaja

different languages to express a common meaning. It mattered little which path one took or which language one spoke so long as one honestly tried (through actual deeds) to reach the common goal. Another example he gave was that different religions were like different flowers that spread their fragrance in the garden of life. All should be appreciated without one religion trying to displace the other, or any believer diluting one's own personal faith in favor of some other. Gandhiji also expressed the same sentiments and views.

Khwaja had no difficulty in harmonizing his deep Islamic faith with secular nationalism. He often repeated in private and public that he loved Islam as much as he loved India, just as he loved equally his mother and father. He also pointed out the futility of the question that many political sophists enjoyed putting to Muslims before independence and even now: "Are you Indians first, and Muslims second, or is it the other way round?" Khwaja used to reply that he was a Muslim and Indian at one and the same time just as he was the child of both his parents at one and the same time.

Khwaja not only venerated the Gita but went to the extent of openly and repeatedly affirming that the wide spread Hindu practice of idol worship (though a formal violation of Monotheism) should be viewed in the light of the underlying basic Hindu belief that all gods and goddesses are, ultimately, themselves the manifestations of one Supreme Being or Reality. And this is what Gandhi himself believed in and practiced without castigating those to whom idol worship brought solace and inner peace. This is also what the great scholar and savant of the 11th century, Al-Beruni, said after years of study of Sanskrit scriptures during an extended stay in India. And the great *Sufi* writers and poets also give the same verdict. Khwaja was particularly fond of the 13th century Persian *Sufi* poet, Fariduddin Attar. One of his anecdotes is as follows:

"Once the angel Gabriel heard God saying 'labbaik' (I respond). Since this expression is normally used by humans as a response to the Creator rather than by God Himself Gabriel became curious to know what the

matter was. After a lot of suspense the mystery was resolved when Gabriel came to learn that God Himself had responded to an infidel's prayer from Turkey because of its utter sincerity and devotion."

Khwaja also held that the Quran does not specifically contradict the Hindu concept of rebirth based on one's '*karma*'. The Hindu concept of 'repeated rebirths' until the evil *karma* of a soul is exhausted or washed away performs essentially the same function of deterrence as the Islamic concept of Divine punishment on the Day of Judgment. Both beliefs relate to the unseen world and both serve to exhort the doing of good and the avoidance of evil. Hence it is futile to claim exclusive truth for either. The crucial factor is the doing of good and avoidance of evil and both the Quran and the Gita broadly agree as to what is good and what is bad, though social customs and religious rites do vary from religion to religion.

Khwaja often appreciated the tolerance found in Hindu society in respect of creedal matters though not in social intercourse. Hindu thinkers and religious leaders always allowed the individual to think of the Supreme Being as either God with attributes (*saguna*) or as without attributes (*nirguna*). He used to say: let anybody go and ask any Hindu whether there are several supreme Beings or only one Supreme Reality and find the answer.

THE SPHERE OF RELIGION AND THE SPHERE OF CULTURE:

Khwaja was quite clear and repeatedly pointed out that religious faith should not be mixed up with territorial or geo-cultural customs, practices and institutions. Islam originated in Arabia and the Prophet himself was born and brought up in an Arab tribe having its own traditions and customs. He naturally and rightly continued to follow them even after he was blessed with the gift of Prophethood unless Divine revelation or guidance modified or abrogated some specific feature of the tribal tradition. Thus, the pre-Islamic raw stuff of ethnic Arab culture, namely, personal names, language, dress, music, food

Appendix 2: Some Random Personal Memories of Abdul Majeed Khwaja

habits, marriage customs, family structures and relational patterns, prohibited degrees of marriage, gender relations and ideas of chastity, laws of inheritance, disposal of the dead, and funeral rites etc., were all retained by a general consensus unless some Quranic text or Prophet's word or deed specifically prohibited them, for instance, the early Arabs who converted to Islam did not change their personal names, the men continued to sport beards and the women to cover their breasts, the burial rites remained as they were, the spoken language and poetry remained the same, the love of horses and camels continued and so on and so forth. However, alcoholic drinks, pork, games of chance, adultery, and unlimited polygamy, etc. became prohibited acts as such, though (obviously) violations must have always been present.

Khwaja argued that the above facts show that religion need not spill over into the sphere of social customs and institutions. He held that the early Muslims, in fact, did retain their original cultural traits and institutions in Iran, Egypt, North Africa, Spain and other countries where the Arab Muslims established themselves. Indeed, in the Abbaside period the Arabic substratum of the ruling and culturally dominant classes began to imbibe the much older Iranian and Greek concepts and values to the great annoyance of the Arab cultural puritans. Khwaja pointed out that Iranians retained the old pre-Islamic names, (such as 'Jamshed', 'Parvez', 'Feroze', 'Khursheed', 'Naseem', and so on) as well as old myths and folk tales, proverbs, turns of speech, similes and symbols, such as the tales of Sohrab and Rustam, Shirin and Ferhad and so on. This also happened in the case of the spread of Islam several centuries later in China, Malaysia, Indonesia, etc. But cultural Arabia won, over and above Islamization, was much more obtrusive in India for different reasons, though even here regional differences remained fairly strong in different parts of the great Indian sub-continent. Khwaja was an advocate of cultural autonomy and pluralism. He welcomed the idea that Indian Muslims should take to ethnic Indian names, which they really liked without any religious qualms or fear of losing their religious identity or faith. He applied the same logic to the style of dress, style of living and eating, music, entertainments, architecture, etc.

Appendix 2: Some Random Personal Memories of Abdul Majeed Khwaja

Khwaja was, perhaps, the first Indian Muslim in the Aligarh region to bring out his family out of traditional purdah system. He remained highly sensitive to the virtue of feminine modesty and chastity and also disapproved of women taking to fashion in dress, make-up, free mixing, ball-room dancing, dating, love marriages, etc. But what has ever baffled me is that he disapproved of higher education for women on the ground that it was unnecessary and tended to erode domestic harmony, and the welfare of the children. Unfair to women (to my mind) as Khwaja was in this respect, he was an active campaigner for women's equality with men in respect of the right to divorce, if a married woman so wished.

KHWAJA'S CONCERN FOR REFORM IN MUSLIM LAW OF DIVORCE:

Khwaja strongly held that the traditional interpretation of the Muslim law of divorce deprived the woman of equal rights with the male in respect of terminating the marriage contract if she so desired. While Muslim law permitted the husband to divorce his married partner, unilaterally, at his sweet will, the wife had an extremely qualified right to seek a remedy for an unhappy and unwanted union with her husband. The traditional Islamic apologists made much of this theoretical or qualified freedom of the woman in Muslim canon law in the face of the total helplessness and subjection of women in Hindu society. But the intellectual honesty of Khwaja made him painfully aware of how very difficult it was for the Muslim married woman to translate this theoretical right into practice through the provision of *khula* in Muslim law. Khwaja, therefore, very strongly and persistently advocated that the Muslim marriage contract must always be in writing and should clearly stipulate the equality of the partners to terminate the contract if either or both desire to do so. That this approach was a major step forward in the direction of complete gender equality cannot be questioned. Khwaja not only preached this ideal but also practiced it to the hilt when he sought marriage alliances for his own daughters as well as sons. Indeed, his sticking to this principle even in the case of very close relations led to considerable family discord and alienation between loved ones. However, some members of the younger generation in families and friends close to Khwaja Sahab took inspiration from his principled approach. Indeed, his active advocacy lay behind the passing of the *Kazmi Act* in the late thirties of the 19th century by the then Central government at Delhi. This Act incorporated the view and suggestions repeatedly advanced by Khwaja, though he never put these ideas in writing.

KHWAJA'S APPROACH TO THE ISSUE OF RELIGIOUS INTER-MARRIAGE:

According to the *shariah* a Muslim believer is not permitted to marry a non-Muslim, though a male believer is permitted to marry a female member of the 'people of the Book'. This expression is traditionally applied to Jew and Christians alone. The relevant Quranic verses, as translated by Marmaduke Pickthall, are as follows:

(Quran, 2:221)
"*Wed not idolatresses till they believe; for lo! A believing bondwoman is better than an idolatress though she please you; and give not your daughters in marriage to idolaters till they believe, for lo! A believing slave is better than an idolater though he please you. These invite unto the Fire, and Allah inviteth unto the Garden, and unto forgiveness by His grace, and expoundeth thus His revelations to mankind that haply they may remember.*"

(Quran 5:5)
"*This day are (all) good things made lawful for you. The food of those who have received the Scripture is lawful for you, and your food is lawful for them. And so are the virtuous women of the believers and the virtuous women of those who received the Scripture before you (lawful for you) when ye give them their marriage portions and live with them in honor, not in fornication, nor taking them as secret concubines. Whoso denieth the faith, his work is vain and he will be among the losers in the Hereafter.*"

Appendix 2: Some Random Personal Memories of Abdul Majeed Khwaja

Khwaja's point was that these verses clearly state that a Muslim believer may not marry an atheist, polytheist or idolater. But Khwaja held that whether or not a person who enters into a marriage contract falls in this category should depend upon his or her actual conviction, beliefs and practice, rather than upon putting the individual under any formal or blanket category, as such. Khwaja held that the traditional approach committed the fallacy of categorizing entire groups as monotheists, atheists, polytheists etc. in an arbitrary manner. This approach is invalid on two counts, first, it completely fails to ascertain the actual belies/convictions of the concerned individual, and second, it ignores the internal distinctions between sub-groups within a larger group. Khwaja held that several sects clubbed as 'Hindu' were very far, indeed, from being idol-worshippers, polytheists, and pagans, etc., for example, the members of the Brahmo Samaj, Arya Samaj, the Kabir Panthis, Sikhs and others.

True to this stand or logic, he also disapproved of marriages when one of the partners was a Muslim believer while the other was an authentic atheist or a polytheist no matter what his or her formal affiliation. He also did not approve of inter-religious marriage under the (now) defunct *Special Marriage Act* of British times when the parties concerned were obliged to declare they had no religious affiliation. His basic thesis was that the authentic Muslim must follow the Quran in all matters concerning morality and the articles of faith in the Unseen. However, he rejected, on principle, the branding of entire communities as prohibited groups for the purpose of marriage irrespective of the actual beliefs and convictions and quality of life of the individuals concerned.

Khwaja's permissive approach to Hindu-Muslim marriage flowed from the Quranic concept of marriage as a contract. It is amusing and interesting that he was not much given to appreciating love marriages, since he thought that young people usually mistook infatuation and sexual attraction as love and made a mess of their lives. He thought that parents should select temperamentally suitable marriage partners from families of more or less equal social standing and wealth, irrespective of their formal religious affiliation. The children should be taught to respect all religions and make their own authentic choice when they come of age.

Khwaja was very clear, indeed, that an open minded spiritually oriented secularism was not opposed to religion as such. A clash develops only when it is claimed that the jurisdiction of religion covers every aspect of life. He was clear that the essential function of religions (including Islam) was inner purification and respect for the moral law (seeking nearness to and the pleasure of God) rather than the external regulation of political or economic behavior. In short, he had fully integrated his commitment to secular politics in a free and united India (on the basis of joint electorates with suitable safeguards for all minorities or weaker sections) and his commitment to Quranic Islam and universal tolerance. His passionate loyalty and devotion to his mentor, Gandhiji, and his deep admiration and reverence for the *Bhagwad Gita* were, thus, firmly rooted in his Quranic faith that the Creator had sent Divinely inspired messengers to all nations with a common message, and that Divine mercy and guidance was a universal phenomenon. Khwaja, therefore, pleaded that the Quranic references to the *"people of the Book"* should not be confined to Jews and Christians alone. Indeed, he often used to refer to the Quran and the Gita in the same breath. I recall with a sense of pride and gratitude to my father that he had encouraged me to read the Gita when I was still a youth.

Khwaja often drew attention to the numerous Quranic verses saying that the Creator had sent His messengers and Warner's to all peoples in all ages though only a few had been named in the Quran. He never tired of observing that how could people think and behave that such a large and centrally located country like India had not been blessed with Divine guidance.

KHWAJA'S APPROACH TO INDIAN POLITICS:

Khwaja's political thinking was formed by his study of modern history and British political institutions. He held that the British

Appendix 2: Some Random Personal Memories of Abdul Majeed Khwaja

Imperial policy was to prepare the Indian masses for self-governance under the imperial umbrella. As a first step the British rulers formed statutory bodies for local self-government in the large cities and towns and they were given limited powers subject to veto by the state governments. Members were elected to these bodies from out of local residents on the basis of qualified adult franchise. The entire concept of representative governance was, obviously, strange to Indian thinking. Moreover, getting elected to a public body required exposure to modern ideas and institutions apart from a measure of economic strength. It was hardly surprising; therefore, that very few Muslims got elected to these bodies, to begin with. Many conservative Muslim minds developed a fear that the same might happen at higher levels of governance, since the Hindu majority was far more financially secure and ahead in western education than the Muslims who stood totally demoralized and shocked after the debacle of 1857.

With the notable exception of a few forward looking and professionally established Muslims in Calcutta, Bombay and Madras the feudal minded landlords and the small town Muslim nobility could not look at the concerned issues from a sound sociological perspective. They developed fears that the British rulers and the western educated *'Bengali Babus'* might totally marginalize them in the fast emerging colonial Indian society. But it would be futile to blame them since it was hardly an easy matter for the demoralized and defeated Muslim gentry to acquire a sound sociological perspective on the Indian situation after having undergone the awesome atrocities of the British army reprisals after 1857.

Under the leadership of one of Sir Syed's successors as Secretary of the MAO College Trustees and the Nawab of Dacca a select delegation of the Muslim gentry presented a memorandum before the Viceroy, Lord Minto, in 1906 praying that there should be constitutional provision of a quota for Muslim seats on the basis of separate electorates at all elected bodies, present and future. This policy was, pretty obviously, politically advantageous for the Muslims in the short run. But Khwaja was deeply concerned with the long-term interest and concerns of the common man, both Hindu and Muslim. However, at that point of time the short term interests of the Indian Muslim leadership and the long term interests of the imperial British power definitely converged. And the fateful principle of separate electorates won the day.

When this happened the young Khwaja was studying at Cambridge. Though he had imbibed Sir Syed's liberal approach to Islam, the young dynamic and romantic Khwaja always had a mind of his own. He did not hesitate to develop new dimensions in the legacy of Sir Syed. He deeply felt that separate electorates went against the grain of liberal democracy and that it led to the politics of community and caste. From the very beginning he valued emotional integration of different groups as a principle rather than as a mere strategy or political necessity. No wonder he forged such warm friendships with numerous non-Muslims.

Khwaja, along with Dr. Ansari, and Tassaduq Sherwani, *et al*, was convinced that, despite appearances to the contrary, separate electorates would weaken and dilute the actual and potential status arid power of the Indian Muslims in the governance of the country at large. Muslims will tend to develop a 'minority complex' and the approach of seeking concessions instead of enjoying the dignity and pride of being absolutely equal citizens along with others. Khwaja stood for equal opportunity in the mainstream of Indian polities with all its risks rather than the safety and security of a pressure group watching from the shore. It was in the same spirit that he so resolutely fought against partition. When the controversy over partition was at its height and he heard some people say that if Pakistan is created it will be the biggest Muslim state in the world he retorted that this will at the same time make India into the biggest Hindu state, and this was not acceptable to him. He wanted neither a Hindu nor an Islamic state but a secular state based on Gandhian principles. When some pro-Pakistan Muslims referred to Jinnah as the great leader (*Quaide Azam*) of Muslims he retorted that Jinnah was, rather, the great benefactor (*Mohsine Azam*) of Hindus. In all humility, I submit that this insight of Khwaja Sahab bears the stamp of both his sharp wit and political insight. At another occasion somebody (not very close to Khwaja) rather mischievously asked him to answer clearly whether he was a Muslim or Hindu, and also how could one call Gandhi as both a Hindu and a Muslim. Khwaja replied that if the questioner thought that Gandhi was a Muslim he could, as well think that Khwaja was a Hindu. The questioner was left puzzled and speechless.

KHWAJA ON COMMUNAL RIOTS AND THE PROTECTION OF MINORITIES:

The recurring pattern of communal riots and the great loss of life and property together with a looming sense of insecurity in one's own motherland greatly depressed Khwaja. But he never lost faith in the essential goodness of the vast majority of his Hindu brothers or in the strategy of common action against evil forces irrespective of religious labels. He categorically ruled out vicarious retaliation or revenge against any out-group. He was well aware of the sociological and economic forces at work and the temptations to seek power and short-term gains by exploiting religious sentiments. He was also quite clear that Muslims should not turn communal minded, or become demoralized but that they should fully cooperate with secular and peace loving elements that constituted the silent majority in the country and was bound to prevail in the long run. Khwaja held that while periodic consultations among the aggrieved Muslim minority could effectively help in overcoming the problems faced by Muslims after partition, the politics of separatism, as a strategy, would prove counter effective in the long run, for the simple reason that it would inevitably polarize the mixed Indian society. He was convinced that this was a national task and that the Indian people as a whole, sooner or later, would rise to the occasion and success would come along through constructive work from common platforms.

Khwaja, however, never held the Westminster model of secular democracy as the last word in matters of governance. He was highly critical of the principle of territorial franchise, and at times he even expressed disillusionment with the idea of unconditional adult franchise as such. Khwaja was also at a loss how to reconcile a possible or actual conflict between a law enacted by a sovereign legislature and a clear injunction of the Quran. Though his views on Islamic dogmas and jurisprudence were considerably forward looking and radical in relation to his times, he did not or could not keep up, in his later years, the once extensive reading habits of his Cambridge days. Several post-Victorian advances in Western knowledge and wisdom, went unregistered by his sharp mind. The implications of the seminal work done by Western creative intellects such as Darwin, Marx, Freud, and Einstein *et al*, did not engage his attention. However, Khwaja's genuine admiration for Gandhiji, his natural goodness and ethical approach to life, warm friendships, cutting across differences of religion, region or caste, and above all his firm commitment to pure Quranic Islam devoid of all temporally conditioned accretions, theologies and local superstitions, his indifference to worldly recognition or success led him to remain a steadfast nationalist patriot as well as a committed follower of Quranic Islam. He remained a fearless, untiring and selfless worker for the causes dear to him: Islam, respect for all religions, communal harmony and national interest of the greater Indian family, though strongly advocating suitable safeguards for the legitimate interests of all minorities and weaker sections of Indian society.

KHWAJA'S APPROACH TO THE ISSUE OF BANK INTEREST:

Khwaja concurred with the general line of Islamic liberalism on this subject. He held that the Quranic term '*riba*' referred to usury as it was practiced in early times. Usury was, indeed, highly exploitative and pernicious since it entailed exorbitantly high costs of borrowing money subject to very severe penalties for default. Modern banking was different and therefore it did not violate any Quranic injunction. However, it could degenerate into usury due to human greed. It was, therefore, essential that state and society be ever vigilant in safeguarding the interests of society as a whole rather than merely be content with promoting the welfare of the rich.

Some Other Social Issues:

To the best of my knowledge Khwaja Sahab was not very vocal on some social issues, like Quran's non-abolition of slavery, some aspects of Quranic penology, such as corporal forms of punishment for theft and adultery, gender inequality in inheritance and the laws of evidence, and some other matters. This, I submit, has been the predicament of almost all liberal Muslims throughout the modern era. This difficulty can be overcome, without nullifying the concept of the infallibility of Quranic revelation, on the basis of a holistic study of Quranic semantics. But so far the Muslim community has not undertaken this very fundamental and vitally important task. The early creative religious thinkers threw up remarkable insights, but the Islamic state and society did not tolerate free inquiry into such delicate matters. It would, therefore, not be fair to single out Khwaja for some limitations to his brave and honest approach to understanding Islam in the modern age.

Khwaja's Veneration for Gandhiji:

Khwaja used to say that of all persons he had known in his life he found Gandhi to be nearest to Prophet Muhammad in actually practicing and pursuing truth, righteousness and justice. After his mentor's martyrdom Khwaja regularly offered '*fatiha*' in memory of the Mahatma. During the period when Jinnah Sahab had veered to accepting the incredible 'Two-nation theory' of Indian history Khwaja used to say that Gandhi was closer to Islam than was Jinnah. When some of his critics challenged him to answer whether he was prepared to be placed in the ranks of non-Muslims like (Gandhi) on the Day of Judgment, he readily answered that he would prefer this than to be placed with Jinnanh.

In all humility, I submit that this sentiment of Khwaja Sahab contrasts sharply with the reply Muhammad Ali, (then President of the Indian National Congress) gave to a rather mischievous query from a press reporter, in 1923, whether a morally virtuous and saintly non-

Appendix 2: Some Random Personal Memories of Abdul Majeed Khwaja

Muslim was superior or not to an evil or immoral Muslim believer? Muhammad Ali answered that, according to the *shariah*, the formal Muslim was superior spiritually though not morally, but avoided giving his own opinion in the matter. I mention this incident, not to glorify my father at the expense of his own venerated leader and friend, but merely to bring out the fact that Khwaja had tremendous moral courage and clarity of thought and that that he sincerely admired Gandhiji. His integration of the Islamic faith with the principle of secular democracy and Indian nationalism was more clear and consistent than the thinking of most of the *Khilafat* leaders well known and rightly respected for their patriotism. He boldly affirmed the concept of religious pluralism without any dilution of his own faith in Islam.

This was the foundational insight and guiding maxim of Mahatma Gandhi.

APPENDIX 3

About The Author

Jamal Khwaja was born in Delhi in 1928*. His ancestors had been closely connected with the Islamic reform movement, inaugurated by Sir Syed Ahmad Khan, the founder of the famous *M.A.O. College*, Aligarh in the second half of the 19th century, and the Indian freedom movement under Gandhi's leadership in the first half of the 20th century. After doing his M.A. in Philosophy from the *Aligarh Muslim University*, India, he obtained an honors degree from *Christ's College University of Cambridge*, UK. Later he spent a year studying the German language and European existentialism at *Munster University*, Germany.

At Cambridge he was deeply influenced by the work of C.D. Broad, Wittgenstein and John Wisdom, apart from his college tutor, I.T.Ramsey who later became *Professor of Christian Religion* at Oxford.

It was the latter's influence, which taught Khwaja to appreciate the inner beauty and power of pure spirituality. Khwaja was thus led to appreciate the value of linguistic analysis as a tool of philosophical inquiry and to combine the quest for clarity with the insights and depth of the existentialist approach to religion and spirituality.

Khwaja was appointed Lecturer in Philosophy at the *Aligarh Muslim University* in 1953. Before he could begin serious academic work in his chosen field, his family tradition of public work pulled him into a brief spell of active politics under the charismatic Jawahar Lal Nehru; the first Prime Minister of India. Nehru was keen to rejuvenate his team of colleagues through inducting fresh blood into the *Indian National*

---

* Jamal Khwaja was born in Delhi on August 12, 1926. However, most official records mistakenly show 1928 as the year of birth.

Congress. He included young Khwaja, then freshly returned from Cambridge, along with four or five other young persons. Khwaja thus became one of the youngest entrants into the Indian Parliament as a member of the *Lok Sabha* (Lower House) from 1957 to 1962. While in the corridors of power he learned to distinguish between ideals and illusions, and finally chose to pursue the path of knowledge rather than the path of acquiring authority or power. Returning to his *alma mater* in 1962, he resumed teaching and research in the philosophy of religion. Ever since then Khwaja has lived a quiet life at Aligarh.

He was Dean of the *Faculty of Arts* and was a member of important committees of the *University Grants Commission* and the *Indian Council for Philosophical Research* before retiring as Professor and Chairman of the *Department of Philosophy* in 1988. He was a frequent and active participant in national seminars held at the *Indian Institute of Advanced Study*, Shimla.

His works include, *Five Approaches to Philosophy*, *Quest for Islam*, *Authenticity and Islamic Liberalism*, *Living The Quran In Our Times*, and numerous articles and scholarly essays. He was invited to deliver the *Khuda Bakhsh Memorial Lecture* at Patna. He was one of the official Indian delegates at the *World Philosophical Congress Brighton*, UK, in 1988, and also at the *International Islamic Conference Kuala Lumpur*, Malaysia, in 1967, and the *Pakistan International Philosophy Congress*, Peshawar, Pakistan, in 1964. He has visited the USA and several countries in Western Europe.

He performed *Hajj* in 2005.

Major Published Works:

Jamal Khwaja has written seven major books. Anyone interested in the intersection of Islam and Modernity will find Khwaja to be a reliable guide. His work is magisterial in scope. It is full of passion but remains balanced in perspective. Readers of his work will be in turn, informed, inspired, and intellectually liberated.

As complex issues get illumined and perplexities whither away, Muslim readers in particular, will feel emotionally aligned with the Quran and find themselves empowered to live as authentic Muslims in the heart of the multi-cultural global village.

1. Five Approaches To Philosophy: A discerning philosopher philosophizes about the philosophy of philosophy with wisdom and clarity. (2nd Edition). 158 Pages. ISBN: 978-1-935293-51-4

2. Quest For Islam: A philosophers approach to religion in the age of science and cultural pluralism. (Significantly Enlarged 2nd Edition). 364 Pages. ISBN: 978-1-935293-69-9

3. Authenticity And Islamic Liberalism: A mature vision of Islamic Liberalism grounded in the Quran. (Significantly Enlarged 2nd Edition). 244 Pages. ISBN: 978-1-935293-68-2

4. Essays On Cultural Pluralism: A philosophical framework for authentic interfaith dialogue. 268 Pages. ISBN: 978-1-935293-52-1

5. The Call Of Modernity And Islam: A Muslim's journey into the 21st century. 232 Pages. ISBN: 978-1-935293-94-1

6. Living The Quran In Our Times: A vision of how Muslims can revitalize their faith, while being faithful to God and His messenger. 266 Pages. ISBN: 978-81-321-1046-0

7. The Vision Of An Unknown Indian Muslim: My journey to interfaith spirituality. 326 Pages. ISBN: 978-1-935293-96-5

Khwaja's work is the definitive contemporary discussion regarding the collision of Islam and Modernity. Explore it. You will be profoundly rewarded.

For more information, visit *www.JamalKhwaja.com*

INDEX

A

Abdali, Ahmad Shah, *160, 163*
Abdullah,
- Farooq, *98*
- Shaikh Muhammad, *70, 223*
Abidi, Haji Hasan, *111*
abolition of zamindari, *227*
Abraham, feet of, *103-104*
abyss of uncertainty, *126*
Achint Ram, Lala, *73*
adolescence, *15, 86-87, 152*
Afghani, Jamaluddin, *4*
Afghanistan, *23, 58-60, 160*
Afro-Asian Philosophy Conference, *94*
agonizing decision, *202*
Ajmal Khan, Hakim, *5, 260, 262, 275*
Akbar, Major General Muhammad, *60*
Akbarbhai Chavda, *62*
Al-Beruni, *180, 186, 280*
alcohol, *38, 45-46, 137, 216, 282*
Al-Ghazzali, *53, 89*
Ali,
- Hashim, *116, 121*
- Muhammad, *5, 259, 275-276,*
291-292
alienation, *135, 284*
Aligarh Muslim University,
6, 14, 17-18, 20-28, 47, 51-55, 73,
77-79, 84-85, 88, 90, 95, 97, 106,
112-117, 121, 124, 129, 207-208,
260, 262, 264, 268, 270, 275-276
Aligarh, *3-8, 9, 14-16, 18, 20-29,*
55-56, 70, 77, 109, 124, 259, 264,
268, 270, 272, 274, 277-279
Allahabad High Court, *6-9,*
16, 95, 99, 260, 272
Allahabad, *4, 7-8, 9, 12, 14-16,*
24-25, 98-99, 137, 180, 260, 265,
269, 271-272
Alvi, Dr., *95*
Alvi, Ishtiaq, *111*
ambition vs. integrity, *54, 71, 89*
Amir Ali, *31, 88, 278*
Amir Khusro, *160, 187*
ancestors, *3, 160, 293*
Ansari, Dr. M.A., *5-6, 262, 275, 288*
apologetics, *41, 88*
apostasy, *92, 169*
appeasement, *212, 226*
Arabic, *13, 16, 52, 74, 88-89,*

Index

110, 143, 145, 158, 191-192, 237, 266, 273, 272, 282
Arafat, Yasser, *91*
Arya Samaj, *129-130, 285*
Aryans, *158-159, 183, 236*
Aslam Jairajpuri, *5, 264*
atheist, *18, 33, 42, 52, 67, 70, 115, 117, 134, 137, 149*
Authenticity and Islamic Liberalism, *109, 294*
Azad, Abul Kalam, *9, 24, 31, 57, 63, 68, 88, 133, 196-205, 208, 238, 263, 274-276*

B

Babar, *3, 160-163, 183*
Badshah, Khan Abdul Ghaffar, *203*
Bajrang Dal, *234*
beautiful names of Allah, *143*
Bedar, Dr. A.R., *109*
Bhagalpur communal riot, *122*
Bhagwan Das, Dr., *54*
Bhakti **movement,** *178-179, 245*
Bible Studies, *12*
Birla, G.D., *5*
Brahmo Samaj, *129-130, 285*

C

Cabinet Mission plan, *197-200, 260*
Calcutta, *191-192, 287*
Cambridge,
- Cam River, *105*
- Christ's College, *5, 7, 28, 260,* 273, 293
- College baths, *44-45*
- College dinner, *45*
- tutorial system, *21, 36*
Capitol Hill, *105*
Cariappa, Marshall, *60-61*
caste system, *129, 161, 174, 178, 219, 230, 249*
Chattari, Nawab of, *111*
children's railway, Delhi, *74*
Christian,
- missionaries, *89, 190, 239-240, 243*
- Theology, *49*
clarity, *18, 28, 37, 84, 121, 253, 263-264, 292*
codes of conduct, *213-214*
cognitive,
- analysis, *134*
- vacuity, *80*
common civil code, *232*
Communism, *48, 60, 216-217, 247*
Communist, *48, 52-53, 73, 101, 115, 117, 134, 149, 206, 210, 215, 217-218, 226, 242-243*
comparative Religion, *41, 85, 186, 273*
Congress dog, *23*
Congress Party, *9, 22-26, 28, 53-57, 60, 62-64, 69-73, 77, 97, 101, 116, 132, 183, 193, 195-207, 211, 234, 247-250, 260-261, 268, 274-276, 291*
conventional Muslims, *39, 41, 70, 180*
corridors of power, *71, 173, 211,*

226, 243
creative fidelity, *150*
Cromer, Lord, *4*
cultural,
- diversity, *41, 221, 240*
- fundamentalism, *234*
- impact of Islam, *132*

D

Dalits, *55, 221, 243, 247-248, 252*
Dara Shikoh, prince, *170*
darkness at noon, *203, 277*
Darwin, Charles, *18, 43, 126, 190*
deen-e Ilahi, *169*
democracy, *42, 48, 59-60, 94-95, 100, 126, 132, 190, 193-195, 210-215, 229-230, 234, 237, 248-252, 264, 288-292*
democratic,
- spirit, *214*
- temper of, *27*
demon of caste, *219*
Dev Atma, *129*
Dev Samaj, *129-130*
dharma, *163*
dhimmis, *94, 167, 171*
Divine,
- grace, *141-142, 148, 152*
- Light, *153*
- love, *32-33*
- Presence, *152*
- spark, *153*
dogmatic slumbers, *40, 217*

dream of an Indian Muslim, *245-254*

E

East India Company, *189-190, 193*
Eisenhower, President, *61*
emergency, *95-97, 123, 218*
emotional,
- distance, *232*
- integration, *168, 181, 195, 221-222, 230, 232, 243, 288*
- intelligence, *134*
- responses, *82*
empathy, *21, 119, 233*
empirical enquiry, *217, 242*
ethical approach, *9, 48, 92, 97, 129, 209, 212, 253, 261, 291*
exclusive salvation, *170, 180*
Executive Council, AMU, *112-116, 268*
existential,
- anxiety, *239*
- approach, *89, 101-102, 254, 293*
- beliefs, *33*
- certainties, *87*
- commitment, *39*
- convictions, *82, 251*
- doubt, *33*
- interpretation, *82, 99, 183*
- opaqueness, *41*
- perspective, *87*
- perplexity, *32*
- revolution, *37*

Index

expediency, *149, 213, 247*

F

failure of vision and will, *159*
fear,
-as the mother of hate, *239*
- of commitment, *82*
- of freedom, *102*
- of writing, *84*
Five Approaches to Philosophy, *49, 79, 84, 294*
free enquiry, *19-21, 27-28, 31, 60, 115, 120, 236, 239, 242*
freedom of the will, *18, 33*
Freud, Sigmund, *16, 31*
Fromm, Erich, *28, 101, 131, 152*

G

Gandhi, Mahatma, *5-8, 9-10, 24, 46, 52, 55, 57, 61-63, 68, 92, 95-97, 115, 122, 159, 186, 192, 196, 199-203, 207-208, 209-215, 224, 233, 237-238, 248-250, 253, 259, 261-262, 266-268, 272-277, 280, 286-292*
Gandhi,
- Indira, *8, 62-63, 95-99, 115-116, 211-212, 216, 255, 267*
- Rajiv, *212, 216, 251, 255*
- Sanjay, *96-97*
Gandhi-Nehru vision, *209, 224*
gender,
- discrimination, *126*
- equality, *92, 145, 149, 241, 283*
- inequality, *41*
- relations, *282*
genius of India, *211, 230, 253*
Germany, *5, 15, 37, 39, 42, 45, 221, 260, 276*
Ghalib, Mirza, *153*
Ghori, Muhammad, *160*
Gita, Bhagwad, *10, 133, 280-281, 286*
Gitanjali, *253*
God, *13, 15-19, 31-32, 52, 62, 91, 100, 117, 130-137, 139, 151-152, 156, 179, 215, 242, 247, 269, 273, 278, 280-281, 286*
Goleman, Daniel, *134*
Golwalkar, Guru, *26, 233-234*
Grover, Dr. Sanjay, *131*
Grunebaum, Prof., *88-90*
Gujrat, *62, 98, 187, 237, 252*

H

Habib,
- Begum Muhammad, *8*
- Prof, Muhammad, *8, 19*
- Prof. Irfan, *115, 208*
Haidar, Begun Sajjad, *8*
Haidry, Molvi Abul Hasan, *13*
Hajira, Bibi, *139, 144-145*
Hajj, *46, 139-151, 206*
halal meat, *136*
Hamidia Girls School, *8*
Hamied, Dr. K.A., *5*
Harvard University, *43, 105*
heaven, *11-12, 147, 253*
Hedgewar, Dr., *233*
Hifzur Rahman, Maulana, *203*

Index

Hind, Urdu magazine, *8*
Hindi language, *10, 118, 192, 221, 266*
Hindu/Hinduism, *3, 10, 12, 16, 22-27, 32-33, 39, 57, 62, 67-72, 118, 121, 129-135, 158-187, 190, 192-198, 203-206, 212, 219, 223-244, 245-254, 259, 266, 275-276, 280-289*
hindutva, *183, 226, 230-234, 238, 240, 243, 247-250*
Hira cave, Mecca, *104*
historical causation, *101, 200*
Hitler, *126, 159, 184*
humanistic love, *95, 131, 178, 180*
Husain,
- **Dr. Abid,** *264*
- **Dr. Zakir,** *5-6, 27-28, 52, 55, 78-79, 130, 260, 264, 275-276*
- **Naushad,** *111*
Hyderabad, *7, 26-27, 88, 97-98, 147, 164, 177*
hypocrisy, *48, 111, 135, 137, 198*

I

Ibrahim Qutub Shah, *167*
idealism, *11, 19, 201, 206, 242*
imperialism, *4, 201, 234*
in group/out group, *126, 184*
incarnation, *33, 37, 162*
Indonesia, *90-92, 186, 282*
infallibility, *18, 129, 217, 291*
innocence, *16-17, 31, 34*
interior silence, *147*

International Islamic Conference, *90*
inter-religious, marriage, *57, 285*
intolerance, *47-48, 123*
Iqbal, Muhammad, Allama, *5, 88, 121, 208*
Irfan, Maulana Abul, *92*
isht Devata, *176, 186, 232*
Islam, complete code, *249, 279*
Islamic,
- civilization, *158*
- fundamentalism, *87, 231-232, 238-239, 249*
- hegemony, *249*
- Liberalism, *3, 6, 52, 55-56, 89, 92, 121, 277, 290*
- power bloc, *239*
- wealth tax (zakat), *168, 171*
Islamization of democracy, *95, 217, 282*

J

Jainism, *36, 130, 159, 161, 185, 236-237*
Jalali, Farrukh, *111*
Jamate Islami, *73*
Jamia Millia Islamia, *5-6, 20, 130, 259-276*
Jaspers, Karl, *40, 99, 102*
Jats, *164, 248*
Jinnah, Muhammad Ali, *24-26, 196-208, 238, 271, 275, 288, 291*
jizya, *167-172*

Index

Jung,
- Bahadur Yar, *26*
- Begum Razia Haleem, *141*
- Begum Akhtar Sarbuland, *7, 10*
- Maqsood Ullah, *70*
- Muhammad Ullah, *4*
- Nawab Ali Yavar, *78-79, 88, 111*
- Nawab Sarbuland, *6*

K

Kaba, *103-104, 139-148*
Kabir, Humayun, *56, 63, 77*
Kakar, Dr. Sudhir, *130*
Kanal, Dr., *130*
karma, *32-33, 37-38, 41, 281*
Kashmir, *12, 69, 85, 98, 164, 166, 187, 221-224, 244*
Katju, Kailash Nath, *12*
Khan, Dr. Ajmal Hasan, *8*
Khilafat Movement, *5, 196, 259, 262, 272, 274, 292*
Khuda Bakhsh Lectures, *109, 124, 294*
Khuda Bakhsh Library, *109, 124, 132*
Khwaja,
- Abdul Majeed, *4, 9, 259-292*
- Abdul Qadir, *3*
- Ajmal, *8, 142, 146-147, 262*
- Dr. Raveend, *8, 10, 21-23, 105-107, 125, 261, 267*
- Geeta Anjum, *75, 103, 140, 149, 266*
- Hamida, Begum, *61, 103, 131-132, 140-141, 149-152*
- Jawahar Kabir, *74, 87, 266*
- Moin Uddin, *180*
- Muhammad Yusuf, *3-4, 273*
- Naazneen, *141-147*
- Nasser Navin, *75, 266*
- Rajen Habib, *74*
- Shakira, *147*
- Ubaid Ullah Ahrar, *3*
Kidwai,
- Dr. Hashim, *22, 276*
- Rafi Ahmad, *276*
- Shafiqur Rahman, *5*
Kluckhom, Clyde, *66*
kotwal, *173, 175, 177*

L

Lahore, *25, 85, 88, 129, 160, 177, 196*
Lal, Dewan Chaman, *63*
Lenin, *52, 73, 210*
liberal,
- humanist tradition, *16, 22, 60, 78, 100, 110, 206, 209, 244*
- Islam, *16, 38, 78, 92, 109, 238*
- reformers, *194*
- vanguard, *240*
Library of Congress, *105*
Linguistic,
- analysis, *35-36, 40, 81, 84, 102*
- games, *84*
Lodi, Sultan Ibrahim, *163*
London, *130, 191*
love marriage, *127, 283, 285*

Index

Lysenko controversy, *48*

M

M.A.O. College, *4-5, 7, 207, 275, 287*
Macaulay, Lord, *191*
Madon Report, *122, 244*
Mahmud,
- Dr. Syed, *28, 57, 273, 276*
- Gawan, *166*
- Sultan of Ghazna, *160, 183*
- Syed, Justice, *7, 273*
Mandela, Nelson, *253*
mandir-masjid dispute, *135*
Maqsood, Clovis, *57*
Marathas, *164, 171-172, 189*
Martyrdom, *6, 17, 291*
Marx, Karl, *16, 73, 210, 216, 246, 290*
Marxism, *48, 52, 93, 115, 217, 242*
Mathura, *24, 185*
Maugham, Somerset, *39*
Maulana Azad Library, *111, 117*
Maurya, B.P., *55*
Mawdudi, Maulana, *16, 238*
Mayawati, Dalit leader, *248*
medieval Indian culture, *20, 158, 162, 182-183*
Mehboob Bhai, *137*
Menon, Krishna, *64*
Metaphilosophy, *79*
Metaphysics,
- as a super-science, *81*
- as nonsense, *36*
- Brahmanical, *178*
- fear of, *82*
- positivist rejection of, *36*
Mill, John Stuart, *44, 190*
mixed economy, *100, 217*
monkey menace, *75*
Mother India, *91, 225, 231, 235*
Mountbatten, Lord, *198-202*
Mughal-Sikh confrontation, *132, 172*
Munster University, *39-40, 45*
Muslim Educational Conference, *7*
Muslim League, *20-25, 195-196, 205-2088, 238, 276*
Muslim Majlis, *6, 260*
Muslim,
- homeland, *22, 203-204*
- peasantry, *227*
- perceptions, *226, 239*
- personal law, *206, 212, 232*
- Theology, *84*
Muslims of Indian origin, *166, 186*
Mysore, *164, 177, 189*
mystical experience, *18, 42*
mysticism, *41, 82, 102*
mythology, *67, 82, 121, 130, 133, 158, 187*

N

Nadir Shah, *160, 163, 184, 245*
Naidu,
- Padmaja, *7*

- **Sarojini,** *7, 262*
Nanak, Guru, *132*
Narayan, Jai Prakash, *61, 96-97*
Narendra Modi, *252*
Nehru,
- **B.K.,** *98, 131*
- **Uma,** *56-57*
- **Tyagi exchange,** *64*
Nehru, Jawaharlal, *5-8, 20, 24, 46, 52-57, 61-69, 73, 86, 100-101, 111, 122, 197-203, 207, 209-213, 217-219, 222-224, 238, 255, 260, 265, 271-273*
New Aligarh Movement, *116, 121, 263*
New Servants of India Society, *122*
Nitish Kumar, OBC leader, *252*
Nizam of Hyderabad, *27, 88, 164*
Nizamuddin Auliya, *160, 180*
Non-cooperation Movement, *5, 7, 9*
Non-Resident Student's Centre, *112*
Noorul Arfin, *17, 20, 85*
Norwich, *105, 125*

O

Obama moment, *253*
objective truths, *36, 82*
obligatory prayers, *38-39, 117*
opium of the masses, *16, 217*
opportunistic, *73, 248*
orthodox, *9, 42, 57, 68, 71, 125, 151, 167-170, 179-180, 186, 269, 271, 277*
Oxford, *18, 21, 35-38, 42-47, 78, 86, 100, 107, 120, 208, 275*

P

Pakistan Philosophy Congress, *77*
Pakistan, *6, 20-26, 47-48, 58-61-64, 77-78, 84-85, 90-91, 124, 195, 198-210, 223-226, 238-240*
palm greasing, *211, 214*
Pant, G.B., *54, 72*
partition,
- **Britain's role of,** *200*
- **of Bengal,** *195, 200-202, 207-208*
- **of India,** *6, 21, 25-29, 132-133, 159, 162, 192, 196-208, 224-225, 230, 246, 250, 259-262, 276, 288-289*
- **responsibility for,** *199-200, 206*
Parvez, Dr. Athar, *114*
Patel, Sardar, *200-203, 210*
Patna, *5, 9, 109, 124, 132, 259, 274, 294*
patronage, *164, 225-227*
peak spiritual experience, *142*
Peareylal, Congress leader, *97, 202*
Peareylal, secretary, Gandhiji, *202, 208*
Peck, Scott, *131*

Index

Persian, *10, 12-13, 46, 88-89, 102-103, 110, 117, 158-159, 166, 181, 192, 269, 273, 280*
philosophical,
- climate, *36*
- method, *37, 40, 153*
- theories, *34-35, 80*

Philosophy Congress, Brighton, *123*
Philosophy,
- of history, *82, 101*
- proper task of, *80*

pilgrim tax, *170-171*
plural interpretations, *106, 124, 278*
polygamy, *107, 231, 282*
polytheism, *49, 180*
Pope, *106, 240*
pork, *38, 41, 91, 278, 282*
poverty, *104, 134, 181, 218, 227-228, 243*
Pratap, Raja Mahendra, *23, 56*
price of Pakistan, *26*
procrastination, *15, 119, 146*
Proctor, AMU, *112, 114*
Professor,
- Adhami, Usman, *22*
- Ahmad, Aziz, *88*
- Ahmad, Maqbool, *120*
- Akbarabadi, S.A., *110*
- Ansari, Anwar, *110*
- Arberry, Prof., *48, 88*
- Banerjee, N.V., *207*
- Broad, C.D., *33-35, 293*
- Chaterjee, Margaret, *123*
- Chatterjee, Suniti Kumar, *93*
- Devaraja, *123, 185*
- Farooqui, Qamar, *113-114*
- Gahrana, G.K., *111*
- Gibb, H.A.R., *88*
- Gilbert, *35, 80*
- Hasan, Masoodul, *110-113*
- Hasan, Mohibbul, *110*
- Hasan, Noorul, *85*
- Hasan, Zafrul, *18*
- Hasan, Ziaul, *22*
- Husain Masud, VC, *20*
- Khan, Abdul Baseer, *79*
- Khan, Hamieduddin, *88*
- Khan, Luqman, *131*
- Khusro, A.M., *112*
- Krishna, Daya, *123*
- Mujeeb, Muhammad, *130, 264*
- Mukerjee, Hiren, *56*
- Murty, Sachitananda, *77-78, 92, 123*
- Nasr, Syed Husain, *78*
- Nicholson, *88, 273*
- Niebuhr, Reinhold, *85-86, 253*
- Pitcher, *86*
- Prasad, J.N., *114*
- Prasad, Rajendra, *123*
- Qadri, Jamil, *111*
- Rahman, Fazlur, *47-48, 78, 124*
- Ramachandran, *95*
- Ramsey, I.T., *38-39, 79, 102*
- Ray, Nihar Ranjan, *92*
- Razvi, M.H., *111*
- Ritter, J., *40*

- Rizvi, S.A.A., *88-89*
- Schimmel, Annemarie, *88*
- Shafi, Muhammad, *112*
- Shah, K.J., *123*
- Shareef, M.M., *18, 77*
- Sherwani, R.R., *111*
- Siddiqui, Abdul Aleem, *51-52, 112*
- Siddiqui, Aulad Ahmed, *102*
- Siddiqui, Mujtaba, *79*
- Siddiqui, Rasheed Ahmad, *111*
- Smith, Cantwell, *27, 88*
- Suroor, A.A., *20, 98, 121*
- Troll, Christian, *109*
- Umaruddin, M., *53, 83*
- Verma, Roop Rekha, *123*
- Watt, Montgomery, *88*
- Wisdom, John, *34-36, 80, 86, 102*
- Wittgenstein, Ludwig, *34-36, 40, 51, 80-81, 86, 293*
- Zafar Ahmad, *110*

proof of God's existence, *18-19*
pseudo-secularism, *234, 251*
psyche of the Hindu, *221*
psychic phenomena, *34*
Psychology, *14, 40, 69, 101, 134, 142, 186*
Punjab, *60, 73, 129-130, 180, 189, 198, 200, 202, 204, 208, 221-222, 225, 274*
purdah, *4, 8, 15*
puritanical phase, *15*
purusharthas, *165*

Q

Qadeer Piya, sufi saint, *147*
Qazi Mughisuddin, *164*
Quest for Islam, *49, 87-90, 102, 109*
Quran, *9-10, 16, 62, 74, 88, 94, 103, 106, 121, 124-126, 140-143, 148-150, 158, 167, 264, 278-286, 290-291*

R

Radhakrishnan, Dr. S, *56, 133*
Rai Bareilly, *4, 95*
Rahman, Fazlur, *88*
Rajputs, *163, 176, 182, 186*
Rampur, *20, 54, 57*
Rao, Narasinha, *27, 213*
Rasheed, Babu Abdul, *26*
Ray, Sir P.C., *5*
Razvi, Qasim, *26*
Reade, Winwood, *17*
religious,
- plurality, *230, 237*
- apologetics, *41*
- convictions, *19, 36, 117*
- faith, *17, 29, 37, 41, 93, 107, 151, 161, 229, 264, 277*
- pedagogy, *26*
- piety, *41, 185, 242*
- tolerance, *93, 167-168, 176, 231*
reservation for Indian Muslims, *225, 227*
RSS, *26, 134, 233-236*
Russell, Bertrand, *33, 35, 40,*

Index

80-84, 246

S

Sachhar Report, *251*
Salam, Dr. Abdus, *47*
Samanth, Dr., *137*
Sami Ullah, Moulvi, *3-7, 273*
Sanskrit, *10, 12, 158, 166, 180, 186, 191-192, 280*
Sapru, Sir Tej Bahadur, *6, 12*
Sarabhai, Mridula, *69-70*
Satan, *145, 191, 242*
satyagraha, *122, 196, 215*
Scientific Society, *3*
scientific temper, *65, 93, 209*
secular democracy, *95, 194, 251, 264, 289, 292*
self,
- esteem, *16, 87, 152*
- improvement, *15*

separate electorates, *194-195, 287-288*
Shafiq, Ahmed Khan, *104*
Shakespeare, *43-44, 190*
Shankaracharya, Adi, *159, 236*
shariah, *16, 124-125, 164-171, 238, 250, 284, 292*
Shastri, Prakash Vir, *66*
Sher Shah, *163, 166*
Shervani,
- Mustafa Rasheed, *100*
- T.A.K., *6, 273, 276*

Shia Islam, *89, 117-118, 172, 174, 268-272*
Shibli, Nomani, Allama, *4, 88, 263, 278*
Shivaji, *163-164, 172*

shunya, *140*
Siddiqui, Jameel, *22*
Sikhs, *131-137, 159, 164, 172, 237, 285*
Sind, *160, 189, 204, 208, 225*
Singh,
- Amrik, *122*
- Fateh, Maharaja of Baroda, *69*
- General Gobinder, *131*
- General Rajendra, *60*
- Khushwant, *131*
- Prithi of Bharatpur, *132*
- Raja Dinesh, *54, 65, 67-68*
- Rajendra, MP, *67*
- S.K. (Bachhan Babu), *70*
- Shailendra Kumar, *114*
- U.N., Dr., *98-99*

Socialism, *100, 210, 212, 216-218*
socialist, *47, 100-101, 210, 212, 215-218*
Socratic discussion, *21, 31*
Solan, *129-136, 140-141*
Soviet Union, *101, 222*
spirit of the age, *81, 157*
spiritual,
- ecstasy, *141, 145, 186*
- Geography, *85*

St. Mary's Convent, *8, 12*
Sufis, *10-11, 20, 42, 70, 89, 103, 134, 142, 145-147, 160, 162, 166, 168, 179-181, 186-187, 245, 269, 279-280*
Sulaiman, Sir Shah, *5*
Sultan of Bijapur, *163, 167*

Index

Sundarlal, Pandit, *10, 46, 266*
Supreme Being, *10, 186, 280-281*
sura Fatiha, *143*
Svetlana (Stalin), *69*
Syed, Sir Ahmad, *3-4, 7, 24, 31, 68, 84, 110, 116, 121, 193-195, 208, 263-264, 273, 275, 277-279, 287-288*
syllabus, *17-18, 21, 84, 86*

T

Tagore's prayer, *253*
Taj Apa (Begum Taj Hafeez Ahmad), *8, 11*
Tajuddin Feroze, Sultan, *166*
Tehzibul Akhlaq, *116*
terrorism, *91, 223, 239, 249*
Thanvi, Maulana Ashraf Ali, *12*
Theistic *bhakti*, *130*
Tipu Sultan, *164*
tolerance, *27, 55, 60, 70, 93, 124-125, 131, 133, 147, 167-168, 176, 180, 209, 231, 264, 268, 278, 281, 286*
tomb, *148, 175, 279*
total revolution, *62, 96*
transcendental meditation, *102, 134*
Two-nation theory, *20, 22, 25, 195, 208, 225, 239, 260, 276, 291*
Tyabji, Badruddin, *78, 193, 207*
Tyagi, Mahavir, *56, 64-65*

U

ulema, *92, 110, 124, 164-165, 168-169, 179-181, 186, 197, 203, 277*
ultra-orthodox believers, *125, 151*
umra, *103, 139, 141, 145-146*
University Grants Commission, *53, 118, 120, 294*
Upanishads, *170, 178*
Urdu Centre, Solan, *130*
Urdu, *8, 12, 17, 20, 26, 84, 88-89, 102, 111, 114, 116, 121, 153, 192, 206, 262-263, 268-271*

V

vedanta, *158*
Vedic,
- Brahmanism, *159*
- wisdom, *235*
vertical mobility, *161, 166, 221, 231*
vicarious punishment, *32, 289*
vipasna, *144*
Vivekananda, Swami, *233*
vote-bank politics, *183, 251-252*

W

Warris, Ghulam, *111*
Washington, *49*
Wasim, Muhammad, *19, 25, 273*
Wavel, Lord, *197-198, 208*
West Asia, *91, 158, 161, 174, 227*

wisdom of,
- **humility,** *71, 75, 153*
- **the East,** *190*
- **the Vedas,** *235*

Y
Yogi, Mahesh, *102*

Z
Zaheer, Ali, *90*
Zaidi, B.H., *54-55, 264*
Zam Zam spring, *103, 145*
Zaynul Abidin, Sultan, *166, 187*

To learn more about the author - Jamal Khwaja, and his various works visit:

www.JamalKhwaja.com

Download free Digital Books, Lectures, Essays, browse links to related sites and much more...

Publishers website can be found at:

www.AlhamdPublishers.com

www.ingramcontent.com/pod-product-compliance
Lightning Source LLC
Chambersburg PA
CBHW021139080526
44588CB00008B/127